Peripheral Visions in the Globalizing Present

Thamyris/
Intersecting: Place, Sex and Race

Series Editor

Ernst van Alphen

Editorial Team

Murat Aydemir
Maaike Bleeker
Maria Boletsi
Isabel Hoving
Esther Peeren

VOLUME 31

The titles published in this series are listed at *brill.com/tham*

Peripheral Visions in the Globalizing Present

Space, Mobility, Aesthetics

Edited by

Esther Peeren
Hanneke Stuit
Astrid Van Weyenberg

BRILL

RODOPI

LEIDEN | BOSTON

Cover illustration: Klaipèda, Lithuania (2014). Image by Astrid Van Weyenberg.

The Library of Congress Cataloging-in-Publication Data is available online at http://catalog.loc.gov
LC record available at http://lccn.loc.gov/2016027437

Want or need Open Access? Brill Open offers you the choice to make your research freely accessible online
in exchange for a publication charge. Review your various options on brill.com/brill-open.

Typeface for the Latin, Greek, and Cyrillic scripts: "Brill". See and download: brill.com/brill-typeface.

ISSN 1570-7253
ISBN 978-90-04-32144-1 (paperback)
ISBN 978-90-04-32305-6 (e-book)

Printed by Printforce, the Netherlands

Contents

Thamyris Mission Statement

Thamyris seeks to initiate alternative forms of criticism by analyzing the ways in which cultural and theoretical discourses intervene in the contemporary world. This criticism should pursue a re-politicizing and remobilizing of theoretical perspectives and cultural practices, preferably through case studies. *Thamyris* hopes to contribute to the productive interaction between art, activism, and theory. We understand cultural practices to include those of literary, visual, digital, and performance arts, but also social practices related to gender, sexuality, and ethnicity. In short, *Thamyris* aims at exploring the ways in which varying cultural practices, separately or in interaction, can be effective as agents of social and cultural change.

List of Illustrations

Notes on Contributors

Paulina Aroch-Fugellie

is Visiting Professor at the Humanities Department, Universidad Autónoma Metropolitana, Unidad Cuajimalpa, in Mexico City. She is part of the research group Cuerpo Académico Expresión y Representación. In 2012–13 she was a Fellow at the Cornell University Society for the Humanities, where she taught and conducted research on the production of value in contemporary art from the perspective of the global periphery. Her background is in postcolonial theory, critical theory, African studies and English literature. She obtained her PhD in the Humanities from the University of Amsterdam in 2010. Recent publications include "Leverage: The Art of the Mexican Student Movement" in the *Journal of Latin American Cultural Studies*, "Anecdotes of an Obsolete Object" in *A Journal of Literature, Culture and Literary Translation*, and "Movement and the Paradox of Resistance" in *Cosmos and History: The Journal of Natural and Social Philosophy*.

Paula Blair

is a Lecturer in Film Studies at Lancaster University, and holds a PhD in Film and Visual Studies from Queen's University Belfast. Her research interests lie in mediatized conflict and convergences between cinema and visual art. She is particularly drawn to the ways marginal or hidden events and experiences are brought to light by artists and filmmakers who themselves operate on the peripheries of production, distribution and exhibition systems. Her publications include *Old Borders, New Technologies: Reframing Film and Visual Culture in Contemporary Northern Ireland* (Peter Lang, 2014), "Panopticons Within Panopticons: Surveillance Inversions in Willie Doherty's Video Installations" in the *Journal of Postcolonial Writing* (2013) and "Newsreel Politics: Early American Non-Fiction Film and the Irish Question" in *POST SCRIPT: Essays in Film and the Humanities* (2013).

Sudeep Dasgupta

is Associate Professor in Media Studies at the University of Amsterdam. He is the co-editor of *What's Queer about Europe? Productive Encounters and Re-enchanting Paradigms* (Fordham UP, 2014) and has written numerous essays on visual culture and critical theory in the fields of globalization, postcolonial, feminist and queer studies. His publications include "Permanent Transiency, Tele-visual Spectacle, and the Slum as Postcolonial Monument" in *South Asian Studies* (2013), "The Spiral of Thought in the Work of Jacques Rancière" in

Theory & Event (2013), "Detours, Delays, Derailments: La Petite Jérusalem and Slow Training in Culture" in *Paris-Amsterdam Underground: Essays on Cultural Resistance, Subversion, and Diversion* (Amsterdam UP, 2013) and "Conjunctive Times, Disjointed Time: Philosophy between Enigma and Disagreement" in *Parallax* (2009).

Matthieu Foucher

holds an MSc degree from the Iéseg School of Management, where he wrote his thesis about new business models in the media industry. In 2015, he finished the Research MA in Media Studies at the University of Amsterdam with a thesis in which he used queer theory and the notion of spectrality to analyze queer representations in the French art magazine *La Revue Monstre*. He has held several positions in the media industry, working as a production assistant, a program development officer and as a cultural journalist and writer specialized in queer cultures and politics. A prospective PhD candidate, his research interests include queer and critical theory, spectrality and urban culture.

Ena Jansen

studied at the universities of Stellenbosch and Utrecht. She taught for sixteen years at the University of the Witwatersrand, where she obtained her PhD in 1992, before moving to the Netherlands in 2001, where she teaches and is a researcher in the Literature & Society department at the Free University. She is also Professor of South African Literature at the University of Amsterdam and research fellow at the University of Johannesburg. Her inaugural lecture on constructions of Jan van Riebeeck's translator Eva/Krotoa is available on the internet. Her publications include *Afstand en verbintenis. Elisabeth Eybers in Amsterdam* (1996 and 1998 – in Afrikaans and Dutch editions), as well as books and articles on the Boer War, migrant literature, city novels and the representation of families in literature. *Soos familie* (Like Family), her book on the representation of domestic workers in South African city texts, was published in May 2015 by Protea. The Dutch translation was published in 2016 by Cossee.

Geli Mademli

is a PhD candidate at the Amsterdam School of Cultural Analysis at the University of Amsterdam, as a scholar of the Greek State Scholarships Foundation, working on the intersection of media studies, archival studies and film museology. She studied Journalism and Mass Media (BA, Aristotle University of Thessaloniki), Film Theory (MA, University of Amsterdam) and Cultural Studies (MA Cum Laude, National University of Athens). For the last few years, she has been working for the Thessaloniki Int'l Film Festival as a program assistant, catalogue coordinator and editor of its annual publications, and she is also a freelance journalist, specializing in film and media. She is a member of the editorial board of the Journal of Greek Film Studies *FilmIcon* and a founding member of the non-profit organization Greek Architecture Syndicate.

Esther Peeren

is Associate Professor of Globalization and Media Studies at the University of Amsterdam, Vice-Director of the Amsterdam Center for Globalization Studies (ACGS) and Vice-Director of the Amsterdam School for Cultural Analysis (ASCA). She is the author of *The Spectral Metaphor: Living Ghosts and the Agency of Invisibility* (Palgrave, 2014) and *Intersubjectivities and Popular Culture: Bakhtin and Beyond* (Stanford UP, 2008), and co-editor of *The Shock of the Other: Situating Alterities* (Rodopi, 2007), *Representation Matters: (Re)Articulating Collective Identities in a Postcolonial World* (Rodopi, 2010), *Popular Ghosts: The Haunted Spaces of Everyday Culture* (Continuum, 2010) and *The Spectralities Reader* (Bloomsbury, 2013).

Paula Pustułka

has a PhD in Sociology from Bangor University. Her doctoral project (2010–2014) was dedicated to Polish migrant mothering in the United Kingdom and Germany. Her other research on migration includes projects on Polish Schooling in the UK (PAU, 2012) and "Nothing About Us Without Us," a study on migrant participation (ISP, 2013). She is currently a Researcher in the TRANSFAM project (Jagiellonian University, 2013–2016). Her scholarly interests encompass qualitative inquiries into the migration/family nexus, connections between mobility and personal lives, contemporary feminism, as well as postmodern framings of identities and belonging.

Luca Raineri

is a PhD candidate at the Sant'Anna School of Advanced Studies of Pisa and a member of the Oslo Research School of Peace and Conflict. He is currently working on a project that explores the link between border practices, international security and organized crime in the context of the conflict in Mali, in order to critically reconstruct the specificity of the geopolitics of the desert. His articles have appeared in *African Security* ("State, Secession, and Jihad: The Micropolitical Economy of Conflict in Northern Mali," with Francesco Strazzari) and in Italian reviews of international politics such as *Il Mulino – Rivista* online and *Limes*.

Ksenia Robbe

is Assistant Professor at the Leiden University Centre for the Arts in Society, University of Leiden, specializing in African and comparative literature. She received her PhD in English and American Literature and Culture from the University of Giessen with a dissertation on South African women's writing. She also holds degrees in African literatures and English language and translation from the University of St. Petersburg. Before Leiden, she taught at the universities of Giessen and Münster, and was a visiting scholar at the Faculty of Social Sciences in Freiburg and at the African Studies Centre in Cape Town. Her recently published book *Conversations of Motherhood: South African Women's Writing Across Traditions* is a comparative study focusing on ways of re-figuring history through the tropes and representations of motherhood in contemporary English and Afrikaans prose. Other publications include essays on the production of cultural theory in South Africa and on nostalgia and the re-writing of "transition" in the work of Antjie Krog. Her current research explores comparative perspectives on memory and social transformation in contemporary Russian and South African literature and art.

Mireille Rosello

is Professor of Literary and Cultural Analysis (LCA) at the University of Amsterdam. Within cultural studies, her main focus lies on gender studies and on diasporic, (post)colonial and globalization studies. Her most recent book publications include *What's Queer About Europe: Productive Encounters and Re-enchanting Paradigms* (co-edited with Sudeep Dasgupta, Fordham UP, 2014), *The Reparative in Narratives: Works of Mourning in Progress* (Liverpool UP, 2010) and *Postcolonial Hospitality: The Immigrant as Guest* (Stanford UP, 2001).

Magdalena Ślusarczyk

has a PhD in Sociology from Jagiellonian University (2005) and a Bachelor of Arts in German Studies (2002). She is Assistant Professor in the Department of Population Studies at the Institute of Sociology of Jagiellonian University. Research projects she has worked on include FeMiPol (focused on the integration of female migrants in the labor market and society) as well as research for the Ombudsman Office concerning migrant return issues and their reintegration into Polish society. Currently she is a researcher and WP leader in the TRANSFAM project "Doing Family in a Transnational Context," realized by a Jagiellonian University-led international consortium. Her main research interests are migration, family and educational systems.

Durgesh Solanki

is an MPhil Scholar at the Centre for Inclusive Development and Social Justice, Tata Institute of Social Sciences in Mumbai. His research areas include urbanization, spatial segregation and the manifestation of caste and race in cities in the global south. He has worked as the project coordinator for the Tata Institute of Social Sciences on a comparative research project exploring socio-spatial transformation and emerging forms of structural violence in three cities in the global south: Mumbai, Rio de Janeiro and Durban.

Hanneke Stuit

is Assistant Professor at the Literary and Cultural Analysis Department of the University of Amsterdam and a member of the Amsterdam School for Cultural Analysis (ASCA). Her book *Ubuntu Strategies: Constructing Spaces of Belonging in Contemporary South African Culture* (Palgrave, 2016) provides a new perspective on the Southern African concept of ubuntu that addresses the role of representation in its cultural production, studies its global dissemination and critically assesses the various approaches to ubuntu from different disciplines, including its recent commodification. She has published on ubuntu in the journal *Krisis* (2014) and in the edited volume *Representation Matters: (Re)articulating Collective Identities in a Postcolonial World* (Rodopi, 2010). She was also guest editor of the special issue "Shadow Histories: Transculturation and Narrative in Afrikaans" for the Dutch journal *Tijdschrift voor Nederlandse Taal- en Letterkunde* (2015).

Astrid Van Weyenberg

is Lecturer in Literary Studies at the Film and Literary Studies Department of Leiden University and a member of the Leiden University Centre for the Arts in Society (LUCAS). She is the author of *The Politics of Adaptation: Contemporary African Drama and Greek Tragedy* (Rodopi, 2013), which analyzes six South African and Nigerian dramatic texts through the thematic lenses of resistance, revolution, reconciliation and mourning. The focus is on how the politics of adaptation is constituted by the tension at play in the two-directional dynamic between adaptation and pre-text. Her current research focuses on narrative constructions of Europe in European cultural projects.

Doro Wiese

is Lecturer of Comparative Literature and Gender Studies at Utrecht University. She was trained in Film Studies and Literary Studies at the University of Hamburg. She received her PhD from Utrecht University, where she was a Marie Curie doctoral research fellow and a Junior Teacher in the Gender Studies Program/Media and Culture Studies Department. Her monograph *The Powers of the False: Reading, Writing, Thinking beyond Truth and Fiction* (Northwestern UP, 2014) reflects on how literature can make it possible to represent histories that are otherwise ineffable. Her current research aims to address forms of untranslatability in the globally circulating oeuvres of American Indian authors Leslie Marmon Silko, N. Scott Momaday and James Welch. In particular, this research will explore how their fictional configurations of time and space remain incommensurable for Western readers. Further interests include the relationship between literature and historiography, New Comparative Literature and untranslatability, intermediality, theories of affect and critiques of (neo-)colonialism.

Introduction: Peripheral Visions in the Globalizing Present

Esther Peeren, Hanneke Stuit and Astrid Van Weyenberg

Does it still make sense to speak of centers and peripheries? Globalization discourses, whether proposing a flattened world (Friedman) or one traversed by disjunctive flows (Appadurai), tend to stress the inadequacy of center-periphery models.[1] Yet it seems impossible to understand the globalizing present without making some distinction between what is (becoming) central and what is (becoming) peripheral in geographical, political, economic, social or cultural terms. People tend to be aware of whether they or their environment, communities, activities and creations are considered – from particular perspectives and in specific respects – as central or peripheral, and they understand that this has concrete, material effects, especially in terms of the capacity to effect changes in their own position or in the world at large. The intensification of global connectivity has not done away with inequalities and hierarchies, even if their distribution across the world has shifted as a result of, for example, the rise of the BRICS economies and the recent destabilization of the European Union. Calls have arisen, too, to acknowledge other epistemologies by provincializing and decentering Europe (Chakrabarty; West) or by turning Asia into a method (Chen). Consequently, as Mary Louise Pratt insists, to reject the terminology as outdated does not diminish the degree to which power relations continue to play out across center-periphery divisions at various levels of everyday life, from the local to the global. Such a move would only make these power relations, and especially the privileged position of that which is deemed or constructs itself as central, less accessible to analysis and critique:

> To deploy the terms *center* and *periphery* is of course to revive a vocabulary now seen as anachronistic, supposedly replaced by an unaligned

---

1 It should be noted, however, that Appadurai's oft-quoted statement that "the new global cultural economy has to be seen as a complex, overlapping, disjunctive order that cannot any longer be understood in terms of existing center-periphery models (even those that might account for multiple centers and peripheries)" (32) does not preclude the development of new center-periphery models for capturing globalization processes, perhaps not just by multiplying centers and peripheries but also by rendering them dynamic, relational and perspectival, as we aim to do in this volume.

concept of globalization. I wish to suggest, however, that it is arbitrary and unnecessary to regard the concept of globalization as replacing a center-periphery perspective. Indeed, to do so reauthorizes the center to function unmarked as a center.

PRATT 23

In this volume, we follow Pratt in insisting on the continuing relevance and explanatory force of thinking through the ways centers and peripheries are constituted in relation to each other, and seek to explore the implications of this for how people live their lives in the contemporary globalizing world. Because in most considerations of center-periphery relations the emphasis is placed on the influence – whether beneficial or detrimental – of the central on the peripheral, we shift the focus to the peripheral in order to ask where today's peripheries are located and what visions of past, present and future emerge from them. In doing this, we take up the peripheral in its broadest possible sense as referring to spatial locations, social, political and economic formations, identity constructions and cultural and aesthetic practices.

We view present-day peripheries, first of all, as dynamic, shifting realities that mark changing political, economic and cultural power relations. In the context of globalization, significant transformations are taking place with regard to which parts (of the world, of a particular region, nation or city) are considered to be at the core and which are becoming more tangential. The consequences of such transformations are far-reaching and include, for example, the rise of populist nationalism in states whose centrality is perceived as being under threat, or the ways in which everyday uses beyond the purposes of business or tourism are increasingly pushed to the periphery of metropolitan cities. At the same time, contact is intensifying across the board: not just between centers and peripheries, but also among centers and among peripheries. As Walter Mignolo and Freya Schiwy point out, peripheries come into contact with each other and provide alternative perspectives on presumed centers of cultural domination, even if crucial differences between these peripheries still exist. The Zapatista movement offers an example of such a "change in directionality" in terms of translation and transculturation: the translations between its four main languages (Tojolabal, Tzeltal, Tzotzil and Chol) and the Spanish of the Marxist-Leninist theories mobilized by the movement result in a profound mixture of cosmologies entering global political discourse: "dichotomies are dissolved because these multiple others challenge the center and critically engage with each other, on its interior and exterior borders" (Mignolo and Schiwy 21, 28). In order to gain better insight into these kinds of increasingly dynamic relations, it is imperative not only to investigate the

complex relationships of peripheries to centers, but also those between different (emerging) peripheries.

Secondly, we conceive of peripheries as complex and perspectival constructs fulfilling a variety of functions. Peripheries may be discerned on global, continental, national or local scales, and a place that is peripheral on one
scale, may be central on another. Similarly, what appears as peripheral from
one point of view may seem central from another. In terms of their function,
peripheries can manifest and be mobilized, among other possibilities, as zones
of exclusion (borderlands, ungovernable regions, media black spots), exclusivity (gated communities, off-the-beaten-track tourist sites, niche cultures and
media), extraction (of resources, labor or cultural forms), expression (creative subcultures, spiritual movements) or contestation (cultural or political
counter-movements, social media networks). While it is important to establish
what different peripheries have in common, it is therefore equally important
to consider particular peripheries in their specificity.

A third dimension of contemporary peripheries that requires careful reflection is their status as evaluative and affective modalities. Being deemed peripheral has profound consequences for the organization and assessment of
beings and matters, especially in terms of warranting attention, investment,
care or protection. Peripheries may be valued as sites to escape the pressures of
globalization, but can also become associated with less desirable effects of national, transnational and corporate policy, such as waste disposal, resource extraction, tax evasion or the containment of prisoners and unwanted migrants.
We want to suggest that peripheral spaces, social structures, cultural forms and
media practices yield different forms of subjectivity, affective investments and
political imaginations than central ones. At the same time, peripheries emerge
from specific contexts or encounters and can therefore neither be understood
as necessarily nostalgic or reactionary nor as inherently progressive.

The main aim of this volume is to shed new light on how today's peripheries are lived, imagined and mobilized in the context of rapidly advancing
globalization processes, and to take seriously not only external perspectives on
peripheries but also those emerging from within them, as well as the interplay
between the two. In concentrating on peripheral *visions*, moreover, we seek
to highlight how the peripheral – as that which, physiologically, can only be
partially, furtively and vaguely perceived – is not necessarily any more incon-
sequential or opaque than what lies in the center of the field of vision; in fact,
it can almost always be brought into focus by a change in viewing position or,
in narratological terms, a refocalization (Bal). Peripheral visions also imply a
sense of revelation, innovation and futurity, countering the lingering association of the peripheral with stagnation and backwardness.

This introduction begins by probing the etymology of the word "periphery" in order to lay bare its most salient characteristics and tensions, before outlining the dominant ways in which the peripheral has been theorized in world systems theory, postcolonial studies and globalization studies. Next, we develop our own understanding of peripheral vision and peripheral thinking. Finally, we provide an outline of the sections of this volume and the chapters they contain.

What is a Periphery?

Etymologically, "periphery" can be traced back to the Ancient Greek περιφέρεια (circumference, rounded surface, curve, arc of a circle), formed after the verb περιφέρειν (to carry round).[2] It is, thus, in origin, not so much a term of fixed location as one of movement that, significantly, implies a sense of burden. The *Oxford English Dictionary* primarily defines "periphery" as a boundary, circumference or perimeter. The periphery is what marks inside from outside, but it is difficult to say whether it is itself inside or outside, whether it is part of what it circumscribes or not. It is said to refer to the "external boundary or surface of a space or object" and to "the region, space, or area surrounding something," yet, when applied to the human body, it can refer not only to "the superficial or outer parts of the body," but also to "an organ," which would place it firmly on the inside. This question of whether the periphery is inside or outside is deeply relevant: when power relations are articulated through center-periphery distinctions, whether the periphery is considered part of the center (albeit distant from it) or whether it constitutes its border or is external to it has significant implications for the functions assigned to the periphery and for its ability to redefine the relationship to the center.

Notably, the OED definition of "peripheral" pairs its general meaning as "of, relating to, or situated on a periphery; constituting or characteristic of the circumference or external surface of something" with a figurative meaning of "marginal, not of direct concern."[3] The notion that what is peripheral is inessential and less vital than the non-peripheral is made explicit in the use of "peripheral" for "equipment that is used in conjunction with a computer *without being an integral or necessary part of one*" and in the use of "peripheral" for "the part of the nervous system other than the brain and spinal cord" (emphasis added). Here, the peripheral is useful, like a mouse or the ability to feel

---

2   *Oxford English Dictionary*, Third Edition (2005): periphery, *n.*

3   *Oxford English Dictionary*, Third Edition (2005): peripheral, *adj.* and *n.*

pain through the nerves in our extremities, but also expendable. If necessary, we can control the computer without the mouse and it is the central nervous system – particularly the brain – that separates life from death. Whereas in the case of computers and, to a lesser degree, the nervous system, it may be accurate to associate the peripheral with the supplementary, the transposition of this association to other types of peripheralities (geographical, political, economic, social, cultural) is what symbolically comes to legitimate relations of oppression, exploitation and neglect. It also problematically obfuscates how the peripheral does not necessarily live off the center (like a mouse powered by a computer), but is, on the contrary, often what the center lives off and profits from. In a profound sense, this parasitic position of the center with regard to the periphery in economic and other terms is a structural aspect of the relations between them, as is evidenced in the study of colonialism and, more recently, globalization.[4]

The *OED* recognizes the periphery as that which is exploited by the center – and simultaneously marginalized in order to conceal this exploitation – in the illustrative quotations it gathers under the definition of "periphery" as "the region, space, or area surrounding something; a fringe, margin." These quotations refer to "Spacious Peripheries of Enrichment" and to "the metropolis suck[ing] capital out of the periphery and us[ing] its power to maintain the economic, political, social, and cultural structure of the periphery." Curiously, however, a contradictory emphasis on the periphery's independence from the center is placed in the sentence that follows the above definition: "Now chiefly: the outlying areas of a region, most distant from or *least influenced by* some political, cultural or economic centre" (emphasis added). None of the quotations provided, however, actually endorse this supposedly current and prevalent sense (the entry was last updated in 2005). The closest one – "The marginal tribes on the periphery of an area are no longer truly representative of it" – pertains to a lack of likeness rather than a lack of influence between center and periphery.

Crucially, this incongruous definition points to a possible reading of the periphery as having a very different relation to the center than subordination or supplementarity. The peripheral becomes that which is most able to escape

---

4   As Comaroff and Comaroff argue in their introduction to *Theory from the South*, "the edges of empire" were "fertile staging grounds for ways of doing things that were not possible elsewhere"; they point to experiments in urban planning, brutally profitable methods of labor discipline, socially engineered regimes of public health and untried practices of "governance and extraction, bureaucracy and warfare, property and pedagogy" (5). They also emphasize that none of these ways of using the global South as a "petridish" are in the distant past (Comaroff and Comaroff 5).

the center's impact and thus potentially capable of developing independently from it. Significantly, the *OED* refrains from defining this type of peripherality solely in terms of spatial distance – it is "most distant from *or* least influenced by the centre" (emphasis added). With many border zones across the world ever-more tightly controlled and contested, it is important to realize that the periphery may also be located elsewhere than on the borderline and may manifest as that which the center cannot (or does not want to) touch and which, consequently, may be defined or may define itself as a space of potential freedom. While such spaces may be politically progressive and inclusive (communes, artist colonies), they can also be retrogressive and exclusive (cults, militias). The idea that the periphery is located at a considerable distance from the center is complicated, however, by the fact that center and periphery are often coextensive. Individuals, things or ideas can be both peripheral and central at the same time. In Alejandro González Iñárritu's film *Biutiful* (2010), for instance, the main character Uxbal can be said to be peripheral, considering that his name suggests a Roma background, he lives outside the city center of Barcelona and he considers himself a spirit medium. Yet, especially in relation to other peripheral (or perhaps subaltern) characters in the film, he occupies a central position, running a dubious yet profitable scheme hiring out illegal Asian workers to sweatshops and "managing" the African migrants who sell the goods produced there at the heart of Barcelona's city center.

The peripheral, then, can be inside or outside, and can be a space of dependency, oppression and exploitation as well as of independence and potential freedom. In addition, the *OED* recognizes that, especially in figurative uses that do not refer to a spatial relation, peripherality is less a fixed status than the result of an active process driven by established or emerging power structures. Thus, the entry for the transitive verb "peripheralize" defines it as "to consign to the fringes or periphery; to marginalize." Because of its transitivity, "peripheralize" always has a subject and an object: someone or something that peripheralizes and someone or something that is being peripheralized. One of the aims of this volume is to illuminate the workings, motivations and effects of peripheralization from both perspectives. How do peripheralizations unfold, what drives them and how and why are they perpetuated? Conversely, how do those who are (being) peripheralized experience and respond to this? Going one step further, we also ask whether there is such a thing as self-peripheralization, where subject and object coincide, and, if so, what might drive such a process of choosing to become or to remain peripheral. Before developing our approach to thinking the peripheral/ized further, however, a brief overview of how the center-periphery relation has been thought in world systems theory, postcolonial studies and globalization studies is apposite.

Theorizing Center-Periphery Relations

Immanuel Wallerstein's world systems theory sees the capitalist world economy dividing the globe into cores with "high-profit, high-technology, high-wage, diversified production," peripheries with "low-profit, low-technology, low-wage, less diversified production" and semi-peripheries with some characteristics of each (1976: 462).[5] The most dynamic of these categories is that of the semi-periphery, which, especially during global economic downturns, is able to exploit its in-between position to ascend to the core. But cores and peripheries are not stable either. While Wallerstein considers the system of "unequal exchange" that exists between and defines cores, peripheries and semi-peripheries as inherent to global capitalism and therefore as structural (1984: 38), his more recent work, in response to charges of "'nation-state centrism' and 'state structuralism'" stresses that, within this system, core and periphery are "a relation, not an essence" (2012: 525, 526). Particular countries, then, rather than *being* cores or peripheries, harbor different quantities of "core-like" and "peripheral processes" that may change over time. In other words, there may be "a seeming geographical correlation but geography does not define coreness or peripherality" (Wallerstein 2012: 526). Semi-peripheries are different in that there is no such thing as a "semi-peripheral process"; instead, semi-peripherality marks the position of a state in which core-like and peripheral processes roughly balance each other, prompting political decisions aimed at tipping this balance in favor of the core-like processes (Wallerstein 2012: 526).

World systems theory is committed to understanding the workings of the world capitalist order in order to challenge the inequalities on which it is founded and which it perpetuates. Thus, Janzen argues that the contributors to the 2011 edited volume *Immanuel Wallerstein and the Problem of the World: System, Scale, Culture*, including Wallerstein himself, suggest that "we would do well to reflect on the relationship of the contingent to the system, lest we end up celebrating the peripheral without making room to conceptualize the way out of the periphery" (7). However, while there indeed seems very little to celebrate about being peripheral within the capitalist world economy and it is certainly necessary to try to conceive of an economic system that would not require core-periphery inequalities, intersections between different forms of peripherality (spatial, economic, social, cultural) may also produce attachments and affordances that complicate a view of peripherality as always to be

---

5   For an overview of Wallerstein's world systems theory and its emergence as a critique of modernization theory influenced by the *Annales* school (Fernand Braudel), Marx and dependency theory (Fernando Henrique Cardoso), see Mishra.

opposed or escaped, as Sudeep Dasgupta, Durgesh Solanki, Luca Raineri, Doro Wiese, Geli Mademli and Matthieu Foucher variously suggest in their contributions to this volume.

Partly in response to world systems theory, postcolonial theorists have pointed out that the inequalities produced by the capitalist world economy cannot be fully understood without exploring its historical reliance on colonial exploitation, which should be seen as thoroughly intertwined with and in fact preceding the discourse of modernity that divided the world into economic, social, cultural and political centers and peripheries. According to Walter Mignolo, "modern world-system analysis brings colonialism into the picture, although as a derivative rather than a constitutive component of modernity, since it does not yet make visible coloniality, the other (darker?) side of modernity" (2002: 60). Crucially, Mignolo sees coloniality, or "the irreducible colonial difference,"[6] appearing in the dependency theory of Enrique Dussel and Anibal Quijano as "the difference between center and periphery, between the Eurocentric critique of Eurocentrism and knowledge production by those who participated in building the modern/colonial world and those who have been left out of the discussion" (2002: 63).[7] Here, the peripheral is at once a space of exclusion – or, in Mignolo's terms, exteriority (2002: 75) – and a privileged space of and for material and epistemological transformation, since for those living in the periphery the relations of dependency and exploitation forged by the expansion of coloniality/modernity are not to be denied. Only from a peripheral

---

6   The colonial difference is defined as "a connector that, in short, refers to the changing faces of colonial differences throughout the history of the modern/colonial world-system and brings to the foreground the planetary dimension of human history silenced by discourses centering on modernity, postmodernity, and Western civilization" (Mignolo 2002: 61–2).

7   Mignolo uses the center-periphery opposition while also suggesting it may no longer be adequate for the late twentieth-century face of colonial difference: "If dependency in the modern/colonial world-system is no longer structured under the center/periphery dichotomy, this does not mean that dependency vanishes because this dichotomy is not as clear today as it was yesterday. On the other hand, *interdependency* is a term that served to restructure the coloniality of power around the emergence of transnational corporations" (2002: 62). Like Appadurai's statement quoted in footnote 1, Mignolo's formulation is ambivalent: in his view, the center/periphery dichotomy has not disappeared, but has become less clearly defined. At the same time, the colonial difference now expresses itself as also structured along relations of interdependency that run across the center/periphery dichotomy. In a later work, Mignolo proposes thinking in terms of internal and external borders – "not discrete entities but rather moments of a continuum in colonial expansion and in changes of national imperial hegemonies" (2012: 33) – as an alternative to the linear, territorial logic of world systems theory's triad of center, periphery and semi-periphery.

perspective, then, can the colonial difference be apprehended, capitalism be looked at otherwise and "alternative futures" imagined (Mignolo 2002: 76). This is not to say that a critique from the center is impossible or without value – Mignolo praises Wallerstein for mounting precisely such a central critique (2002: 78) – but that certain dimensions of the capitalist/modernist/colonialist organization of the world are only accessible from a peripheral point of view.

The emergence of a distinct peripheral perspective, which Mignolo elsewhere conceptualizes as "border thinking" or "border gnosis" (2012), from places exteriorized as lacking modernity and, consequently, the capacity to produce valid knowledge, is a complicated process, as Paulina Aroch-Fugellie's chapter on Africa's continuing exclusion from global circuits of intellectual value emphasizes. In her seminal text "Modernity and Periphery," Mary Louise Pratt discusses how the colonizing center defined modernity as emerging and diffusing from its (European) location, so that the colonized periphery could be constituted as spatially outside and temporally behind it in order to be forced into a "condition of imposed receptivity" (Pratt 35). Under this condition, the periphery cannot refuse what the center chooses to disseminate; it can only decide *how* to receive what arrives from the center, with each choice having particular, more or less dispossessing consequences. Arguing that the prevalent attitudes of contradiction, complementarity and differentiation do not escape the logic of imposed receptivity, Pratt distinguishes three aesthetic strategies that go some way toward redefining the periphery's lack (as defined from the center) as a plenitude: Oswald de Andrade's anthropophagist manifesto's resolve to absorb only the useful and expunge the rest; the way frontier aesthetics positions the periphery as a "site of creative authenticity"; and the way Latin American literature's engagement with the rural and the popular shows how the center's notion of modernity can only enter the periphery through "the very things that at the center are defined as its others" (Pratt 42–3).

Benita Parry equally rejects the reduction of peripheral modernities to entirely passive "shadow imitations" of metropolitan modernity (17), arguing, in stronger terms than Pratt, that the center's "message, bearing exploitation, inequality and injustice, was refused by significant numbers of the literate and illiterate" in the periphery (16). The secularly educated, in particular, are seen as capable of developing a nuanced position towards metropolitan modernity that, in imaginative texts, registers as "an affection for and a dislocation from tradition, a propulsion toward but not an integration into the modern as this had been received by way of a predatory colonialism" (Parry 16–7). The work of Leslie Marmon Silko, discussed in this volume by Doro Wiese, may be considered as a powerful example of an ambivalent mobilization of a peripheralized tradition that, in its cultivation of untranslatability, constitutes a refusal of the center's construction of modernity, while at the same time challenging Parry's privileging of the secular.

What remains in both Pratt's and Parry's account is the inability of the periphery to completely evade the center's influence: it has to relate to the center in some way, as even a refusal constitutes an acknowledgment of the center's power to incite a response. However, perhaps complete autonomy is not a viable aim. If we follow Mignolo in seeing the periphery as a constructed exteriority rather than as a true outside, it makes sense that, being part of the same world-system as the center, the periphery would neither be able to function independently nor to return to some untouched, unspoiled state before modernity/coloniality.[8] Mediating between the extremes of cultural preservationism and cultural imperialism, Kwame Anthony Appiah offers "contamination" as a counter-ideal to romantic notions of cultural purity and as a way of understanding how cultural influence actually works on a local level (111). Not only do "people in each place make their own uses even of the most famous global commodities," he explains, but to overstate the influence of the center on the periphery also reveals a false and patronizing gesture which treats the latter as a tabula rasa "on which global capitalism's moving finger writes a message" (Appiah 111, 113).

While the periphery cannot totally ignore the center, neither can the center fully disavow the periphery – not under colonialism, where the center also received from the periphery in unanticipated never entirely controllable ways, as accounts of colonial intimacy have shown,[9] and certainly not under contemporary conditions of globalization. Nowadays, there is not only intensified mobility from peripheries to centers and between different peripheries, but centers have also multiplied so that they can be played off against each other: under certain circumstances, peripheries can now refuse what one center (Europe or the US) has to offer by entering into a relation with another center (Russia or China). One of the emphases of this volume is that while, on the one hand, centers often impose themselves on peripheries with extreme gravity, so that dismissing the center-periphery model altogether would mean losing a powerful way of accounting for "dramatically uneven development,"

---

8   Thus, Mignolo sees border epistemologies "emerging from the wounds of colonial histories, memories, and experiences" (2012: 37) rather than from what came before. Parry, while stressing that peripheral modernities rely on "reverberations of rediscovered histories," also cautions that "this respect for the past cannot be dismissed as nativist and regressive" (21, 17).

9   On colonial intimacy, see, for example, Homi Bhabha's *The Location of Culture*, Ann Laura Stoler's *Carnal Knowledge and Imperial Power: Race and the Intimate in Colonial Rule*, Heike Ingeborg Schmidt's "Colonial Intimacy: The Rechenberg Scandal and Homosexuality in German East Africa" and Neville Hoad's *African Intimacies: Race, Homosexuality, and Globalization*.

center-periphery relations are, on the other hand, always to some extent multidirectional. They exhibit a reciprocal dimension that is foregrounded and en-
hanced under contemporary conditions of globalization (Young 615).

Timothy Brennan motivates the importance of continuing to think globalization's uneven development in terms of center-periphery relations by
pointing to the way peripheries yield profit for global capitalism's centers
not just materially, as "physical spaces where cheap manufacturing and resource extraction flourish," but also in the form of an idea (101). He calls
this the periphery's "image-function," seen to convey "a sense of the rules of
perception – those demands made under capitalism in a phase when production has come prominently to include information as one of its commodities"
(101). As long as the periphery serves a material economic function, the idea of
it will be "preserved by way of a fiercely defended set of regulations governing
what can and cannot be said about it" (Brennan 101). In Brennan's view, postcolonial critiques miss the mark by challenging the idea of the periphery without
acknowledging the material economic relations that require it to be kept in
place. At the same time, he chides economic theory (both from the imperial
myth school and dependency theory) for ignoring cultural theorists' insistence
on the role played in economic behavior by affect, desire and ideology – by that
which is not immediately observable or quantifiable, yet exerts considerable
influence on global economic exchange.

For Brennan, the image-function of the periphery in the globalizing world is
essentially to obscure; it works to create a zone of invisibility characterized by
"blindness to the recidivist elements of the new economy, suppression of first
world material dependencies, and ignorance of the warehousing of labor" (112).
The way the dominant discourses of the global economy picture capitalism as
having reached a phase in which "production has come prominently to include
information as one of its commodities" conceals the vast quantity of industrial
labor still provided by the periphery, as well as its essential value as a source
of cheap exploitable resources (accessed through, among other practices, land
grabbing and biopiracy) and a site of "soft" corporate regulation (Brennan 101).
In literature, desolate portrayals of the global periphery, even when intended
as critiques of global capitalism, play into the image-function afforded to the
periphery by "remind[ing] the denizens of tenement halls that they are, for all
that, members of the winning side" and thus keeping the underprivileged of
the center from rebelling against their own peripheralization (Brennan 117).
In this way, the periphery as a carefully managed and circumscribed idea veils
the actual workings of global capitalism and pre-empts solidarity between the
dispossessed of the center and the periphery.

Brennan's view of the image-function of the periphery is, however, not
wholly pessimistic. Much like Pratt and Parry, he sees avant-garde art as one

of the "important psychological and emotional outlets" related to the image-function of the periphery (Brennan 118). It allows the periphery to act as a "repository of counter-modernity" capable of providing different values from those propagated by the capitalist center and even of generating hope (Brennan 118). For Jean and John Comaroff, the periphery pluralizes the idea of modernity in an even more radical way. Rather than linking peripheries to notions of "counter-modernity" or "alternative modernity," they insist on the fact that Afromodernity, for instance, is a *vernacular*, just like Euromodernity itself. The idea of "alternative modernity," even though it was coined to "move beyond the premodern and the modern," obscures that modernities from the South, the East and elsewhere in fact developed at the same time as Euromodernity did, albeit not independently from it (Comaroff and Comaroff 9–11). In the context of contemporary world-historical processes, these modernities are "disrupting received geographies of core and periphery, relocating southward – and, of course, eastward as well – some of the most innovative and energetic modes of producing value," as well as altering "the lineaments of global modernity *tout court*" (Comaroff and Comaroff 7).

There is, then, a possibility for multiple image-functions of the periphery to coexist and contest each other. The periphery may be imaged from the center so that, as an idea, it comes to support its own material exploitation, or it can be imaged from the periphery (in accordance with Mignolo's notion of decolonization) as a site promoting

> the art of conversation, the decrease of speed, the altruistic act of hospitality, and the decommercialization of artistic performance, all of them important psychological and emotional outlets for the negative energy overwhelming a metropolis characterized by anxiety, fear, and restlessness.
>
> BRENNAN 118

Although this particular citation seems to once again put the periphery in service of the center, as offering potential relief to those occupying global cities, we want to take up Brennan's suggestion that the periphery's image-function, though heavily policed in dominant discourse, maintains a certain flexibility that aesthetic creation is particularly adept at exploiting. As the chapters by Paula Blair, Ksenia Robbe and Matthieu Foucher insist, it is through aesthetic techniques that different meanings and values may be assigned to the periphery, and that those dimensions obscured by the zone of invisibility Brennan sees produced by the dominant image-function of the periphery may be brought to light.

One particular work of art that extensively explores the image-function of the periphery is J.M. Coetzee's novel *Waiting for the Barbarians* (1980), which will be briefly discussed in order to outline what is at stake in theoretical, cultural and social uses of the periphery. Coetzee's novelistic treatment of peripherality lays bare a spatial, discursive, physical and emotional placement of the periphery that is decidedly normative in its connotations. *Waiting for the Barbarians* takes place in a nameless settlement on the border of "the Empire." The settlement is run by the Magistrate, an elderly man who spends his time hunting, philandering and studying the remnants of an ancient civilization he discovers in the desert around the outpost. The novel opens at a moment when a number of officials from the Empire's capital visit the town in order to investigate the threat emanating from the "barbarian" people living in the direct vicinity of it – officially across the Empire's outer border, but in and close to the settlement in practice. Over time, the investigation escalates into a military campaign meant to push the barbarians back further, so the Empire's provincial periphery (here seen as lying inside the border) can continue to share in the civilization diffused by the Empire's center. As the Magistrate, who functions as protagonist, narrator and focalizer, signals early in the narrative, the barbarian threat seems rather elusive, at least from his perspective: "Of this unrest I myself saw nothing ... Show me a barbarian army, and I will believe" (Coetzee 9). Whether or not the barbarians actually pose a threat to the settlement or the Empire at large remains a matter of who is looking at the situation and depends on a particular politics of vision; in the end, the outpost is never attacked. The military campaign does a lot of damage, however, to both the settlement and the barbarians in its deployment of rampant violence against anything that is considered not Empirical or "not central."

Coetzee's novel negotiates and complicates the center-periphery dynamic in powerful and suggestive ways, particularly in its description of how the people in the town – its inhabitants, the soldiers that come from the center of the Empire to defend it and the Magistrate himself – respond to the barbarian threat from outside the border. This response is characterized by a powerful mix of disgust, (sexual) fascination and fear:

> There is no woman living along the frontier who has not dreamed of a dark barbarian hand coming from under the bed to grip her ankle, no man who has not frightened himself with visions of the barbarians carousing his home, breaking the plates, setting fire to the curtains, raping his daughters.
>
> COETZEE 9

This citation lays bare the disconcerting emotional, psychological and social structures that underpin the construction of and response to the category of the barbarians. The latter are constructed in the public imaginary as a threat that can, at any moment, violently invade the settlement, while this imaginary simultaneously glosses over the fact that many barbarians already participate in everyday life there; the town's inhabitants trade avidly with them and the barbarian prisoners who happen to be held captive by the Magistrate when Empire arrives are held prisoner in the town itself (40–1, 4).

In portraying the liminal position of the barbarians as, in the Empire's eyes, too close for comfort and as leading to a violent campaign of externalization, the novel traces what Mireille Rosello in this volume calls the "grammar of peripheralization." According to this grammar, the center wields and seeks to consolidate its power by actively distancing those elements that it deems undesirable, confining them to a periphery that may lie inside the border or that may be pushed outwards beyond it. Revealing and describing the rules of this grammar, as both Coetzee's novel and Neill Blomkamp's film *District 9* (discussed by Rosello) do, is crucial in any attempt to revisit the idea of the periphery as potentially productive.

Peripheral Vision

Coetzee's novel sticks to the point of view of the Magistrate, so a sustained perspective of the barbarian side remains absent. Yet, in its portrayal of the Magistrate's relationship with a barbarian girl, who, as a result of torture by the Empire's investigators has lost central focus in her sight, the novel also engages this volume's focus on the idea of peripheral vision and on how the biases of vision may be otherwise imagined. As feminist philosopher Donna Haraway explains, vision is not just something we do in a biological and neu- rological sense. In "The Persistence of Vision," she argues that vision "is *always* a question of the power to see – and perhaps of the violence implicit in our visualizing practices" (680). In order to look at such violence responsibly, it is necessary to undo Western cultural narratives about objectivity, which are "allegories of the ideologies of the relations of what we call mind and body, of distance and responsibility" (Haraway 678). The Magistrate's attitude to the barbarian girl aligns closely with this critique on the ideological repercussions of regarding "vision" as an objective and neutral denominator of knowledge, because it complicates the relation between vision and understanding.

In the middle of the girl's vision is a blurry spot, because of which she can only see from the corner of her eyes. Despite this visual impairment, however, she is perfectly capable of "seeing" and understanding the Magistrate for what he is. Discerning that his interest in her and her scars revolves around a scrupulous attempt to decipher and understand her, which causes him to lose himself in his own dislocated desires, she resists his intrusive inquiries about her torture at the hands of the Empire. The Magistrate, on the other hand, has "normal" or "full" vision, and his assumption that the girl can be seen objectively at all renders him blind to the acuity of her alternative perspective. Throughout their liaison, he fails to see the girl in any other way but as a tortured and domesticated body to which he should, but is ultimately unable to gain full access:

> I look into the eye. Am I to believe that gazing back at me she sees nothing – my feet perhaps, parts of the room, a hazy circle of light, but at the centre, where I am, only a blur, a blank? I pass my hand slowly in front of her face, watching her pupils. I cannot discern any movement. She does not blink. But she smiles: "Why do you do that? Do you think I cannot see?"
>
> COETZEE 33

Significantly, what is most disturbing to the Magistrate is that he, who is supposedly at the center (of her vision, but also of civilization and power), may appear to the girl only as a "blur" or even a "blank." His obsession with the scars on the girl's eyes is driven by his curiosity about what she can see *of him* and is thus ultimately not about her at all. Most notably, despite her repeated reminders that she can actually see, he keeps referring to her as "blind" (see, for example, 27, 31, 33, 64, 77). In the course of the novel, however, his centrality is revealed to be an illusion not only in relation to the girl but also in relation to the Empire itself. When he returns the girl to "her people" (even though there is no evidence that she has ever met these particular barbarians before), she has no qualms about leaving him. Upon his return to the settlement, moreover, his marginal position as Magistrate of a border town who has unauthorized contact with the barbarians leads to his own incarceration and torture at the hands of Empire. Ultimately, then, the Magistrate's own vision is as peripheral as the girl's, and the metaphorical affliction of his central sight undoes any straightforward relation between seeing and knowing.

From a psychophysiological perspective, peripheral vision, also known as eccentric vision, is a part of the vision of humans located on either side of the fovea, a small groove at the back of the eyeball covered with light receptor cells. Foveal vision covers everything within two degrees of the center of the eye, while anything outside this range is called peripheral vision. This limit is more gradual than absolute, however, as the part of vision up to eight degrees from the center is still referred to as the central visual field (Strasburger, Rentschler and Jüttner 3). The light receptor cells covering the fovea are mostly cone cells, which are attuned to bright light and allow people to see color and fine details. They are also sensitive to movement. Rod cells, which are prevalent in peripheral areas of the eye, function better in dim light, enabling people to see in the dark (albeit without much color). Peripheral vision, however, is not just the result of the distribution of cone and rod cells in the eye. Other, more complex cells also determine how we see, and there are strong indications that sustained attention to particular objects influences vision. Strasburger, Rentschler and Jüttner suggest, for instance, that human vision seems to be particularly biased towards the center of vision and explain that viewers, much like Coetzee's Magistrate, tend to assume that the most important information is presented at the center of any image (41).

The Magistrate's inability to see is even more poignant in this context, since even though what is peripheral to him is in fact looking and speaking back at him, he seems unable to process this information. As such, he displays a non-physiological blind spot for what is going on in the periphery of his conceptual, discursive, social and visual world, which remains closed off to him even as he is staring right at it. In contrast, the barbarian girl is able to see eccentrically, both in the technical sense and in the sense of seeing differently or otherwise. With regard to the girl's ability to see sidelong, it is noteworthy that peripheral vision seems to provide more diagnostic information about a person's surroundings than the center of human sight, if only because eccentric vision covers a much larger part of the field of vision. Especially important in this respect is peripheral vision's function in "gist recognition" (Strasburger, Rentschler and Jüttner 41). Taking into account that the recognition of individual images or graphs in peripheral vision tends to be negatively influenced by crowding (by the fact that these images occur within a particular spatial distance from each other that makes it difficult to discern them from the corner of one's eye), peripheral vision is actually "better" at recognizing, for instance, the gist of landscape scenes than central vision is. Although the reasons for this are not yet well understood, Strasburger, Rentschler and Jüttner do suggest that a coarse categorization and unification of fragmentary information about scenes, objects, words and emotional expressions on faces takes place in peripheral vision, even when measured at larger distances from foveal vision (43–4). Thus, it seems that peripheral vision is crucial in recognizing shapes, patterns and textures in ways that support, complement and perhaps even makes possible the detail, color and movement perception in foveal vision.[10] This foregrounds one of the main claims of this volume, namely that periphery and center exist in a dialectic relation in which each is influenced by the other, even if not always to an equal extent.

Crucially, peripheral vision can be improved through training: "Of particular relevance for basic *and* clinical research is the possibility of improving peripheral form vision by way of learning ... Perceptual learning may enhance elementary functions such as orientation discrimination, contrast sensitivity, and types of acuity" (Strasburger, Rentschler and Jüttner 3). This suggests that the ability to see – or not to see – something is not fixed, but susceptible to exercise and to habituation. In more conceptual terms, peripheral vision can be taught to recognize and process information that was difficult to recognize before, and this information could potentially also be made available to central vision if it causes us to turn our head.

Ultimately, however, the aim of this volume is not necessarily to turn what is peripheral into what is central. What may be much more crucial is to validate the peripheral alongside the central as offering something not inherently worse or better, but something different that should be taken into account as we try to understand the world and its ongoing globalization. Learning from Coetzee's novel, we should not dismiss the barbarian girl's impaired vision or even try to fix it, but look into the specific insights it has to offer. Accordingly, the chapters in this volume all, in different ways, address the consequences of taking the binary between center and periphery, and its metaphorically charged normativity, for granted. They propose to take visions developed in the periphery as seriously as visions of the periphery that originate from the center.

Peripheral Thinking

Similar to how peripheral vision in the physiological sense, when not properly understood, is taken as inferior or at best supplemental to central vision, the

---

10   Strasburger, Rentschler and Jüttner do not draw this conclusion in the article discussed here. We are building on the fact that peripheral vision is important for gist *recognition*, a term which implies that "new" information is difficult to perceive and that better sight is based on recognizing shapes one has already seen before. Nonetheless, central and peripheral vision do seem to "need" each other, and appear to be mutually constructed in a constant oscillating movement, with central vision filling out the details provided by peripheral vision's gist recognition and framing.

notion of peripheral thinking has been used in social psychology to denote a lesser form of cognitive engagement. Richard E. Petty and John T. Cacioppo distinguish two routes by which people may be persuaded of something: a central one where changes in attitude result "from a person's careful consideration of information that reflects what that person feels are the true merits of a particular attitudinal position" and a peripheral one where such changes "do not occur because the person has diligently considered the pros and cons of the issue; they occur because the person associates the attitude issue or object with positive or negative cues or makes a simple inference about the merits of the advocated position based on various simple cues in the persuasion context" (70).[11]

Here, the peripheral is associated with a lack of care, diligence and complexity. Peripheral thinkers are people whose "ability to scrutinize the message arguments is relatively low" or who are "unmotivated" to do so, for example because the message's personal relevance is low (Petty and Cacioppo 71). In being designated "*cognitive misers*," the latter group, moreover, is associated with a deliberate withholding that carries connotations of immorality rather than, for example, with a sensible desire to conserve cognitive energy for more pressing issues (Cacioppo et al. 1033, emphasis in text). Instead of seeing central and peripheral thinkers as differing "chronically in their tendency to engage in and enjoy effortful cognitive endeavors," this difference might just as well be seen as incidental or even strategic (Cacioppo et al. 1038).

For social psychologists, however, peripheral thinking is invariably dangerous because it opens people up to being manipulated and duped. By deliberately creating "limited-thinking situations," even those who are not normally cognitive misers can be made to privilege peripheral cues over substantive arguments, as has been shown with regard to the use of familiar phrases in commercial messages (Howard 231) and the marketing practices of online pharmacies (Orizio et al.).[12] While in a consumer-protection context, revealing such practices is necessary and laudable, the generalized dismissal of peripheral thinking is based on the debatable assumption that it is always possible to

---

11   Petty and Cacioppo later specify the "simple" inferences and cues mentioned here as the presumed expertise or likeability of the one making the argument, the sheer number of arguments presented or information about how others felt about the issue.

12   Orizio et al. conclude that, by focusing on peripheral cues, "online pharmacies sell the promise of providing the desired products in an easy and inexpensive way, focusing the consumers' attention on aspects that they might find attractive, but which are irrelevant, secondary and fundamentally distorting in the perspective of being autonomous in the management of their health" (975).

determine, in an objective manner, which arguments are strong, relevant and valid, and which are not. In addition, such dismissal relies on unquestioned notions of rationality and information, and a blanket rejection of, for example, emotions, which, according to Orizio et al., "distract from critical thinking" (974).

Instead of dismissing peripheral thinking as not really thinking at all and therefore as inevitably treacherous, it is also possible to conceive of it as a different form of thinking with its own merits. This is exemplified by South African artist William Kentridge in a recent lecture on "Peripheral Thinking." Drawing on his own practice, Kentridge relates how every attempt to focus on a singular, coherent subject or thought is immediately disturbed because of all the peripheral thoughts that arise. As an example of a creative process in which "every encounter with the world is a mixture of that which comes towards us, which the world brings to us, and that which we project onto it," he lists all the things that come to mind as he tries to focus on the drawing of a tree (Kentridge n. pag.).

The tree, in Kentridge's example, is at the center and all the other thoughts are at the periphery, "coming down to sit down or weigh down or crack the branches of the tree." Whether these thoughts will make the tree richer or more meaningful, or whether they will change or perhaps ultimately even destroy it, remains unpredictable. Yet, no matter the outcome, "the tree can never just be the tree itself," as histories, memories and associations are always a part of what it is. Such seemingly extraneous thoughts, then, serve as "reminders of the things you are not focused on" and make up a "peripheral vision that is akin to peripheral thoughts." Kentridge also introduces the idea of the "porousness of focus," a paradoxical combination of words, as "focus" implies the stabilization of a single thought that, in part, relies on keeping other, possibly distracting thoughts at bay, while that which is "porous" by definition remains exposed and vulnerable to all that may permeate its surface. Here, this vulnerability is revealed as productive, as allowing for extraneous influences to become part of the focus and thereby preventing knowledge from sedimenting as rigid truth.

Peripheral thinking conceived in this way recognizes that the periphery is always already part of the center and that, in Kentridge's words, "focusing solely on the centre is in fact removing the centre itself," because "the meaning of the centre is made by the periphery" (n. pag.). Kentridge's is a creative and aesthetic model, but can also be seen as ethical in the way it calls for openness to what comes to us from beyond the borders of what we think we already know. Revisiting the periphery from this perspective allows for a renewed understanding of the center by virtue of what was initially excluded from it. Peripheral thinking, in short, rather than opening us up to manipulation may, when we open ourselves up to it, propel our thinking in unforeseen directions, just as peripheral vision can lead us to see more rather than less.

Outline

The thirteen chapters that make up this volume develop new accounts of the peripheral – in terms of how it comes into being; its functions, meanings and effects; its relation to what is deemed central or also peripheral; and the eccentric visions of the past, present and future that may emerge from it. They do so by analyzing case studies from different parts of the world involving a range of social and cultural processes and practices. The chapters are grouped into four sections: theorizing the peripheral, peripheral spaces, peripheral mobilities and peripheral aesthetics.

The opening section focuses on theoretical conceptions of peripherality. Specifically, its first two chapters explore how peripheries are constructed and maintained as spaces of exclusion and exploitation that should, however, also be seen as constitutive of the center and as harboring a vital potential for thinking and acting otherwise. The other two chapters concretize this potential in terms of, respectively, a politics of indifference that recognizes differences between places, subjects and bodies without reducing them to set identities, locations or oppositions, and a practice of untranslatability that circulates peripheralized meanings in the purported center without rendering them fully accessible. In this way, the periphery is foregrounded less as derivative from or dependent on the center than as a site of irreducible alterity generating its own worldscapes.

Mireille Rosello presents a detailed reading of Neill Blomkamp's 2009 film *District 9*, in which a population of stranded aliens – and the man who gradually becomes one of them – is driven further and further away from the city of Johannesburg and, simultaneously, ever more rigidly separated from the category of the human. The film is seen to draw attention to the way peripheries do not simply exist, but are actively produced by an exclusive and often violent process of spatial and social peripheralization emanating from the center. This process is standardized and, consequently, functions as a grammar encompassing both the rules and their exceptions. Contesting such a "grammar of peripheralization" is difficult, since all attempts to rehabilitate the periphery end up reaffirming the binary it has been placed in. Nevertheless, Rosello argues that *District 9*, by exposing the workings and effects of this grammar to the viewer and by presenting its protagonist and its own genre as mixed (human-alien and science fiction-documentary), creates room for an "anti-peripheralization

counter-narrative." The logic at work here is not one of reversal (periphery becoming center and vice versa, leaving the binary structure in place) but one of
contiguity: if an alien can be, at the same time, a human, and a science fiction
film can be a documentary, then periphery and center can also relate in as yet
unrealized ways.

The second chapter reminds us that the periphery is itself radically differentiated across the globe. Paulina Aroch-Fugellie examines the specific position
of Africa in the post-Fordist capitalist world-system and its circuits of symbolic
capital. Africa, she argues, is not just a periphery in Wallerstein's sense of a
location for cheap production, but also an *infra-periphery*. On the one hand, it
fulfills functions that support the world-system, such as harboring a vast labor
reserve, while, on the other, it is reduced to a useless realm of abjection. According to Aroch-Fugellie, this duality is replicated in the global production
of intellectual value, with Africa systematically excluded from the capacity to
produce theory as self-reflexivity, while also confirming theory's scarcity and
thus its value. In the face of this, Aroch-Fugellie proposes a historiographical
approach able to validate a different intellectual history. The work of Tanzanian political economist Issa Shivji on the neocolonial practices of NGOs in Africa is taken as exemplary of this approach. Shivji is seen to produce theory not
as symbolic capital for speculation, but as a basis for societal transformation.

Whereas Rosello and Aroch-Fugellie stress the dispossessions resulting
from processes of peripheralization set in motion and sustained from the center, Sudeep Dasgupta aims to think the periphery without a center. He does
so by developing, through an analysis of Sébastien Lifshitz's 2004 film *Wild
Side*, the notion of a politics of indifference. This politics is connected to an
aesthetic figuring of the sensuous as the realm that marks the self's inherent
displacement from stable, singular identity. Dasgupta cites Barthes's concept
of the Neutral as that which proposes living aporias as creation and discusses
his account of visiting Morocco, where language (and its penchant for stereotype) is bypassed in favor of images that, because of their vacancy, facilitate a
sensuous, relational understanding rather than a masterful knowing. Through
a similar strategy of figuration, *Wild Side*'s presentation of images as fragments
is seen to generate "an ethics of discretion and respect." The three main characters' ostensible peripherality – in terms of geographical location, nationality,
sexuality and language – is undone as fixed identity by the way these fragments
are set into relation, forming a dynamic process in which new relationalities
constantly emerge. Significantly, Dasgupta insists that this does not constitute
an aestheticization of peripheralization or a denial of its violence, but rather a
way of rendering peripheralized subjects present on terms other than those of
the center without forcing them into full exposure.

The final chapter in this section, by Doro Wiese, also finds value in the periphery holding something back. Developing the notion of untranslatability to include narrative forms and tropes, Wiese explores the work of American Indian author Leslie Marmon Silko to suggest that the relation between center and periphery is transformed rather than merely reversed when what was once peripheralized begins to circulate in the center without rendering itself fully legible. Silko's narratives remain in part opaque for those readers not intimately acquainted with the indigenous culture they derive from. By making this opacity perceptible as significant, yet untranslatable meaning rather than as absence or lack, these texts pre-empt dismissive or exoticizing responses and demonstrate that the periphery produces its own unique, valuable forms of being and knowing. This, Wiese argues, constitutes a democratic project that creates room for "alternative worldscapes." The condition of imposed receptivity Pratt ascribes to the periphery in the colonial situation, as discussed above, is here creatively transformed not just by having the center also receive from the periphery, but by rendering a full, uncomplicated reception impossible and thus forcing readers from the center to experience some of the frustrations peripheralized subjects are routinely faced with.

Although visions from the periphery are as fractional and diverse as those from the center, they allow us to learn about how peripherality is experienced and imagined within particular locales. Of course, such perspectives do not exist in isolation from the center, if only because the lived realities in peripheralized spaces are inherently entwined with the forces of globalization. Still, drawing attention not just to what is projected onto but also to what emerges from within particular peripheralized spaces helps to challenge traditional (often distorted) representations and allows for new visions to arise. The three chapters in the second section do exactly that: by zooming in on particular larger and smaller peripheral spaces (the Sahara Desert, housing quarters in Mumbai and the South African backyard), they give room to the particular practices, values and knowledges that surface from within them.

Luca Raineri turns to the Sahara Desert, which is traditionally qualified as an empty and irrelevant space, romanticized as an empty stretch of sandy dunes or perceived primarily as a border separating sub-Saharan from North Africa. He deconstructs such representations and discusses how military uses of the desert that put the Sahara at the center of global security concerns challenge its supposed peripheral status. These uses, Raineri demonstrates, continue to rely on the idea of an exclusive border (emphasizing national sovereignty and private property) and take into account neither the actual geography of the Sahara space nor the way in which nomadic actors inhabit and use it. Invoking the perspective of such local actors, Raineri reveals alternative patterns of mobility and connectivity, offering a different interpretation of the Saharan space and of its place in the contemporary globalizing world.

Like Raineri, Durgesh Solanki sheds light on how global processes affect a particular, local place. Through an ethnographic study of conservancy workers' quarters in Mumbai, he investigates the ways in which urban spatial planning, marked by processes of neo-liberalization and globalization, keeps the traditional Hindu caste system in place. Housing and occupation emerge as tools that segregate and peripheralize Dalits (formally referred to as "untouchables") not only spatially but also socially, economically and politically. Familiar with the area and belonging to the same caste group as the people whose experiences he examines, Solanki uses self-ethnography to try to understand what it means to live in a state of inherited peripherality. This chapter, then, is also about the specific position of the analyst in relation to what he or she is analyzing, and about the insights that this might generate.

Ena Jansen zooms in even further in terms of locality, namely on the South African backyard, or *agterplaas* in Afrikaans, the outdoor space of a house where black domestic workers and the white families they work for meet. Jansen considers this a "very local peripheral space" that continues to occupy a central place in South Africa's racial divide, in many ways functioning as a microcosmos of the power relations at work in South African society at large. Looking at a selection of (semi-)autobiographical texts by both black and white authors (Ezekiel Mphahlele, Rian Malan, Griselda Pollock, Mark Gevisser, Elsa Joubert and Antjie Krog), Jansen demonstrates that the backyard is a space of complex negotiations between domestic workers and their employers, which involves domination, but also ambivalent relations of care and affection. While, to some extent, the South African backyard functions as a "contact zone" (Pratt) between white and black, urban and rural, and rich and poor, Jansen draws on the historical and literary archive to demonstrate that it is more appropriate to view it as a frontier or border zone instead – a space marked by intricate power relations, where violence and degradation continue to govern.

Jansen describes the paradoxical situation of black domestic workers who, when they go to work, physically move out of the periphery of the city, but nonetheless carry their social peripherality with them. In fact, their bodily presence within the center even reinforces their peripheral position in relation to that center. Mobility, then, is by no means a guarantee for escaping from spatial or social peripheries, as cases of racial, class or gender discrimination demonstrate. At the same time, one's peripheral position or status need not per definition hinder one's (upward) mobility, and may in fact be used strategically, for example in the fight for minority rights or in the quest for cultural belonging. Clearly, then, a more complex understanding of how periphery and mobility might relate needs to be developed. The three chapters in the third section each shed light on this relation, as well as on how the peripheral, usually thought of as a static notion, can become mobile and mobilized itself.

Magdalena Ślusarczyk and Paula Pustułka demonstrate that, while the conceptual distinction between center and periphery is important to migrant identities (since it determines how different groups of migrants are framed as welcome or not), in practice it plays out in very different ways. Investigating a wide range of individual biographies and trajectories of Polish migrants in the United Kingdom, Germany and Norway, they reveal peripherality as a conceptual frame that can, indeed, signify marginalization, but may also be strategically employed to lead to empowerment. As the variegated experiences of the migrants show, moving out of Europe's periphery does not automatically mean leaving peripherality behind; while those migrants occupying a geographically and economically central position in Poland are often able to move to globally recognized central locations, those from Polish peripheries tend to end up in the peripheries of these centers. Even such moves from periphery to periphery may, however, give migrants significantly better lives. This highlights how, in the current age of globalization, not all peripheries (or centers) are equal, and how mobility occurs in complex patterns that cannot be captured in a simple assumption that everyone will be able to or wants to move to global centers.

Forces of peripheralization and centralization may also conflict with each other, as is clear in the two European cultural projects Astrid Van Weyenberg analyzes: the House of European History, planned to open in Brussels in 2016, and the Via Regia, promoted by the European Institute for Cultural Routes. While the House of European History acknowledges the ongoing dynamic between shifting centers and peripheries, even announcing "centre and periphery" as the permanent exhibition's leitmotiv, it builds on a problematically static center-periphery model in order to keep the unifying European story on display intact. The Via Regia cultural route also seems designed to overcome the division of Europe into centers and peripheries: promoting cross-European mobility, it draws a line from Santiago de Compostela to Kiev to connect Western and Eastern Europe in a singular trajectory. As Van Weyenberg demonstrates, however, the continuity and homogeneity propagated by this Europeanizing narrative that seeks to place everything at the center, is undermined by the way locations fulfill different, sometimes conflicting narrative functions within regional, national and supranational frames. Both cultural projects show that the story of Europe is one of shifting multiplicities and cannot be immobilized into a singular history or route that glosses over the differences and inequalities that inhere between (past and present) centers and peripheries.

That the periphery can be mobilized strategically is most explicit in the final chapter in this section. Geli Mademli connects the different uses of the term "periphery" within the contemporary context of the "Greek crisis" to the history of Greece's positioning within Europe, highlighting how the country has conceived of itself as peripheral in relation to shifting centers. As a telling example, Mademli recalls how the first Greek political parties took on the names of the centers of power in modern Europe with which they allied themselves: the Russian Party, the British Party, the French Party. In contemporary Greece, too, a peripheral position is not just imposed from the outside, by other European countries and the so-called troika, but also claimed from within. Mademli's investigation of Greek media coverage of the European debt crisis and, specifically, the Greek bailout referendum of 5 July 2015, shows that the priority in Greek public discourse was not to adhere to a static center-periphery binary, but to articulate Greece's peripheral position in relation to an abstract European center in a way that allowed for the articulation of a shared cultural identity and an active questioning of the "center" and its deficiencies. Peripherality, then, can be employed strategically, not just by the center, but also by the periphery itself. Here, the periphery emerges not only as a mobile and multiple notion (attaching itself to various centers at different times), but also as a mobilizable tool.

The fourth and final section revolves around questions of aesthetics and form in the uses, effects and significations of peripherality. Even though cultural expressions are not directly reflective of or causally related to their historical and material conditions, their performative and constructive potential influences how the topics, themes, people and politics they foreground are framed and regarded in everyday life. The three chapters investigate the ways in which particular peripheralized histories, subjects and spaces are represented in artistic forms that work against the grammar of peripheralization imposed from the center. More specifically, they convey how detailed attention to form and aesthetics can help to better understand peripheral visions as perspectives from the periphery that enable a thinking "otherwise." In all three chapters, this thinking "otherwise" – which is deeply political – takes the shape of a complex relation to a troubled past that, rather than closing it off, seeks to recognize it and to mobilize it for the present and the future.

In Paula Blair's chapter, different layers of peripheral aesthetics come to the fore. Analyzing Willie Doherty's video-installation *Ancient Ground* and Patricio Guzmán's documentary *Nostalgia for the Light*, Blair shows how these works are peripheral in both form and content: they lack commerciality, are not generally accessible and engage with issues "involving minor groups that are often met with denial and exclusion." Revolving around the disappeared of Northern Ireland's Troubles and of Pinochet's regime in Chile respectively, they use their content, media platform and particular aesthetic strategies to counter the "official forgetting" that characterizes these events up to the present day. Focusing particularly on the portrayal of landscape, Blair discusses how Doherty actively confounds and counters the idyllic marketing of the County of Donegal by evoking the disappeared in its depths. Similarly, Guzmán's images of women scouring the Atacama Desert for the physical remains of their loved ones are juxtaposed with the "sky searching" conducted at the space observation center also located there. According to Blair, these works politically contest the center's attempts to bury past troubles by creating a peripheral aesthetics that allows such troubles to be brought to light, albeit, at least at first, only to the limited audiences afforded by the peripheral status of their genres.

In her chapter on post-Soviet narratives, Ksenia Robbe, too, focuses on the ethics and politics of relegating certain histories, socialities and spaces to the periphery. She discusses how, after the demise of the Soviet Union, memories and stories of everyday life were pushed to the peripheries of public discussion and collective memory too quickly and too unambiguously. In careful readings of Ksenia Buksha's *The Freedom Factory* and Igor Saveljev's *Tereshkova is Flying to Mars*, Robbe traces how these novels portray an alternative position in relation to the Soviet past, where the relation is no longer one of outright refusal or dissection, but features instead a productively nostalgic belief in the possibility of commonality. The peripheralized past is considered as "an assemblage of imaginary and material forces" and read through Svetlana Boym's notion of the "common place" as a complex layering of the myths that organized Soviet life, the sites of ordinary life that often evolved counter to these commonplace myths and the creation and enactment of an ideal or utopian horizon. Relying on Serguei Oushakine's notion of post-Soviet aphasia, defined as a reusing of old symbolic forms in the absence of new ones, Robbe examines how, in the two novels, peripheralized locations and discourses from the past are salvaged from their essentialized forms and turned into positive attempts at developing a language comprising past, present and future.

Matthieu Foucher, in his analysis of the French queer magazine *La Revue Monstre*'s controversial call to return to the closet and Michael James O'Brien's photo series *Interiors* depicting Parisian backrooms, is also interested in how the past continues to manifest in the present. Crucially, rather than seeking to sever the long-standing association of the queer spaces of the closet and the backroom with danger and deadly desire, *Monstre* and *Interiors* are seen to evoke this association, aesthetically and politically, as potentially enabling. In line with Dasgupta's and Wiese's contentions that a withholding of full exposure can signify a certain empowerment of the peripheral, Foucher argues that, even if the negative connotations of the closet and the backroom, and their dominant representation from the perspective of the center, cannot be denied, the fact that these peripheral spaces are to a certain extent closed off from the outside world can also make them "expansive space[s] of possibility" for queer communities. This makes it possible to conceive of returning to the closet not as a giving in to the center, but as a radical alternative to the politics of visibility adopted by mainstream queer activism, with the peripheral acting up to reserve the right to remain in the dark on its own terms.

Together, the four sections signal the importance of keeping the peripheral alive as a category while adopting a differentiated stance towards it. This volume is, in the end, not about the emancipation of the periphery into the center – about turning it into something that can be more easily understood in terms mostly dictated by this center – but about looking for ways to regard the periphery as able to negotiate its inevitable relation with the center on a variety of terms that belie its construction as statically "other."

Works Cited

Appadurai, Arjun. *Modernity at Large: Cultural Dimensions of Globalization*. Minneapolis: U of Minnesota P, 1996.

Bal, Mieke. *Narratology: Introduction to the Theory of Narrative*. Toronto: U of Toronto P, 2009.

Bhabha, Homi K. *The Location of Culture*. London and New York: Routledge, 2004.

Brennan, Timothy. "The Economic Image-Function of the Periphery." *Postcolonial Studies and Beyond*. Ed. Ania Loomba et al. Durham: Duke UP, 2005. 101–22.

Cacioppo, John T., et al. "Central and Peripheral Routes to Persuasion: An Individual Difference Perspective." *Journal of Personality and Social Psychology* 51.5 (1986): 1032–43.

Chakrabarty, Dipesh. *Provincializing Europe: Postcolonial Thought and Historical Difference*. Princeton: Princeton UP, 2009.

Chen, Kuan-Hsing. *Asia as Method: Toward Deimperialization*. Durham: Duke UP, 2010.

Coetzee, J.M. *Waiting for the Barbarians*. London: Vintage, 2004.

Comaroff, Jean, and John L. Comaroff. *Theory from the South: Or, How Euro-America Is Evolving Toward Africa*. London and New York: Routledge, 2012.

Friedman, Thomas L. *The World Is Flat: The Globalized World in the Twenty-First Century*. London: Penguin, 2006.

Haraway, Donna. "The Persistence of Vision." *The Visual Culture Reader*. Ed. Nicholas Mirzoeff. London and New York: Routledge, 2002. 677–84.

Hoad, Neville Wallace. *African Intimacies: Race, Homosexuality, and Globalization*. Minneapolis: U of Minnesota P, 2007.

Howard, Daniel J. "Familiar Phrases as Peripheral Persuasion Cues." *Journal of Experimental Social Psychology* 33 (1997): 231–43.

Janzen, Marike. "Immanuel Wallerstein and the Problem of the World: System, Scale, Culture. Edited by David Palumbo-Liu, Bruce Robbins, and Nirvana Tanoukhi (review)." *Comparative Literature Studies* 51.3 (2014): 6–9.

Kentridge, William. "Peripheral Thinking." *Design Indaba*. 3 June 2015. Web. Keynote Address.

Mignolo, Walter D. "The Geopolitics of Knowledge and the Colonial Difference." *South Atlantic Quarterly* 101.1 (2002): 57–96.

———. "Introduction: On Gnosis and the Imaginary of the Modern/Colonial World System." *Local Histories/Global Designs: Coloniality, Subaltern Knowledges, and Border Thinking*. Princeton and Oxford: Princeton UP, 2012. 3–45.

Mignolo, Walter D., and Freya Schiwy. "Transculturation and the Colonial Difference: Double Translation." *Revista científica de información y communicación* 4 (2007): 12–34.

Mishra, Rapti. "World System Theory: Understanding the Capitalist Design." *Asian Journal of Multidisciplinary Studies* 1.3 (2013): 160–8.

Orizio, Grazia, et al. "'Save 30% If You Buy Today': Online Pharmacies and the Enhancement of Peripheral Thinking in Consumers." *Pharmacoepidemiology and Drug Safety* 19 (2010): 970–6.

Parry, Benita. "The Presence of the Past in Peripheral Modernities." *Beyond the Black Atlantic: Relocating Modernization and Technology*. Ed. Walter Goebel and Saskia Schabio. London: Routledge, 2006. 13–28.

Petty, Richard E., and John T. Cacioppo. "The Effects of Involvement on Responses to Argument Quantity and Quality: Central and Peripheral Routes to Perception." *Journal of Personality and Social Psychology* 46.1 (1984): 69–81.

Pratt, Mary Louise. "Modernity and Periphery: Toward a Global and Relational Analysis." *Beyond Dichotomies: Histories, Identities, Cultures, and the Challenge of Globalization*. Ed. Elisabeth Mudimbe-Boyi. Albany: SUNY Press, 2012. 21–47.

Schmidt, Heike Ingeborg. "Colonial Intimacy: The Rechenberg Scandal and Homosexuality in German East Africa." *Journal of the History of Sexuality* 17.1 (2008): 25–59.

Stoler, Ann Laura. *Carnal Knowledge and Imperial Power: Race and the Intimate in Colonial Rule*. Berkeley: U of California P, 2002.

Strasburger, Hans, Ingo Rentschler and Martin Jüttner. "Peripheral Vision and Pattern Recognition: A Review." *Journal of Vision* 11.5 (2011): 1–82.

Wallerstein, Immanuel. "Semi-Peripheral Countries and the Contemporary World Crisis." *Theory and Society* 3.4 (1976): 461–83.

———. *The Politics of the World-Economy: The States, the Movements and the Civilizations.* Cambridge: Cambridge UP, 1984.

———. "Robinson's Critical Appraisal Appraised." *International Sociology* 27.4 (2012): 524–8.

West, Cornel. "Decentring Europe: A Memorial Lecture for James Snead, Introduced by Colin MacCabe." *Critical Quarterly* 33.1 (1991): 1–19.

Young, Paul. "Peripheralizing Modernity: Global Modernism and Uneven Development." *Literature Compass* 9.9 (2012): 611–6.

PART 1

Theorizing the Peripheral

∵

CHAPTER 1

A Grammar of Peripheralization: Neill Blomkamp's *District 9*

Mireille Rosello

Cultural subjects or communities are never peripheral. Yet this whole text is about peripheral cultural subjects and communities, something it claims does not exist. The point of this apparently paradoxical exercise is to highlight the problematic erasure of the metaphorical aspects of the opposition between core and periphery, and the nefarious consequences of that slippage for those subjects essentialized as peripheral.

In geometry, one may calculate the perimeter of a circle without assuming that the center is a privileged site of identity and power and that the periphery is derivative. The trouble starts, however, when that apparently simple distinction is displaced onto cultural values: then, the "periphery" is opposed to the core or the center. Even if "is opposed" seems to describe a stable situation, I hear the verb as an active-passive voice, perhaps a passively aggressive voice: by "the periphery is opposed to the center," I mean that the difference is a process and a construction that wishes to be forgotten. The periphery is constructed as the opposite of power, which, by default, claims the place of the center and defines it as whatever is deemed desirable: the real, the undiluted and the pure, the good, the healthy, the morally right – in other words, the normal.

When the core/periphery binary opposition serves to map the actors of social organizations, then the very existence of the "periphery" is the symptom of an undesirable process of disempowering. And even if the periphery regained power, it would then become a new core. It is hard to argue against voices that claim that it is true that peripheries are peripheral, because such supposedly tautological and therefore self-evident remarks hide that peripheries do not exist prior to a particular social, spatial and metaphorical operation. Peripheries are the effect of an imbalance; they are the result of a felicitous process of peripheralization.

District 9, the 2009 science fiction film directed by South African Neill Blomkamp is a good example of this process of peripheralization. In the story, the "periphery" – or rather, the peripheralized – is figured as a population of aliens stranded in Johannesburg. The two specific research questions that I will let this film guide me through are the following: how does peripheralization function in popular fiction? And what narrative tricks are necessary for

© KONINKLIJKE BRILL NV, LEIDEN, 2016 | DOI 10.1163/9789004323056_003

an audience or a community to accept that a periphery exists and that certain subjects are (imagined as) having a peripheral identity or an essence? I will suggest that the film deploys standard processes of peripheralization in relation to the alien population but also proposes limited tactics of resistance that have to do with the exposure of peripheralization as well as with the framing of an anti-peripheralization counter-narrative.

A Grammar of Peripheralization

First, I focus on the various narrative devices that make it possible to construct a fictional universe in which the process of peripheralization is understood as the precondition of any other political decision. Like any grammar, this system has rules and exceptions, exceptions that never function as the beginning of a new grammar but only reinforce the rules.

Rule # 1: Choose Your Genre Carefully: Peripheralizing and Science Fiction

The first rule that we may want to consider is well-known among narratologists and is called a generic constraint: *District 9* belongs (at least in part) to the genre of science fiction and one of the laws of that genre is to enable the manifestation of a paranoid fantasy of Earth's peripheralization. *District 9* confirms the grammar of science fiction even if, at first, it appears to differ from traditional stories about powerful aliens invading Planet Earth. The originality of the story is that the aliens are not triumphant super-creatures, as, for example, in Robert Emmerich's *Independence Day* (1996). In such traditional declensions of the generic grammar, the plot evokes the Earth's continued fear of being demoted to a less central (less navel-gazing) position.

Historically and realistically, the possibility of relativizing Earth as center or as periphery has, of course, already happened. The Copernican revolution is a discovery that we are not the center but also posits the relationality of the core/periphery model.[1] And apparently, the Galileos of history quickly realized

---

1 On the series of "three great historical wounds to the primary narcissism of the self-centered human subject, who tries to hold panic at bay by the fantasy of human exceptionalism," see Haraway. To the first three humiliating decenterings (first, the Copernican revolution, then the Darwinian's positioning of the human as one of the animals and finally the Freudian's attack on the self-conscious self) Haraway adds a fourth level, "informatic or cyborgian," which "infolds organic and technological flesh" and further troubles the borders around the Human (11).

that their (perhaps detached) reversal of perspective is experienced as a horrific form of humiliation by Man. Spectators of today's science fiction films know that not everything revolves around "us." Yet, the concept of home has adequately re-imagined planet Earth as a center that does not want to be made aware of its potentially peripheralizable status. The "Blue Planet" is "ours," which makes it symbolically if not spatially central. As long as we forget that we once wanted to be at the center of the universe, the dream of centrality is safe.

Stories that imagine aliens arriving on planet Earth activate a paranoid plot: they peripheralize our world. The spectator is asked to concede that, from the perspective of aliens, "we" are the periphery, perhaps the outermost periphery. Part of our pleasure in reading and watching science fiction is to experience the humiliating reminder that our fantasy of centrality is flawed, only to then walk away from the possibility.[2] Just as horror movies terrify us so that we can remember that there is nothing to fear,[3] a good alien scenario reminds us that we are not at the center of the universe but in the end lets us go back to our illusion of exceptionalism.

Films such as *Independence Day* let us toy with paranoid thoughts of our own peripheralization, then propose the annihilation of that possibility (and of the creatures who are blamed for it). We enjoy this return to the reassuring order; they are gone, or defeated, or exterminated. Actually, they were never there, as we do not believe in aliens. When, in science fiction, Earth is peripheralized by the arrival of aliens, the encounter is inevitably described as an "invasion" and the humans are constructed as victims (they are under attack) but also as heroes (they resist and prevail). In *Independence Day*, the President of the US sacrifices his own life to ensure that life on earth is protected against the "Locusts."

In *District 9* the spectator is treated to a different type of myth about the position of Earth as either core or periphery. In this story, the aliens have always already failed. They have not even technically landed on earth. The superior technology that we associate with space travel could metaphorically make their original home central (from the center, one controls access to the

---

2   In films, just to make sure that we protect the fantasy, we make sure that aliens are evil: in *Independence Day*, they are equated with locusts – one of the Biblical plagues but also potentially a self-incriminating metaphor of colonization coming from Western empires that built their modernity on plundering human and natural resources.

3   For the political implications of such a reading of horror movies, see Chris Cleave's *The Other Hand*, in which a young Nigerian refugee equates her traumatic memories to a film from which she can never walk away and from which there is no refuge.

periphery), but they lost that privilege when their mothership broke down. They are stranded and their enormous ship hangs over Johannesburg like a sword of Damocles. The threat, if there is one, is not at all explicit. The aliens did not "invade"; rather, they had to be rescued, cut out of their malfunctioning ship, and brought down to earth as helpless refugees.[4] In *District 9*, the aliens are not conquerors; they are migrants. They are portrayed as helpless creatures, like those whom Edouard Glissant called "naked migrants" (14).

Twenty years later, when the story actually begins, it is clear that the encounter has turned into a tragically unharmonious juxtaposition between species. The representation of the process of peripheralization that is to unfold in the film shows that such a dynamic entails a stubborn refusal of the reality of cohabitation and a deliberate remapping of space that corresponds to the will to segregate. This is what we could call Rule number 2.

Rule # 2: A Periphery is Never Peripheral Enough

At first, the aliens live within the borders of what imagines itself as the core city. Their home is a slum with well-marked limits but difficult to police, and the proximity of the aliens cannot be ignored. Their presence risks troubling the conceptual opposition between core and periphery that serves to protect the humans against their paranoid fear of being like the "Prawns." The structure of the slum is both like and unlike an orderly city grid. The camera lingers on the roofs of shacks, which, seen from above, are a chaos of imbricated shapes. The "architects" have been left to their own (lack of) resources and have done their best or their worst depending on the perspective. The slums are abandoned by the state and this relegation is to be read in the absence of demarcations. For example, the camera focuses on the absence of distinction between what is thrown out and what is to be kept. The definition of waste has lost its contours. Famished Prawns are seen scavenging in dumpsters or in the open-air heaps of garbage. Waste is food and that proximity endangers the illusion that they can (or ought to) be kept separate.

This figural peripheralization goes hand in hand with a spatial movement that aims to deny the obvious presence: the aliens are going to be pushed further and further away. The dramatic engine that launches the story in *District 9* is an administrative decision to "evict" them from their massive shantytown. As the result of riots that break out in the city, the government decides to

---

4 Although it would be absurd to ignore the references to South African history, I am not reading the film as an allegory of apartheid. For interesting and critical analyses of the film in its South African context, see Valdez Moses et al.

forcibly deport them away from Johannesburg.[5] For the peripheralizing logic to be confirmed, the aliens must preferably be made invisible in the physical place that reiterates (and therefore imposes) itself as a center.

In the film, the government hires the multinational security company MNU (mercenaries) to deport 1.8 million Prawns from District 9 to District 10. The increment (from 9 to 10) symbolizes the added distance. The image of District 10 makes it clear that further peripheralizing strategies are at work. District 10, which is visually presented to the public and the viewer in a half-hearted effort to PR the operation, will be surrounded by enormous barbed-wired fences. It will consist of miles and miles of identical small, white tent-like huts. A threatening sign already warns the "non-humans": "No non-human loitering."

The sign cannot be accused of de-humanizing the Prawns to the extent that they are indeed not "humans": like the narrator of Frantz Fanon's *Black Skin, White Masks* who meets people who comment on his skin color, the aliens must concede that it is "true" that they are not humans.[6] Yet, the peripheralization process consists, here, in denying them an identity: they are simply derivative (the reference is the human) and in a negative way (they are non-human), a classic universalist trick endlessly denounced, endlessly repeated. They lack humanness but have not acquired any other attribute that would separate them from other abjected creatures, such as animals for example. The slur "Prawns" has marked them as animalesque, a move justified by a circular logic: "they *look* like Prawns," one character explains, not ever wondering what humans like him may look like to others.

The aliens' assignment to the camp organizes their movement in a way that reiterates and reinforces the creation of the periphery: any movement that might change the border between the periphery and the core is forbidden. If Prawns move outside of the periphery, regardless of whether they move in the direction of the center or away from it, they are seen as "loitering": this describes their direction as aimless, perverse and probably sexually aggressive, as Ross Chambers showed in his study of *Loiterature*.

The aggressiveness of the double negation (no non-) is painfully underscored by the irony of the name given to this alien relocation camp: "Sanctuary Park." Clearly visible control towers that dominate the rows of shelters leave no

---

5   The title of the film and the fact that it was filmed in Soweto makes it impossible to miss the allusion to the ghost of District 6 in Cape Town, a neighborhood from which about 60,000 inhabitants were forcibly removed between 1966 and 1980 (see Hart).

6   When Fanon's narrator is surrounded by white people who comment on his skin color, he tries to react as if he were not hurt: "'Look, a Negro!' It was an external stimulus that flicked over me as I passed by. I made a tight smile. 'Look, a Negro!' It was true. It amused me" (112).

doubt as to the center's ability to enforce their "no loitering" policy. The aliens will be prisoners of the sanctuary. The periphery is now defined as a border surrounded by a border that stabilizes the relationship between that area and the rest. This comes up against another possible definition of the periphery as an away that is never quite far away enough because it is really inside.

To make the aliens as different as possible from the nature or the essence of what has now declared itself as a normative core, it is not enough to move them to a further spatial periphery. It is also necessary to attach "peripheral" as a differential label to their selves, and more specifically to their bodies. Hence Rule number 3.

Rule #3: Peripheralized Bodies: Reformable or Disgustingly Destroyable?

One of the well-known strategies of peripheralization used by former empires is the fictional and political creation of what Rachel Tolen calls the "Criminal Tribesman." Tolen's study of the role of the Salvation Army in India reveals a complicated dialectics of core and periphery, home and abroad, and of abjecting and reforming. She shows that the category of the "dangerous classes" – "composed of the unemployed, vagrants, the poor, criminals, drunkards and prostitutes" (Tolen 81) – was mapped onto bodies assigned to criminal tribes or castes. Once this assignment took a more concrete and physical form (confinement for example), the Salvation Army moved in to ostensibly reform and cure. This charitable institution proceeded to discipline bodies (Foucault) because the only way to redeem these defective social and physical selves was to transform them into productive instruments of labor. "As criminality was manifested not simply in individual acts of crime but also in disposition, gestures, modes of deportment, habitual behaviors, and types of bodily adornment, they were all the focus of methods aimed at deconstructing persons and reconstituting them as disciplined individuals" (Tolen 94). She continues: "One of the central objectives of the system of reform was to transform criminal tribespeople into productive and subjective bodies" able to exploit their own land and their own energy for the benefit of the colony (Tolen 98). In spite of the rhetoric, the bodies of the tribespeople were therefore neither "cured" nor "reformed": rather, they were turned into cogs in a system of exploitation that equated them with their land.

But what if, as is the case in *District 9*, the aliens do not have valuable land? By redefining the colonial metaphor, the film exacerbates the murderous peripheralization already present in the colonial enterprise. Since the bodies of the aliens are not connected to a resource that can be pillaged or to an economy that tolerates the overt use of slavery, they do not need to be reformed. No cynical economic logic justifies the disciplining of bodies. Instead, the construction of a peripheralized alien body involves the kind of rhetoric that leads to segregation and extermination. Ergo, the aliens are diseased and contagious. They are lives not worth living. Within the economy of the film, the massive deportation of the aliens is therefore justified as a reasonable political response to a powerful "truth": the law of human disgust. It is apparently undeniable that the Prawns are disgusting.

A look at the large body of theories on disgust that seek to categorize what elicits disgust in humans makes clear that the aliens have been endowed with all the (few) necessary attributes that makes a creature repulsive (McGinn; Nussbaum; Miller). Disgust is a bodily and mental response to certain tastes and smells that evoke pollution (Douglas), to the transgression of order between what must remain inside and what oozes out of bodies, politic or material. Disgust is located at the intersection between affect and politics. Etymologically, the word "disgust" comes from "gustatory" (*goût* in French), which, like the English "taste," refers both to what our mouth can identify as good, bad, sweet or sour and to what our aesthetic sense will identify as "in good or bad taste," a "distinction" that Pierre Bourdieu has taught us to recognize as the symptom of the policing of distinct social classes (Bourdieu). Disgust is a fear of contamination with this other that we wish to peripheralize but which insists on sitting aberrantly between inside and outside, dead and alive, normal and abnormal, because such categories are themselves a consequence of the peripheralization at work.

The bodies of the Prawns are distinctly alien but also not radically unthinkable or unimaginable. They can therefore be perceived as abnormally situated between species: at least from the point of view of humans, they are neither animal nor human. They walk on their hind legs but they also look like crustaceans and mollusks. Their shell-like exoskeletons reverse traditional notions of inside and outside, flesh and bone, soft and hard. There are too many of them, so that they look like a generic mass of swarming creatures that endangers the very concept of individuality. They evoke the danger of mindless invasion or viral contamination. Not only do they act and look like swarming critters but they are so big that we encounter them as if they were extreme close ups of giant insects. The unfamiliarity of this relationship to size breaks down the comforting border between humans and miniscule lives whose images only become pleasantly threatening if we look at them through our formidable microscopes.

When Charlie Jane Anders interviews David Meng, one of the members of the Weta's design team[7] who was in charge of conceptualizing the aliens,

---

7   David Meng conceptualized and sculpted the creatures. He worked with Greg Broadmore and Leri Greer as concept engineers of the Weta's team who created the universe of *District 9*. http://www.wetanz.com/movies/ (accessed May 2014).

the title of the article posted on the site of the internet journal *io9* is: "Neill Blomkamp Wanted *District 9*'s Aliens To Be as Disgusting as Possible" (Anders). Clearly, a deliberate authoring principle was at work. Such interviews remind us that, in films (and in real life), no pre-existing bodily knowledge can be separated from an epistemology and a grammar that orients our interpretation of certain bodies. In *District 9*, the aliens are (called) diseased and toxic *because* they need to be ghettoized. Otherwise, they could infect us with concepts of neither here nor there, neither center nor periphery, or, perhaps even worse, of one day here, one day there. Embodying such dual positionings is to be a living insult to the forces that thrive on peripheralizing neatly.

Once I know this, of course, I am less likely to completely forget the narrative manipulation. It has now become (perhaps) more difficult to trust my repulsion and to assume that my own body is telling me a truth that my mind would not wish to accept. The trouble with disgust is that it looks like a universal bodily wisdom. When a brain and body have produced a quick and reliable multifaceted and complex reaction, should we not accept that perception of the world? Is our "instinctive" disgust to be disregarded?

The interview with the director reminds me that a controlled exposure to disgust was precisely my desire when I walked into the dark room. I chose to suspend disbelief when I went to see a science fiction film: the law of that genre demands that these aliens be represented as the objects of our disgust. In other words, the Prawns are not disgusting because they eat cat food and raw meat and because they live in and off garbage. They have such attributes so that we can enjoy them looking disgusting. And, as long as the operation occurs within a work of fiction, it is both problematic and interestingly controversial, since we are free to do what we want with our disgust, including resisting it or recognizing it for what it is: a form of reading that is overdetermined by narrative devices and not by the "truth" of affects. "Our" (definition of) disgust has created the Prawns, not the other way around.

Resisting Peripheralization: Mixed Genres and Mixed DNAs

In case that last paragraph has given the impression that it takes special narratological or theoretical reading skills to become aware of the manipulative grammar of disgust, it is now time to slightly reformulate my argument. This second section suggests that the film as a whole is invested in making its audience aware of the grammar of peripheralization by exposing its limits and offering us alternative narrative strategies. Two specific elements are worth analyzing more closely: the mixed DNA structure of the main human protagonist (who is turning into an alien) and the mixed generic structure of a science fiction film which is also a (faux) documentary. While the latter will help me nuance the role played by rule #1 (generic constraints), I argue that the figure of the "becoming-alien" functions as another level of critique of peripheralization. Both are formal and fictional equivalents.

Becoming Alien

While the humans who are hostile to the "Prawns" do their utmost to impose their peripheralization logic, the experience of the main protagonist is an ironic and powerful denunciation of its artificiality. The whole plot of the movie can be summarized as follows: Wikus van der Merwe, whose responsibility was to deport the 1.8 million aliens to District 10, is himself in the process of turning into an alien.

In one crucial scene, we see Wikus clumsily manipulating an object whose function eludes him and that suddenly sprays some strange liquid over his face. The rest of the story will show that this single moment of airborne contact is enough to fuse Wikus's and the aliens' genetic code. From a human (peripheralizing) perspective, he becomes monstrous. From another perspective, his body is learning how to be an alien. He loses apparently needless bits such as teeth and nails but develops the aliens' long claw-like hands, and he slowly metamorphoses until the last scene shows us a perfect alien that we know is Wikus sculpting a flower out of a piece of garbage. This could, after all, be a success story.

From a human perspective, the body that threatens to contest the peripheralizing process must be described as the most unacceptable site of all. And one of the most effective ways of doing so is to map onto the core/periphery binary another level of metaphorical opposition, that of the distinction between health and disease and/or able-bodiedness/disability. The "symptoms" Wikus displays are portrayed as horrifying and disgusting. The camera focuses on the loss of bodily integrity that causes revulsion in both the character and the viewer. Wikus bites his fingernails and they come off, leaving his fingers looking like an open wound (Jansen van Veuren). At his birthday party, he throws up black fluid over the food, making it impossible to ingest. The physical and mental pain that he experiences is represented as something that does not elicit compassion but disgust. When his human hand turns into a huge alien claw, it causes horror and alarm but also greed: he is immediately treated as a guinea pig because his new DNA can now operate the specific kind of alien weaponry that humans cannot use. He is treated as a lab rat by a team of scientists/torturers/doctors who force him to kill animals and aliens. The narrative logic controlled by those who wish to impose the concept of periphery is intended to make sure that the public reads the transformation as the ultimate abject phenomenon.

Remarkably, however, the aliens' perspective, which could justify or explain what happens, is both foreclosed and displayed as evidence through the bodily metamorphosis. As spectators, we can only register the structuring absence of explanations, theories or discourses about integration or segregation, same and others, assimilability or lack thereof. There is no discussion of whether the aliens see Wikus as disgusting, or criminal, or diseased, or capable of productive labor. No voice in the film ever theorizes about whether he should be reformed, cured, integrated, made productive, enslaved or destroyed. The idea of peripheralizing him is apparently irrelevant: no one wants him in, no one wants him out. Only from the point of view of the humans can we describe this episode as the (other, alien) core welcoming him or being assimilationist. The concepts of being "far away" from the center, figuratively or literally, simply do not apply.

The alien substance that sprays Wikus is both like and unlike blood. And it is also both technological and biological. Therefore, we cannot assume that this is simply an allegory of the paranoid racist fear (one drop of blood makes you black once and for all). The mysterious fluid has the ability to turn other living creatures into aliens, for better and also for worse. And while it is important to bear in mind that this transformation is potentially as violent as the humans' tactic of deportation, it does not need a core-periphery politics.

The supposedly degenerate and diseased Prawns are not dangerous for the reasons that Wikus imagines (to him, they are a dirty, powerless, stupid form of life whose only purpose is to reproduce and their proximity is degrading to him and economically costly). As it turns out, they are dangerous to him because they are hospitable to other species in a way that proves that peripheralization is a political invention. Their despised form of civilization could be called an ecology of the relational: unlike the humans, they do not erect fences whose transgression creates panic. Their way of relating to their environment is relatively porous: their genetic interaction with their material surroundings makes it very difficult to put a border between their bodies and their environment. Here science fiction is also political fiction to the extent that it shows the consequences of imagining a species that has a different type of relation to the universe, a different type of ecology.

Science Fiction and Documentary

One of the most relevant features of *District 9* for this argument on peripheralization is its original double generic structure. The plot respects the codes of science fiction (which rearranges the borders of realism) but frames that tale within the conventions of a documentary (a form of fiction that minimizes its own fictional character and insists on telling the truth). Each genre has its own truth and the interesting aspect of *District 9* is that the law of the truth of documentaries and the law of the truth of science fiction are (at least apparently) incompatible. For a science fiction film to be true to its genre, it must ask the viewer to suspend disbelief about, for example, the existence of aliens. The audience of the documentary, on the other hand, gets information and explanation about a given topic and is not provided with escapist fantasies.

Yet the story of Wikus's transformation into an alien is told in a documentary after the character's death (which deprives us of any suspense), in a nonlinear way, through a series of (fictional) interviews with social scientists, members of the military and the police, with comments from the (hu)man on the street, Wikus's wife, parents and father-in-law. News footage and videos from surveillance cameras try to impose their peripheralizing perspective but fail to completely neutralize a supposedly impossible event: the metamorphosis of a human, who remains human, into an alien.

As the violence against Wikus escalates, the more antagonistic the two genres become, revealing the highly problematic character of the peripheralization principle's claims to truth. In one poignant scene, a distraught and starving Wikus, incapacitated by his bloody right arm, tries to find clothes and food. At the same moment, a voice-over pulls us away from what we see. The voice belongs to the documentary and is discrepant in terms of temporality; it comes from the future, talking about Wikus in the past and putting us in a future anterior position as viewers. The Wikus of the realistic story, we understand, is already dead; what we see belongs to the past. We hear a scientist saying: "he became the most valuable business artifact on earth" because he could operate alien weapons.

Immediately after this interruption from the future, the story returns to the diegetic present and shows the "artifact" in question: a desperate, disabled and wounded human being looking for bare necessities. The genre of the documentary does everything it can to describe the process of transition as a form of criminal activity, whereas the science fiction tale talks about the cruelty of Wikus's abandonment as he most needs care or at least compassion. Thus, two authoring scripts that normally mobilize our exclusive attention as spectators coexist uneasily, with their confrontation exposing the grammar of peripheralization as unstable. In this scene, this grammar manifests as a far-reaching high-technology disciplinary apparatus that has access to the most remote outposts of the country: everywhere, TV screens broadcast newsflashes, and the gaze of the surveillance cameras constantly reassesses where the periphery is.

When Wikus walks into a hamburger shack and tries to buy food, a TV screen literally interrupts the banal transaction, presenting him as a dangerous and contagious patient. We are told that he escaped from the "isolation ward." The grammar of the documentary is the relay for an extreme version of Foucault's "carceral system," here presented as the norm (Foucault). Within this grammar, it seems perfectly acceptable that the hospital should also be a prison and a laboratory where killability is the norm. Wikus's crime, we are told, is a (sexually transmitted) disease and the disease is a crime, which means that, for MNU, the "patient" is not so much an object of care as a criminal to be quarantined and therefore pushed to the ultimate periphery: social and/or physical death – the distinction is not even important since Wikus has become ungrievable (Butler).

At the same time, the science fiction story, which has its own grammar, shows that the reaction to Wikus's body is mediated by the narrative provided by the TV screens. In response, the woman behind the counter panics and people move away from him in a collective movement of physical repulsion. Magical thinking is involved: a customer warns others not to look at him. It is as if he has become some petrifying Medusa (which, of course, is not completely absurd in this case because if they were to see things from his perspective, they would indeed be changed and would have to accept not being afraid of him and instead being afraid of the peripheralization forces that govern their lives). Wikus's transforming body is not even visible in this scene, but his queer anti-peripheralizing physical presence is rendered legible by the (visual and ideological) discourse that literally replaces him by words and images. On the screen, the spectator is made aware of the points of focalization that insist on making him diseased and disabled: the black-and-white film that we are supposed to recognize as the output of a surveillance camera and the public TV screen that tells people what to think about what they see.

The scene that we are instructed to see as if we were all paranoid viewers afraid of being contaminated is a banal exchange between humans about the most basic of human needs: hunger. Wikus is hungry and he wishes to buy food. His behavior is quintessentially and stereotypically civilized: he has manners, he is polite, he says please, he has money, and, as he puts it later when the employee wants to call her manager, "you are legally obliged to serve me." But neither his perfectly proper social skills nor his qualifications as a consumer can compete with the interpretation that the forces of peripheralization can impose. When we, as spectators, view this scene, we have to move back and forth between the two paradigms: Wikus is trapped by the logic of peripheralization in the narrative generated by the genre of the documentary and its intradiegetic helper (the TV). On the other hand, the science fiction narrative lets us adopt his point of view as the victim of the other generic conventions.

Conclusion

District 9 tells a bleak and pessimistic story, suggesting that the periphery (or whoever represents the periphery) can never win in a struggle against the core because that battle always comes too late. The conflict is, in itself, the defeat of the periphery: if the periphery has been peripheralized, it means that some power has usurped the right to turn the world into a spatial metaphor where it occupies the position of the core. Once that process has started, it unfolds like the metamorphosis that Wikus undergoes: it is always already too late and something will take its course. And still, from now on, the periphery that should not exist has no choice but to struggle for recognition as an unjustly treated periphery: it will always both exist and remain invisible or at best marginalized because the core will despise it and reject it. Any attempt at highlighting the periphery as such will play the game of power. Letting the periphery speak, listening to the periphery, speaking in favor of, and even worse, speaking for the periphery will only reinforce the perverse structure put in place by the original peripheralization. Periphery, the film suggests, is a process of relationality that must pass as a category. The tension between the genre of science fiction and the documentary, which is just as antagonistic as the cohabitation between aliens and humans, constantly reminds us that power has a vested interest in controlling the definition of what it means to become peripheral: when an entity is put in a position where its ontology becomes relativized and has to be conceptualized in terms of "more or less like" another entity, then that being has become peripheralized.

And yet, the film is not hopeless. I suggested at the beginning of this chapter that *District 9* offers us an anti-peripheralization perspective and I would like to end on the few elements that nuance the bleak scenario outlined above. Firstly, the fact that spectators are constantly made aware of the various grammars that coexist in the film goes in the direction of anti-peripheralization. The generic constraints that govern the science fiction action film and the faux documentary keep drawing the spectator's attention to their conflicting logic and thus expose the process of peripheralization that the center denies even exists. Between the two narrative grammars, there is no bridge and the only aesthetic possibility is to switch abruptly from one point of view to another. The switch refuses the notion of transition: it is abrupt, either/or, except that this particular binary is the opposite of choosing between the alien and the humans. Both aliens and humans are entitled to a point of view, and the incompatible grammars expose the center's attempts at avoiding this possibility.

After Wikus has become unrecognizable to humans, after he has "become" an alien, the film continues to show us the world from his perspective and to treat him as Wikus and not just another generic Prawn. We see one lonely alien, on a heap of garbage, sculpting a flower. And we know what he is doing because the previous scene was an interview with his wife who participated in the faux documentary. The woman was holding a somewhat clumsily folded can in her hands, reminiscing about her presumed dead husband, wondering whether the sculpted object left on her doorstep could have been a message. The voices that surround her instruct her to throw out the object because it is "rubbish." In this way, the film confirms Wikus's inability to reach her directly across the species line created by peripheralization. Yet it has established, for the spectator, the new basis of a literacy that makes us recreate this bridge between the two characters. The Prawn is alone, concentrating on the object, raising it to check its form, or in a gesture that looks like an offering. There is no transition at all between the previous scene and this one: the aesthetic is now radically different. This time, the camera is unmediated by the center's surveillance apparatus or genres. In a different context, we would see one generic Prawn in its sordid environment. Yet as viewers, we are told that this is the other truth, one vision to which we could adhere: it is at least possible.

This scene is a good allegory for the film as a whole: *District 9* adopts a grammar of juxtaposition that denounces the validity of the center's narrative. We see an alien and we suddenly "recognize," not Wikus, but the fact that this can be and probably is Wikus. Wikus is Wikus, he is alive but he is unrecognizable because his embodiment is now indistinguishable from that of the Prawns. All the categories that we previously used to pigeonhole him as one of the members of the center are now irrelevant. He has transitioned. His metamorphosis is complete and yet (and that is where a new politics of disgust starts existing), he is still Wikus. He is Wikus *and* an alien, and he is entitled to compassion as disgusting. And as viewers, we are made aware of that possibility because the supposedly omnipotent center has not been able to banish from the documentary an emerging, embryonic story of a relationship between the center and the periphery. No matter what the grammar dictates, a link exists that other people call "rubbish" or impossible. Like the aliens and the humans, the grammar of the (fake) documentary and the grammar of the (fake) realist camera cannot talk to each other. But put next to each other, in a relationship of contiguity, they represent, for the spectator, unrealized possibilities.

Works Cited

Anders, Charlie Jane. "Neill Blomkamp Wanted District 9's Aliens To Be as Disgusting as Possible." *io9*. 17 July 2009. Web. 15 Aug 2015.

Bourdieu, Pierre. *Distinction: A Social Critique of the Judgment of Taste*. Cambridge, MA: Harvard UP, 1984.

Butler, Judith. *Frames of War: When Is Life Grievable?* New York and London: Verso, 2010.

Chambers, Ross. *Loiterature*. Lincoln: U of Nebraska P, 1999.

Cleave, Chris. *The Other Hand*. London: Sceptre, 2008.

District 9. Dir. Neill Blomkamp. Metropolitan FilmExport, 2009.

Douglas, Mary. *Purity and Danger: An Analysis of Pollution and Taboo*. London: Routledge, 1966.

Fanon, Frantz. "Concerning Violence." *The Wretched of the Earth*. Preface by Jean-Paul Sartre. Trans. Constance Farrington. New York: Grove Weidenfeld, 1963. 35–106.

Foucault, Michel. *Discipline and Punish: The Birth of the Prison*. Trans. A. Sheridan. New York: Vintage Books, 1977.

Glissant, Edouard. *Introduction à une poétique du divers*. Paris: Gallimard, 1996.

Haraway, Donna. *When Species Meet*. Minneapolis: U of Minnesota P, 2008.

Hart, Deborah. "Political Manipulation of Urban Space: The Razing of District Six, Cape Town." *Urban Geography* 9.6 (1988): 603–28.

Independence Day. Dir. Roland Emmerich. Twentieth Century Fox Film Corporation, 1996.

Jansen van Veuren, Mocke. "Tooth and Nail: Anxious Bodies in Neill Blomkamp's *District 9*." *Critical Arts: South-North Cultural and Media Studies* 26.4 (2012): 570–86.

McGinn, Colin. *The Meaning of Disgust*. Oxford: Oxford UP, 2011.

Miller, William Ian. *The Anatomy of Disgust*. Cambridge, MA: Harvard UP, 1997.

Nussbaum, Martha. *Hiding from Humanity: Disgust, Shame, and the Law*. Princeton and Oxford: Princeton UP, 2004.

Tolen, Rachel J. "Colonizing and Transforming the Criminal Tribesman: The Salvation Army in British India." *Deviant Bodies: Critical Perspectives on Difference in Science and Popular Culture*. Ed. Jennifer Terry and Jacqueline Urla. Bloomington: Indiana UP, 1995. 78–108.

Valdez Moses, Michael, Lucy Valerie Graham, John Marx, Gerald Gaylard, Ralph Goodman, and Stefan Helgesson. "District 9: A Roundtable." *Safundi: The Journal of South African and American Studies* 11.1–2 (2010): 155–75.

CHAPTER 2

The Infra-Periphery and Global Circuits of Symbolic Capital Accumulation

Paulina Aroch-Fugellie[1]

In the so-called post-industrial era, symbolic capital plays a key role for the global economy. Pierre Bourdieu has distinguished three major types of capital: cultural, economic and social. While each of those categories accounts for a set of resources, Bourdieu also introduces the notion of *symbolic capital*, which refers to a particular *dimension* of any of the three sets. This other dimension is the socially legitimized representational value of material resources. Since the conditions of transmission and acquisition of cultural capital are more disguised than those of other forms of capital, cultural capital is particularly "predisposed to function as symbolic capital" (Bourdieu 245). In other words, it is most likely to "be unrecognized as capital and recognized as legitimate competence, as authority" (Bourdieu 245). Endowing its possessors with distinction, cultural capital thrives on its existence as a scarce value.[2]

In this chapter, I want to focus on that disguised, yet fundamental form of capital in so far as it contributes to the differentiation of center and periphery in the contemporary world order, with specific reference to the position of Africa. Furthermore, I want to introduce the concept of *infra-periphery* and explore the ways in which it participates in the global dynamics of production and the uneven circulation of symbolic capital. Informed by the world-systems theory of Immanuel Wallerstein (2004), we might think of the "periphery" in post-Fordism as the industrialized backyard of the core countries. Yet Africa does not fulfill that role in the same way as, say, Latin America does. I propose that we think of Africa as straddling the divide between periphery and "infra-periphery." While extractive enclaves in the continent are highly integrated into the world-system as peripheral nodes of production, the rest of Sub-Saharan

---

1 I thank Brían Hanrahan for his important collaboration in this piece.

2 Bourdieu clarifies that symbolic capital is "capital – in whatever form – insofar as it is represented, i.e. apprehended symbolically, in a relationship of knowledge or, more precisely, of misrecognition and cognition." It "presupposes the intervention of the habitus." The habitus is the introjection of objective social structure into a personal set of cognitive and somatic dispositions. In other words, the habitus may be understood as a "socially constituted cognitive capacity" (255).

© KONINKLIJKE BRILL NV, LEIDEN, 2016 | DOI 10.1163/9789004323056_004

Africa is excluded even from direct forms of capitalist exploitation, while continuing to provide utility to the world-system by acting, among other things, as a large reservoir army of potential labor, which, while remaining unrealized, depreciates its overall value. Thus, infra-peripheral terrains regulate the system by exerting pressure on it. The infra-periphery is thus outside yet inside the world-system, and therefore cannot be equated to Wallerstein's "external arenas," which refers to zones of production articulated into *another* system of production (at different moments in history). External arenas do not play a substantial role in the system under consideration (see Wallerstein 1980).

Furthermore, while the infra-periphery plays an indirect yet fundamental role in the material economy, it also plays a major role in producing and reproducing the semiotic values that the world-system requires for its stabilization and endurance. The primary function of the infra-periphery, in terms of global flows of symbolic capital, is to render the work – especially the *dirty* work – of capitalism invisible. In what follows, I aim to explore this thesis by analyzing how Africa has been represented in contemporary popular and academic discourse, to then focus on the critiques that such uses of Africa as an idea have given rise to in the context of contemporary African critical theory, particularly in the work of Tanzanian intellectual Issa G. Shivji.

Africa as Infra-Periphery

After a couple of pages dedicated to reducing Africa to the fetishistic mind, to the incapacity of its inhabitants to attain the level of abstraction proper to monotheist religions or to Western art, G.W.F. Hegel, in his *Philosophy of History*, solemnly declares: "At this point we leave Africa, not to mention it again. For it is no historical part of the world; it has no movement or development to exhibit" (199). Although this view of Africa is supposed to have been superseded long ago, it remains present in both academic and popular discourse. Mass media equate the continent to abjection and lack, to a violent space of lawlessness, to famine and pernicious disease. Africa is reduced to the sphere of mere biological – indeed, animal – survival, below and beneath civilization and history.

At an apparently opposite end of the spectrum, speculative capital has managed to popularize a coexisting idea of Africa as the land of capital's future, a land of potential, of virtuality, and above all, of mobility. Going over the last two years of the coverage that the popular British weekly magazine *The Economist* has given to the continent, we find a bombardment of story after story about IBM, Google or Microsoft penetrating Africa, about Chinese capital venturing in and gliding through, about potential markets ready to be tapped only by those entrepreneurs savvy enough to have the necessary foresight.[3] It draws my attention that of all the new information and communication technologies, it is precisely mobile phones, with their connotations of flexibility, mediation and mobility, that have become so widely popularized in Africa, and that this fact is so heavily advertised.

In sum, today Africa is shoveled out of history in two ways. First, by way of absolute abjection, by being produced and reproduced as the realm of the infra-human: infra-human meaning here both a precariousness that reduces people at the very best to mere survival and modes of life not yet codified according to the liberal humanist ideals that are the very same ones to co-structure these conditions in the first place. Second, we are confronted with mobile, hyper-fluid African outposts of futurity, with forts and bridgeheads of a kind of clean de-historicized next-wave capitalist future, in what is otherwise a swamp of disease and war.

So long as we understand history not as a particular moment in time but as the dialectic invocation of one moment in and through another, then we may say that history continues to be systematically denied to the continent. It is with this expulsion from history in mind that I want to examine how Africa's place (or rather its displacement) in the global imaginary today at once depicts the continent as lacking symbolic capital and allows that "lack" to produce symbolic capital as a scarcity value elsewhere. In order to do so, I would now like to invoke a key moment in the history of the continent from a global perspective.

In the 1960s there was a shift that reorganized the spatial logistics of the global political economy. New transport, information and communication technologies made it cheaper to subdivide "manufacturing processes into a number of partial operations at different industrial sites throughout the world" (Fröbel, Heinrichs and Kreye 45). Countries of the North Atlantic now focused on the service sector and geared towards consumption, while Asia and Latin America became increasingly interpellated as providers of cheap industrial labor power rather than suppliers of raw material (Fröbel, Heinrichs and Kreye

---

3   See, for example, the February 2013 article "Innovation in Africa: Upwardly Mobile" (http://www.economist.com/node/21560912), where both text and image convey the idea of Africa's direct passage from a land of absolute wilderness to one of technologized futurity. Another example, among many, of both image and text playing into such a view of the continent is the August 2012 article "Information Technology in Africa: The Next Frontier" (http://www.economist.com/news/business/21571889-technology-companies-have-their-eye-africa-ibm-leading-way-next-frontier).

403). With the emergence of this New International Division of Labor, the differentiated roles of each were clearly demarcated: the Global South was to be the ground for the valorization of capital, producing surplus value in industry, while the North Atlantic would be consolidated as the place of value's appropriation and accumulation.

Yet it is only catachrestically that Africa as a homogenous whole can be included in that Global South. As James Ferguson has argued, today most industry in Africa is set up in the form of extractive enclaves that are alienated from their immediate surroundings. These are capital-intensive mining and oil sites, walled off from neighboring society, insulated from the local economy and often guarded by paramilitary forces (Ferguson 34–8). As Ferguson elaborates, the French colonial distinction between "useful" and "unusable" Africa is pertinent now more than ever:[4]

> Usable Africa gets secure enclaves – noncontiguous "useful" bits that are secured, policed, and ... governed through private or semiprivate means. These enclaves are increasingly linked up, not in a national grid, but in transnational networks that connect economically valued spaces dispersed around the world in a point to point fashion.
>
> The rest – the vast terrain of "unusable" Africa – gets increasingly nongovernmental states ... open to banditry and warlordism.
>
> FERGUSON 39

This "unusable" and, even, "useless" part of Africa constitutes the vast majority of the continent, in terms of territory, but mostly in terms of population. Whereas earlier work-intensive industrial capitalist mining (as in the case of the Zambian copper belt) brought with it a social investment in housing, schools and hospitals required for its own fulfillment, contemporary capital-intensive enclaves are socially thin, bringing little employment to Africans and hiring only a reduced amount of foreign high-skilled workers (Ferguson 36–7).

The inhabitants of "unusable Africa" are thus paradigmatic of what Michael Denning has, in a different context, referred to as the precariousness and disposability of human life for contemporary capitalism (79).[5] "Useless" Africa is not a zone beyond the grasp of the global economy, but constitutive of the latter. Just as Walter Rodney's historiography has established that the dependent, export-oriented economies were produced in tandem with, in, by and

---

4   Ferguson's distinction is via the work of William Reno. He refers to "the two different Africas that French colonialism once distinguished as '*Afrique utile*' and '*Afrique inutile*' – or 'usable/ useful Africa' and 'unusable/useless Africa' as Reno (1999) has reminded us" (39).

5   See also Butler 2006.

for colonialism itself, today, the steep relief of contemporary African economies is not an aberration of the norm, but the required inequality that allows for the norm: the norm of competition amongst zones of differentiated taxing regulations, of differentiated prices of labor, of differentiated life expectancies.

It is with these insights in mind that we can conceive neo-liberalism as operating on a triadic geo-economic structure that concentrates accumulation of surplus value in the North Atlantic and industrial production in Asia and Latin America. Africa appears, then, as the infra-periphery of an economy that is nonetheless fundamentally dependent on it. The vast terrain of Africa's "useless" territories, its "disposable lives," its "precarious lives," provide an excess labor force in permanent indebtedness that underscores the speculative logic of the global economy, embodying a state of abjection such that it indexes exploitation itself as a privilege.

Global Circuits of Accumulation of Symbolic Capital

I have signaled Africa's role as the infra-periphery of an economy that produces exploitation as a scarcity value by presenting (African) lives as disposable and at the same time negating this status quo as internal to the global system of exploitation. Let me now argue that a parallel mechanism underpins global circuits of *intellectual value* production, a kind of production deeply intertwined with symbolic capital. The North Atlantic concentrates Theory in the universal sense, while Latin America and Asia's role is to yield an intellectual production of the particular (for example, fiction or theory considered of exclusively local interest). In this reading, Africa is shown to be the land of the *infra-theoretical*, on whose exclusion the value-as-differential of Theory, Theory's scarcity value, ultimately rests. Thus, if, at the time of Hegel, Africa was the place of absolute *absence* – the foundational foreclosure that allowed for the emergence of History elsewhere – in today's hegemonic imaginary, Africa is deployed as a place of such absolute *presence* that it remains unable to enter the second order discourse appropriate for self-reflexivity.

As Edward Said and Gayatri Spivak have elaborated, second order discourse is a paradigmatic place for the constitution of the subject status. Africa operates as the negative space allowing Western Theory as a Universal to achieve its closure. Deployed as the land of the infra-theoretical, Africa fulfills the need for what in mathematical Set Theory would be called the "Theory Complement" (T'), that is, an exterior to the set "Theory" (T), within a given "Universe" (U = T + T'). Serving merely a structural function to delineate the contours of theoretical production elsewhere, the deployment of Africa as pure absence is not only a violence to African intellectual history, but also a violence to history as such: it is the largest scale testament to how the idealist tradition in Western thought has been erected at the cost of and on the basis of a radical separation between history and theory.

The disassociation between Western Theory and its historical specificity is what has always allowed Theory to operate as a universal, yet that disassociation is more heightened today than ever before. In his book *Considerations on Western Marxism*, Perry Anderson writes that the bond between theory and practice even in Marxist intellectuals began to quiver after the First World War and "[b]y the ... Second World War ... the distance between them was so great that it seemed virtually consubstantial with the tradition itself" (29). Anderson is particularly critical of the professionalization and academic affiliation of most contemporary intellectuals.[6] He also criticizes attempts such as Theodor Adorno's in *Negative Dialectics* to find a perfectly closed autonomous systematicity that was not there in Marx's own work to begin with – Anderson therefore refers to this trend of Marxism as an "esoteric" one.

In sum, for Anderson, postwar Western Marxism "had no anchorage within the social class for whose benefit theoretical work in Marxism alone has ultimate meaning" (44). I appreciate Anderson's emphasis here on the importance of approaching theoretical production not only in its own self-legitimating terms. Anderson deploys the pragmatic dimension of theoretical discourse as vital for the completion of its meaning. I believe that both the semantic and the pragmatic dimensions of theory are important to consider as we analyze Africa's infra-theoretical role towards the production of symbolic capital elsewhere. Since theory is one of the most consecrated modes of circulation of contemporary intellectual production, its historical purpose, reason and function in context cannot be ignored.

Historiography is capable of actually producing theory. A historiography of intellectual practice in Africa produces theory *post facto* because economic and semiotic values in capitalism pivot around the sphere of production, but are only *realized* as values in circulation. By engaging in a historiography of African intellectual practices, we legitimate and set into circulation a *pre-existing* intellectual history, the value of which has not yet been actualized as such in North-Atlantic circuits of symbolic capital.

---

6   Anderson goes on to elaborate on the changing historical conditions that cut the ties between social struggles and intellectual practice in the countries of the North Atlantic. One of the most striking features that Anderson detects "about the whole tradition from Lukacs to Althusser ... is the overwhelming predominance of professional philosophers within it," an academic emplacement of theory that, as he observes, was emphatically scorned by earlier Marxists of the Second International, such as Rosa Luxemburg (52).

Crucial here is the fact that, although African cultural production has been increasingly present in academic spheres outside the continent for the past few decades, it has been mostly limited to the role of object enunciated, exotic fetish, or commodity for the mere appropriation and accumulation of symbolic capital for scholars in the North Atlantic. An intellectual history of Africa can serve to legitimate the continent as a site for self-reflexive and critical enunciation, for the production of theory in the aforementioned sense.

Let me now turn to the work of contemporary Tanzanian political economist Issa Shivji since his work is solid ground from which to argue that, while wanting admittance to the enabling global circuits of production and consumption of cultural capital, African intellectual production is, on the other hand, in a privileged position when it comes to the production of meaning, the socially relevant and historically transformative function of theory that Anderson finds so poignantly absent in postwar Western Marxism, not to mention in contemporary theory in general.[7]

In 2007, having been involved in NGO activism for over fifteen years, Issa Shivji published *Silences in NGO Discourse: The Role and Future of NGOs in Africa*, a book that examines NGOs in Africa as a key element of the neocolonialist project. After a historical account of the advance of NGOs on the continent – an advance traceable in figures such as the 400 percent British government increase for funding NGOs overseas between 1984 and 1994 – Shivji puts forward the thesis that "the proponents of neoliberalism saw in charitable development the possibility of enforcing the unjust social order they desired by consensual rather than coercive means" (ix). Therefore, he argues, NGOs are to the neo-liberal project what Christian missionaries were to the colonialist one: the human face at the forefront of the imperialist enterprise. Let us not forget also that NGOs are the form of governmentality that prevails in all of "unusable Africa," in the zones of widespread banditry and warlordism to which Ferguson referred.

The first of the "five silences" of NGOs that Shivji addresses is their unrevised emergence as a reaction of the international donor community to the nation-state centered period in African history (30). Secondly, the author addresses

---

7 I have stressed contemporary Marxism's lack of a social anchorage to adequately produce meaning because a maxim of this philosophical tradition is the transformation (rather than mere interpretation) of the world. Yet this lack of anchorage is a widespread characteristic in contemporary thought and by no means limited to Marxism. While Jonathan Culler, for example, elaborates on post-structuralism's derailment into hyper-formalist and self-referent acrobatics of thought in a number of First World academic niches, Jameson speaks of a basic break between signifier and referent in postmodern society.

NGO activists in Africa, who are mostly urban elites, with only a small sub-portion of them acting out of desire for genuine political transformation. Another subset, argues Shivji, is constituted by altruistic or morally motivated individuals who nonetheless tend to be ignorant of the complicities implicit in the actions in which they engage. Yet, by far the largest subgroup of NGO activists is formed by career-driven individuals. In a continent in which work opportunities in the private sector are lacking and in which governments are thinning out, NGOs increasingly function simply as a source of income (Shivji 31).

The third silence Shivji mentions is that, being donor-funded, NGOs must follow donor agendas. These donors, legitimated as "civil society," are at worst foreign government agencies and at best a non-African civil society. Given that in countries such as Zambia, seventy percent of government revenue consists of foreign aid, national sovereignty is seriously put into question. But it is with regard to the last two "silences of NGO discourse" that Shivji directly addresses the function of the intellectual and the historical purpose of knowledge production as critique.

What the author terms the "fourth silence" is that NGOs are issue-based. In true identity politics style, the organizations target the surface symptom of a problem such as gender violence or child malnutrition and, in disavowing the larger structural ties of such issues in society and history, allow for the problem to continue reproducing itself. This myopic approach can be maintained so long as there persists a rift between academic research and activist agendas. That divorce between critical thought and political action is by all means deliberate. As Shivji bluntly puts it: "our erstwhile benefactors tell us: 'just act, don't think; and we shall fund both'" (35). The fifth silence also relates to the disablement of praxis and the de-historicization of discourse. Shivji refers here to the vagueness of the missions written out by NGOs. In their vagueness, NGO mission statements celebrate moral principles in the abstract; their floating signification is what allows for the naturalization of neo-liberal values.[8] This hegemonic appropriation of terms such as "freedom," "self-governance" or "civil-society" as understood by neo-liberalism can only be counteracted by being historicized.

---

8   See Laclau. Despite later variations, in 1997 Ernesto Laclau holds that floating and empty signifiers are, for all practical purposes, the same: "In the case of a floating signifier we would apparently have an overflowing of meaning while an empty signifier, on the contrary, would ultimately be a signifier without a signified. But if we analyze the matter more carefully, we realize that the floating character of a signifier is the only phenomenal form of its emptiness" (306).

Shivji describes how NGO discourse seems to have internalized Fukuyama's idea of the end of history, the idea that we live in a "permanent present" in which "the hegemony of the imperialist North is declared permanent" and "[a]ny historical understanding of our present state is ridiculed and dismissed," "reduced to a blaming exercise" or "tolerated as a token to ... create the illusion of diversity" (37, 38). Shivji interrogates the NGO slogan that summons us to "Make Poverty History" by asking, "but how can you make poverty history without understanding the history of poverty?" (37). As he elaborates, only in understanding the present as history can we have any hope of changing it (38). Hence, what contemporary hegemonic discourse as articulated in NGO rhetoric forecloses is the political force of history as a *function* of the present.

By historicizing the notion of civil society, Shivji questions the widespread presupposition of "civil society" as a "harmonious whole" (28). Such an assumption comes from both activist and scholarly locations in the West, particularly in Anglo-America today. I am thinking, for example, of the work of Canadian political philosopher Richard Day. In his book *Gramsci is Dead*, which had a direct impact on the Occupy Wall Street movement, Day attributes the failures of the contemporary left to their retrograde forms of organization in political parties and trade unions, and proposes instead to follow the informal modes of organization proper to civil society, which he views as "non-universalizing, non-hierarchical, non-coercive relationships based on mutual aid and shared ethical commitments" (9). Shivji questions the possibility of such uninterested and unmarked forms of organization, since he understands civil society historically, as the realm of economic relations emerging with the birth of the bourgeoisie, and examines the re-emergence of the concept, also historically, in terms of its growing popularity in public discourse in the era of structural adjustment programs. He is thus able to conceive of civil society as a "terrain of contradictory relations" (Shivji 28). By questioning the artificial division of state and civil society, Shivji reassesses the nationalist period in Africa and, in direct opposition to the World Bank's diagnosis of African states as the villains responsible for the continent's declining economic performance, actually proposes to understand the nationalist moment in African history as the constitutive contradiction, the exception, the relative outside, or what he terms "the fundamental antithesis" to the imperialist project (1; see also 20).

Thinking of Adorno's proposition that ideology is based on constitutive exclusions and that to contest an ideology is to negate its negation, to push it towards the realization of its own promise, Shivji's persisting praxis in NGO activism (in and through his severe critique of it), as well as his invocation of the nationalist project as a history to be owned, in the full sense of the term, are carried out in true negative dialectical fashion. They are a way of invoking a particular history to actualize its promise in the present. While conscious of the "politically authoritarian, economically rapacious, internationally compradorial and nationally dictatorial" degenerations of African nationalisms over the course of time, Shivji is still able to build upon the intellectual and political legacy of his countryman, Julius Nyerere, to call forth an exception to that project that was nonetheless possible, however provisionally (11–3).

Thus, in working to destroy the system by pushing it to fulfill its own promise, Shivji is following the path of negative dialectics. Yet, unlike Adorno's negative dialectics, this is not a finished project, not an "esoteric" one, to use Perry Anderson's term. Shivji's project is not hermetic insofar as intellectual production for him is above all else a historically specific use value, a use value of great political force. In that sense, he does not seek to realize African theory as symbolic capital; his concern is not with the socially legitimized representational value of intellectual production, but with its transformative potential, its capacity to bring the past to bear upon the present.

Conclusions

African theory has a history. Its intellectual praxis is not an absent but a peripheralized tradition; and yet this disavowal is precisely what hinders its participation in global circuits of symbolic capital production and accumulation. Symbolic capital, by definition, can only be constituted retroactively. It is in our own reception of African theory that we render it infra-valuable. Since Theory itself, as symbolic capital, relies on its existence as a scarce value, the foreclosure of African intellectual production as theory is a sine qua non requirement for the emergence of Theory as such.

Shivji's *Silences in NGO Discourse* entails a theoretical praxis that contributes to undoing the meaning of Africa as infra-peripheral space and, in so doing, may help undermine – even if in the most circumscribed of manners – the whole triadic structure of core, periphery and infra-periphery. The intersections of intellectual reflection and political action in Shivji's trajectory also relativize the alleged escape from instrumental reason of much contemporary Theory in the North Atlantic tradition. Yet, this has only been a case study with a much broader bearing. Reassessing Shivji's work, but also that of other African theorists, is a way to push for the entrance of African knowledge production into valued global circuits of symbolic capital, and also to question the nature and function of these circuits themselves, to ask what the uses of symbolic capital are to the status quo, and to recall the contingency of that history even as we participate in its production.

Shivji also exposes how NGOs render the work – the dirty work – of neo-liberalism invisible. They do so by allowing donor countries to gain traction in terms of symbolic capital, while foreclosing the possibility for intellectual production in the continent to operate as a use value. Africa as infra-periphery is thus not only excluded from direct modes of capitalist exploitation but also marked as a terrain whose access to the symbolic is once again foreclosed. If Africa as theoretical and economic infra-periphery legitimizes the apparent self-sufficiency of the core-periphery as a hermetic whole, it also constitutes a relative outside from which to break out of the hegemonic imagination of the politics of space in a world that rewrites exploitation at the periphery as privilege.

Works Cited

Adorno, Theodor W. *Negative Dialectics*. 1966. Trans. E.B. Ashton. New York: Continuum, 1983.

Anderson, Perry. *Considerations on Western Marxism*. London: Verso, 1979.

Bourdieu, Pierre. "The Forms of Capital." *Handbook of Theory and Research for the Sociology of Education*. Ed. John G. Richardson. Westport: Greenwood Press, 1986. 241–58.

Butler, Judith. *Precarious Life: The Powers of Mourning and Violence*. London: Verso, 2006.

Culler, Jonathan. "Structure of Ideology and Ideology of Structure." *New Literary History* 4.3 (1973): 471–82.

Day, Richard J.F. *Gramsci is Dead: Anarchist Currents in the Newest Social Movements*. London: Pluto Press, 2005.

Denning, Michael. "Wageless Life." *New Left Review* 66 (2010): 79–97.

Economist, The. "Information Technology in Africa: The Next Frontier." *The Economist*. 23 Aug. 2012. Web. 1 May 2015.

———. "Innovation in Africa: Upwardly Mobile." *The Economist*. 14 Feb. 2013. Web. 1 May 2015.

Ferguson, James. "Globalizing Africa?: Observations from an Inconvenient Continent." *Global Shadows: Africa in the Neoliberal World Order*. Durham: Duke UP, 2006. 25–49.

Fröbel, Folker, Jürgen Heinrichs, and Otto Kreye. *The New International Division of Labour*. Cambridge: Cambridge UP, 1980.

Hegel, G.W.F. "Introduction to *The Philosophy of History*." *Great Books of the Western World*. Ed. Robert M. Hutchins. London: Encyclopedia Britannica, 1952. 151–201.

Jameson, Fredric. *Postmodernism or the Cultural Logic of Late Capitalism*. London: Verso, 1991.

Laclau, Ernesto. "The Death and Resurrection of the Theory of Ideology." *MLN* 112.3 (1997): 297–321.

Rodney, Walter. *How Europe Underdeveloped Africa*. London: Bogle-L'Ouverture and Tanzanian Publishing House, 1972.

Said, Edward W. *Orientalism*. 1978. London: Penguin Books, 2003.

Shivji, Issa G. *Silences in NGO Discourse: The Role and Future of NGOs in Africa*. Nairobi: Fahamu, 2007.

Spivak, Gayatri Chakravorty. "More on Power/Knowledge." *Outside in the Teaching Machine*. New York: Routledge, 1993. 25–51.

Wallerstein, Immanuel. "Africa in a Capitalist World." *Issue: A Journal of Opinion* 10.1–2 (1980): 21–31.

———. *World Systems Analysis: An Introduction*. London: Duke UP, 2004.

CHAPTER 3

Fragments in Relation: Trajectories of/for an Unbound Europe

Sudeep Dasgupta

> Making the logic of the figure sensuous...
> SPIVAK 22

Herta Müller opened her acceptance speech on receiving the Nobel Prize for Literature in 2009 with the words "I stand here, as I often do, beside myself."[1] Originating from the German minority in Romania, growing up in the countryside before moving to Bucharest and finally settling in Germany, Müller's trajectory could be described as one from the periphery to the center. The crowning of her literary work in Stockholm with the Nobel Prize is an occasion where she outlines a figure displaced within and between itself. She disperses herself into a composition of figures standing beside each other. The figure of the writer arrives alongside her multiple selves at the center, which acknowledges her. What logic manifests in a self discursively figuring itself simultaneously next to itself? What logic is manifested in a discourse which figures a centered self simultaneously dispersing itself?

This counter-intuitive logic can be better understood as making the figuration of the self sensual and aesthetic, in this case through the agency of words. By making logic sensuous, a path can be laid for the sensory apprehension of a reality where selves figure themselves in relation to each other. Analyzing the figurations of selves in relation to themselves and others through images and sounds, movement and stasis in Sébastien Lifshitz's *Wild Side* (2004), this chapter sketches a politics of indifference which confounds the logic of both a centered self and its peripheral others. Through a reading of the sensual construction of the film and its sensorial apprehension, I draw the outlines for a politics and aesthetics of figuring contemporary Europe. Figurations of the self in the film construct a sensual acknowledgement of the presence of difference while eschewing the logic of identity and identification which underwrites center-periphery distinctions.

---

1 "Ich stehe (wie so oft) auch hier neben mir selbst." The official translation on the Nobel Foundation website reads: "Here too, as is often the case, I am standing beside myself." http://www.nobelprize.org/nobel_prizes/literature/laureates/2009/muller-speech_en.html.

© KONINKLIJKE BRILL NV, LEIDEN, 2016 | DOI 10.1163/9789004323056_005

Determining the self through identification is one way of logically confirming its stability. Multiplying the self is one mode of figuring the self and acknowledging its sensual disfiguration – the many *in* oneself next to other selves which are also one's own. In English, "to be beside oneself" connotes losing control of oneself, overcome particularly by the senses and perhaps emotions of grief and joy. This formulation is one way of figuring the self's displacement – not the displacement effected by a stable self moving from one place to another, from the periphery to the center or the other way around, but a displacement intrinsic to the self, producing a multiplication of selves rendered indeterminate by this dispersion which is affective and sensorial as much as it is counter-intuitively logical. To rephrase Gayatri Spivak's formulation, the logic of the figure of the self is undone by the sensuous, by the sensory reverberations of the self's dispersal and multiplication. Müller's decentered self is both the speaking subject and the figural subject(s) standing next to her. This is one way of thinking the periphery without a center. Lifshitz's *Wild Side* triangulating a shifting relationship between three uncertainly-figured protagonists, intensifies this displacing logic through figurations of the multiplied self as fragments in relation with others within a transnational European space.

Müller's formulation is aporetic, for who is the self speaking if it acknowledges its self standing beside it? Yet such an aporia is put into language by the formulation, and begins to point to the central focus of the argument below. Undoing language's identificatory drive through the senses – "this is the center, and that the periphery, you belong there, in the periphery, for here is the center" – must pass through language too. Deployed against the logical certainty of making figures knowable through their *location*, language instead acknowledges sensory presence without ascribing meaning and knowledge. Alexander García Düttman's (2000) emphatic separation of recognition from re-cognition is based on this difference in the function of language. Recognition (*Erkenntnis*) deploys cognition to erase the instability which threatens a demand for recognition. Recognition (*Anerkennung*) acknowledges, rather, presence as a sensuous figuration without identifying, naming and locating its difference from the same. This sensuous figure, acknowledged but not identified, divided from within and multiplied alongside itself, is the subject of a politics of indifference.

The same/other, center/periphery division has been one powerful way of neutralizing the disturbing power of "the periphery." The politics of difference is predicated on the production of distinctions and the identification of identities, and location is one parameter for stabilizing such identified subjects. Once ascribed a clearly identifiable physical, geographical or historical location, the periphery functions in different ways to shore up a fictitiously transparent center while stabilizing the relational dynamic between the two. (The preceding sentence testifies to this aporetic dimension of language, which can only undermine a center/periphery division by calling it up.) Acknowledgement of presence rather than knowledge through identification, however, marks the basis of a politics of indifference. The politics of indifference framed through language's potential for *figuring the sensuous* unmakes logic's stabilization of difference. Figural acknowledgement is a disfiguration of knowledge. "Indifference" is the simultaneous acknowledgement of the presence of difference without the logical reduction of it to a definite meaning or location (the periphery).

Sensory Aesthetics and Multiple Peripheralisms

The aesthetic dimension is crucial in living through the conflictual and dynamic border-shifting coordinates of political imaginaries, including those of Europe. Lifshitz's *Wild Side* gestures in the title towards both the wildness and unpredictability of borders, as well as towards the subjects whose life trajectories crisscross multiple transnational spaces. The film, in other words, constructs sensual figurations of subjective trajectories which call center-periphery distinctions into question. Aesthetics itself can be understood as precisely the *sensorial* breaking down of borders between subjects and objects, bodies and the spaces they move through, certain self-knowledge and destabilizing partial knowledges. Aesthetics is the name for the sensorial displacement of the given quality of borders. The politics of indifference must pass through aesthetics as the sensorial construction and apprehension of boundary-crossings to be sensed and apprehended. Susan Buck-Morss underlines these two dimensions of aesthetics as sensory experience and of embodied border-crossing succinctly:

> *Aisthisis* is the ancient Greek word for that which is "perceptive by feeling." *Aisthisis* is the sensory experience of perception ... It is a form of cognition achieved through taste, touch, hearing, seeing, smell – the whole corporeal sensorium. The terminae of all of these ... are located at the surface of the body, the mediating boundary between inner and outer. This physical-cognitive apparatus ... is "out front" of the mind ... prior not only to logic but to meaning as well.
> BUCK-MORSS 6

This specific understanding of aesthetics centralizes the displacing potential of sensory perception, which is irreducible to logic and meaning. The surface of the body being "out front" of it harbors the potential for shifting the embodied self "beside itself" because the senses can undo their subsumption to logic and meaning. The sensual figuration of difference and the politics of indifference are intrinsically linked. In the reading of *Wild Side,* the aesthetic is understood doubly. A sensorial understanding of the aesthetic stages both the experiential dimensions of film viewing and the lived realities of traveling bodies in Europe. Firstly, for the viewing subject the film produces sensually apprehended figurations of purportedly peripheral subjects populating the wildside of contemporary Europe. Secondly, by aesthetically rendering the corporeal experience of the multiple subjects populating locations in Europe, the film renders indeterminate the boundaries of outside and inside, citizen and non-citizen, male and female, homo- and heterosexual, and center and periphery. The aesthetics which furthers a politics of difference exploits and sensorially intensifies the destabilizing mediations which undermine inside and outside, not just of spaces in Europe but also of the viewing body which sensuously registers this disruptive mediation. The bodies on screen and the viewing body are the grounds on which this unstable geography of center and periphery plays out.

Roland Barthes's musings on his experiences in Morocco help frame the first dimension of aesthetics as filmic figuration. As an economically-privileged traveler from Europe in a country with complex links to France, Barthes's observations are located somewhere between center and periphery, and mediate how others observe him. He notices:

> In Morocco, they evidently had no image of me; my efforts, as a good European, to be *this* or *that* received no reply: neither *this* nor *that* was returned in the form of a fine adjective; it never occurred to them to *gloss* me, they unwittingly refused to feed and flatter my image-repertoire ... this matte quality of human relationships ... gradually came to seem a triumph of civilization or the truly dialectical form of erotic discourse.
>
> BARTHES 2010: 43, emphasis in text

The absence of a reply is nevertheless a response. It is a refusal to produce "a fine adjective" which would gloss the centrality of the subject. Instead, the "matte quality" of human relationships displaces established image-repertoires and produces a sensorial and relational understanding of selves acknowledging each other rather than knowing each other through adjectives. Barthes provocatively calls this "a triumph of civilization," overturning a Western prioritization of language as communication and tool of reason for the productive vacancy in the image returned to the traveler. Similarly, the images that construct *Wild*

Side deploy temporality "gradually" to wipe out the adjectival slowly and render vacant the space bordered by the image. Through the construction of images as fragments set into relation, the film's de-populating of image-space produces a sensorial figuration of the political power of acknowledging presences.

The vacating of the image's fullness does not mean the disappearance of the image, but its transformation. The functional transformation of the image from vehicle for meaning-production to the registering of presences engenders an ethics of discretion and respect. Discretion is an acknowledgement of the value of presence without the measuring of its worth through adjectives (the "good European") such as economically desirable immigrant or well-educated foreigner, which populate much discourse issuing from the centers of national and European state power. Barthes's figuration of the image is not iconoclastic but disruptive, productive and transformative. That is why he argues, displacing himself and adopting the position of a third person:

> He is troubled by any *image* of himself, suffers when he is named. He finds the perfection of a human relationship in this vacancy of the image: to abolish – in oneself, between oneself and others – *adjectives*: a relationship which adjectivizes is on the side of the image, on the side of domination, of death.
>
> BARTHES 2010: 43, emphasis in text

Disfigurations of Presence

Wild Side is an exploration of a triadic relationship between Stéphanie/ Pierre, Djamel and Mikhail/Mishka. Moving back and forth in time between their individual and collective histories while spreading out across border-confounding spaces, the presencing of their figurations outlines a complex historical and geographical map. Stéphanie *is* transsexual and presumably French. Pierre names a self that is dead to her and consigned to her past prior to her new gender identity. Djamel *is* French, of North African origin and presumably from Paris or somewhere near it; Mikhail is a Russian army deserter with a traumatic past in Chechnya whose multiple names register his scattered personal history (and geography) between Russia, Chechnya and France, and between his mother and his lovers, who come to form a new family. The film's figurations undo the identifying violence of the verbal construction ("is") which I am obliged to produce above.

Immediately, one could "identify" the three as peripheral to any normative understanding of Europeanness, if by that we mean the stability of identity

based on region, nationality, sexual identity and orientation, and legal citizenship. But in two ways this identification fails. The linguistic translation of their
visual construction does not match the neutrality – that is, the non-classificatory
language – of the film and its perceptual experience. The images produced
through film are not fulsome, and glossed adjectival renderings of categorical
presence are absent. The images, in their own relation to other images and to
the multiple selves continually relating to each other, produce what Barthes,
above, called the "matte quality of human relationships." Secondly, the image-
enabled mediation of inside and outside which the aesthetics of presence produces confounds the boundaries between center and periphery, self and other,
and refuses the clear equations between body and identity usually captured under demographic categories like gender, nation, sexuality and language.

Barthes's somewhat provocative equation of adjectival renderings of the
self with social "death" can now be linked to the sensorial perception of images as the acknowledgement of life in indeterminately located spaces through
his notion of the "neutral." "Tell me how you classify and I will tell you who you
are," is how Barthes ventriloquizes the demand for identification emanating
from a centering and space-ordering power:

> [T]he neutrality of an order ... becomes an esthetic problem ... society
> has always given an exorbitant privilege to charged signs and crudely
> identified a zero degree of things with their negation [that is, zero degree,
> the neutral is uncharged]: for us, there is little place and little consider-
> ation for the neutral, which is always felt morally as an impotence to be
> or to destroy.
> BARTHES 1972: 85–6

The threat of the neutral as a strategy of figuration emerges here. If the word
"neutral," which conjures up the "neutered," is seen normatively as impotent,
then the urge to destroy it through the classificatory function of language seems
paradoxical. Why feel the need to destroy that which is impotent? Precisely
this paradox is a symptom of the threat posed by acknowledging presence.
The neutral figuration of presences *seems* impotent, but its power can only be
neutered if language's rightful function is identified as that of identifying and
classifying.

The task of speaking about the Neutral, Barthes says, is

> how to recognize the world as a tissue of aporias, how to live until death
> by going (painfully, pleasurably) through the aporias, without undo-
> ing them by a logical, dogmatic blow of force? ... how to live aporias as

creation ... by the practice of a text-discourse that doesn't break the aporia but floats it as speech that tangles itself in the other ... ?

BARTHES 2005: 69, emphasis in text

Floating the aporia between order and disorder, the cinematography of the
neutral figures bodies – in – relation as they displace identities and topogra-
phies. Neutral images in that sense vacate the image of the gloss of meaning.
This filmic language flirts with but refuses the intended putting to death of
the subject by reducing it to stereotyped and stabilized categories of gender,
sexuality and citizenship.

Living in a world comprised of a tissue of aporias here could mean many
things: falling in love with a dead boy who is a very alive woman (Pierre and
Stéphanie), living one's sexuality through a doing that metamorphizes one's
identity as a fragment in relationality (Djamel, Mikhail), living in a location
that is both interior and exterior to the city (highway, hotel room, park) and
to the nation and *supra*-state (France and Europe). The mediation of center
and periphery is always incomplete because their relation to each other is continually destabilized. The construction of "vacant" images whose unlocalizable
presence crosses inside/outside coordinates of sensory presence and signifying
presence undoes a strict division between interior spaces and intimate practices on the one hand, and between publicly recognized and socially categorized
actions and locations on the other. These "matte" image constructions of human relationships emphasize what Lauren Berlant (1998) exposed as the shaky
contours of what counts as the "public" with regard to intimacy, and relationally
float images as fragments across boundary-defined forms of cultural legibility.

By "tagging" the body, its identity is stabilized by equating its location in the
periphery with a definite meaning. The aporia any language, including film,
confronts is how to figure this body, and its relation to other bodies, without
tagging it. This is the aporia *Wild Side* confronts and floats in Barthes's sense
by, firstly, *fragmenting* the body's visualization and, secondly, setting its pro-
liferating presences in *relational* constellations within and between its own
images and those of other bodies and selves, thereby producing contingent
acknowledgements across language, bodies, non-communicated histories and
unstable geographies.

Fragments

To spin the web is not to twist sensations into an embroidery in order to
capture ... it is to make of these sensations points of departure ...

RANCIÈRE 2011b: 243

The title sequence of *Wild Side* is sensorially apprehended as a series of fragments. The curve of a full breast and the soft molding of a waist by hairless
flesh is accompanied by an image of a penis nestled between slim hips. The
body emerges (it is Stéphanie/Pierre) but does not merge, image to referent,
into male or female. The status of the image as fragment is produced by a
shadowed image of a part of a body whose gradual apprehension is temporally
produced by the progressive viewing of images of its multiple parts. The
body is not visualized complete, in one image; it emerges through image fragments that do not merge into a normatively recognizable sexed body. The
temporal production of a body through images thwarts the desire to locate
a normative, "charged" meaning at the end of the sequence of images. This
strategy of fragmentation, which acknowledges presence yet fails to definitive-
ly establish a clear relation between the temporal succession of images and
a narrative culmination of the meaningful visualization of a totality, spreads
from the title sequence across the entire film and its sensorial viewing experience. The fragment in movement produces the first limnings of the aesthetic
production of a politics of indifference. The film orchestrates a sensory fabric
which embroiders an indeterminate design. The temporal succession of fragments produces a perceptible experience marked not by images captured and
then stabilized into identities, but as points of departure that set relations
adrift.

The visualization of sex between Stéphanie, Djamel and Mikhail takes place
in the intimate, domestic spaces of their home, contrasted with the often public spaces in which their bodies function in sexual commerce. (All three sell
sex at some point and with varying frequency throughout the film.) Yet the
significance of this interiority – sex within the triadic relationship – is not always visualized through an identificatory logic which makes sexual difference,
gender stability or sexual desire visually identifiable. The extreme close-ups
of their bodies make it often difficult to identify who is doing what to whom.
Arms, legs, mouths, hands clearly tangle and untangle but which body part
belongs to which self remains unclear. If visualizing and presenting sexual intimacy between the three would be one privileged place to locate the intimate
chemistry of their symbiotic relationship, the close-up here fragments their
bodies and eschews identification. Further, the absence of non-diegetic music
(something of a staple in most of Lifshitz's work) does not overlay the images
of intimacy with meanings such as tenderness or urgent desire. In other scenes
where sex is traded for money (Djamel with a woman, and later two men in
the toilets of a train station, Stéphanie in a car, Stéphanie and Mikhail at their
first meeting in a hotel room performing for a client), the camera keeps a
definite distance to set the physical context and identify client, consumer and
exchange. The intimate vantage point of the camera in the private physical

encounters between the three might seem to mirror their actual emotional intimacy. But the extreme closeness of the camera works precisely in the opposite way: by making it hard to identify the "owners" of the bodies, the tangle of limbs visually floats the aporetic relation between image and meaning, body and identity, or, in Barthes's words, text and discourse. The entanglement of bodies floats the aporia of their ex-centric identities which affirm fleshly presence disentangled from meaning. Conversely, the distanced gaze of the camera that identifies bodies, sexual acts and their meaning identifies their public if clandestine work rather than the intimate truths of their private selves. The visual strategies of proximity and distance switch the functions of visible identification and concealment.

The visual construction of bodies as fragments in motion is accompanied by the sounds of words. The *language of words* rather than words in language is one way in which language's identifying logic is neutralized and the image made vacant. By *language of words* I mean the construction and dispersion of words whose relational transfer between the protagonists does not communicate the literal meaning of words. Rather, their words communicate a *willingness to communicate* and connect. Further, this communication of the language of words does not proceed from a central location such as the French language, even though two of the three protagonists are French speakers in a film set in France. Given that Stéphanie, Djamel and Mikhail must negotiate differences in personal history, sexuality, gender and language, for example, none of them occupies a stable position from which the others can be addressed. Mikhail's ignorance of the French language requires Djamel and Stéphanie to speak in heavily accented broken English. With hands and feet, and through the game of football, Djamel and Mikhail mediate their reciprocal linguistic differences as they express their growing affection and sexual desire. When Mikhail meets Stéphanie's mother for the first time, on hearing that he is Russian, she sings a few lines of the song "Kalinka." The sounds of the song do not communicate the literal meaning of the words. Rather, the sonority of the images which Mikhail and Stéphanie's mother share sensually mediate their differences while acknowledging her desire to welcome him. Djamel's ambivalence around Stéphanie's gendered body, articulated in stumbling words, places her in a seemingly subordinate position but the intense affective connection between them overrides the power he might have as being normatively "male." The meaning of voice and sound is the acknowledgement of each other's presence and the expression of a willingness to form a connection, rather than transferring information toward identifying difference. The sensual figuration of images and their intertwined relation to sounds, songs and voices make their fragmentary sensory figurations perceptible as occasions for bridging center-periphery distinctions and relaying affect, desire and affection across boundaries of gender, sexuality, nation and language.

In her reading of Benjamin's *Berliner Chronik* and its specifically fragmentary montage-like structure, Crystal Bartolovich argues: "(E)ach fragment ... is at once threshold and network of intertwinings, incomplete in itself, but nevertheless evidence of, and the route to, a totality that remains beyond our full imagining, both because it is a process, not a stable 'thing', and because of its complexity" (94). The fragment is always en route to somewhere else and hence a center-periphery model is undone by movement. The image fragments in *Wild Side* travel along a continuing journey scattered across multiple non-synchronous times and heterotopic spaces. If the fragment is sensorially experienced as a threshold pointing to an unimaginable totality (Transnational Europe), this is not an alibi for pathos or an announcement of times to come or messianic returns. Instead, the fragment marks the threshold of a "network of intertwinings" of bodies, words, images, spaces and times. The poetics of the image at play in the interval between pure presence and signification generates disjunctive totalities of mobile fragments in relation.

Fragments Set into Relation

The film constructs images visualized as fragments and vacated of identifiable substance. But rather than fragments that lie passively to be arranged into an organic totality, the fragment is by definition dynamic and unstable. Jacques Rancière, for example, drawing inspiration from German Romanticism, understands the fragment not as a to-be-totalized thing. Instead, the fragment sets a process in motion. Following Hölderlin's statement that "all ash is pollen," Rancière argues: "A fragment is not a ruin, it is more of a seed." Rather than the "mark of an unfinished and detotalized status," the fragment, for Rancière, "is the unity in which every fixed thing is put back into the movement of metamorphosis." It is a "finite figure of an infinite process" (2011a: 56) and contingent relationalities are precisely one potential which fragments can invite. In *Wild Side*, the images and sounds set into movement figurations of a non-totalizing series of relationalities which take root and germinate across the normative privileging of a centralized location in the nation or its language and culture. Culture, rather, is the fertile ground for the dissemination of these boundary-confounding relations between selves.

The mobility of images of fragments of bodies is marked early in the film. "People keep coming and going," mutters a middle-aged woman in Russian to Mikhail, who has arrived at a rundown flophouse somewhere in Paris. She is referring to the itinerant and often "illegal" men, primarily from the former Soviet bloc, who stop temporarily in this flat before moving on elsewhere. The location of such arrivals and departures suggests a train station or an airport perhaps. What if this apartment might also be a way of seeing a home, and a transnational one at that? The location of the house in Paris is "central," in the capital of a nation, yet its status is indeterminate. It does not stabilize the movement of those from the "periphery" by housing them permanently. This central location which facilitates further movement in and out of the center undoes the center-periphery distinction as providing the primary coordinates for understanding movement. The presence of the woman on screen, which lasts only a few seconds, is typical of the fragmentary appearance of characters without introduction. Rendering spaces as fragments of moving images and sounds which set people and histories into relation, the film destabilizes the identification of place with spatial location. The physical desire and ambulatory bodies of the three protagonists are figured precisely in this relational setting – into – motion of fragments. Each fragment marks a transfer point between possible trajectories around terms like home, family and love. Extending Müller's multiple selves, which disperse her identity, the perceptible experience of the film sets the multiple selves of each protagonist in relation with those of the other two, and others. Relationality is thus intensified beyond an authoring self's multiplication "besides herself" to multiple selves in relation across different bodies, histories and locations.

The sequence of close-ups of naked bodies in sexual intimacy described above will connect sexual intimacy later on in the film to a metamorphosis of the meaning of family. Mikhail's loss of his family is compensated by Djamel's suggestion that he and Stéphanie could now become both Mikhail's father and mother. The lost mother, physically separated from Mikhail and accessible only through her voice heard through a payphone, becomes related, through Mikhail's lover, to an extending family across multiple spaces. Djamel's offer of a queer familial intimacy (the lovers as parents) is linked within a few seconds to a flashback which is not understandable at first – of a man with a young boy playing in an open field, figures we will later understand to be Stéphanie's father with her when she was a child and a boy, Pierre. The film temporally presents asynchronous fragments from the protagonists' lives chronologically without framing them. Their significance in terms of meaning is not immediately apparent – Pierre's father's sudden appearance is not introduced earlier in the "narrative" and thus his link to the adult Stéphanie is not decipherable easily in relation to the other image fragments of familial transformation and sexual intimacy. The fragments derive their power from being stitched together in a non-associative way, since the stagings of these fragments are not causally connected. Chronology and causality are delinked. The queer extension of family relations offered by Djamel to Mikhail is immediately followed by another sort of queerness: the identifiable father and son from the past pointing to a woman's past in another gender.

Bodily identity and integrity, sexual identity and orientation, the sexual and the familial, metamorphose in uncertain ways, asymptotically touching meaning before swerving away from narrative grasp and germinating in other moments of the narrative in different form. This is why the identification of the protagonists produced earlier in the language of sociology and demography does little justice to the trajectory they draw or are pulled along through images. Instead of a voyeuristic exhibition of a gallery of deviants – traumatized illegal Russian deserter, sexually confused bisexual *beur* hustler, tragic transsexual prostitute – the film produces experiential figurations of their knotted presences through silences, by bodies that move but do not speak, by faces that express but do not name, by stuttering and failed translations that still work. Barthes describes traditional descriptions as "major ideas [which] are coined into 'details' without for a moment entertaining the notion that major ideas can be generated from the mere arrangement and disposition of 'details'" (1972: 85). The images of *Wild Side* are just such dispositions of fragmentary details set in relation, and the ideas they generate are the effect of their temporal and spatial apprehension through visuality rather than through any intrinsic "gloss" which coins major ideas of normalcy or deviancy. Barthes goes on to argue:

> By destroying within discourse the notion of "part," [Michel Butor's *Mobile*] refers us to an infinitely sensitive mobility of closed elements. What are these elements? They have no form in themselves; they are neither ideas nor images nor sensations nor even notations, for they do not emerge from a projected restoration of experience ...
> BARTHES 1972: 88

The film, of course, is replete with images and sensations, yet the part fragments it produces are precisely *not* arranged towards the accomplishment of the goal of restoring, completing and identifying the experiences of the protagonists. Instead, the images and sensations acknowledge presence in two ways. Refusing any intrinsic meaning "in themselves," the forms they outline are relationally constructed. Further, the relation between these images-fragments does not stabilize the center/periphery division into a coherent whole ("a projected restoration of experience"). The projected images are instead a sensorially apprehended movement of fragments which figure presences, generating ideas without stabilizing knowledge. Displacement, desertion, gender and sexual transformation, and forced exile are experiences increasingly intensified (and turned into spectacle) in contemporary global conditions of precarity. The cinematically produced figurations of presence in *Wild Side* undermine stock stereotypes whose volubility often glosses presences into images as easily read-able commonplaces. The diegetic temporality of the film text and the asyn-chronous sensorial apprehension of the protagonists' lives scattered across Chechnya, a highrise in the *banlieu*, the parks where sex is bought and sold, and Stéphanie's familial home, among others, produce a prismatic spatio-temporal experience of the "wild side." The film asserts, through a potent neutrality, that normativity is not "all one can experience" – while sensorially registering the shocks reverberating across the social body and the bodies consigned to the margins of normative discourses of nation, race, sexuality and gender.

Conclusion

The relational dynamic of the film's textuality and its perceptual experience is fleshed out by constructing images as fragments set into motion. Their presences are audio-visually discernible, yet this form of acknowledgement is contingently based on whatever medium (sounds, words, bodies) facilitates their relations to each other. Given the temptation to classify through visual signifiers such as clothing and skin color who does and does not belong in transnational Europe, the film refuses to catalog and explicate in detail the interior psychic realities of the three protagonists who confuse gender and sexual identity. Because the individual might not give itself up so easy to visual translation, those who populate transnational Europe have the power to affirm their presence in the abyss that separates the concept in the image and the im-age's pure material presence.

   The resistance to naming on which a politics of indifference is based runs the risk, however, of implying an obfuscating aestheticism, particularly when "deviant" subjects ("illegals," sexual minorities, asylum-seekers, among oth-ers) are the currency through which Europe profitably deploys its discursive power. By constructing aesthetic experiences which swerve away from knowl-edge-production based on the clarity of meaning, the film, and my reading of it, could be seen as a mode of evading the urgent tasks of bringing into the light through vision the multiple subjects forced to occupy zones of precarity. A politics of indifference, however, does not ignore the presence of subjects shunted to the periphery. Rather, it acknowledges their presence and asserts their value without *measuring* their worth through strategies of identification prescribed by normative discourses. The aesthetics of a politics of indifference

emphatically acknowledges disturbing presences figured in sensory constructions of images, words and bodies. The figuration of such presences cannot be
charted along a continuum of explicit or implicit inscriptions, or manifest and
latent content. Rather, this form of aesthetics is visually very direct in terms of
showing bodies and sexualities but reticent in telling the "truth" of their presumed peripheral status.

An aesthetics of the politics of indifference is neither a refusal of recognition nor a reticence of self-affirmation. Rather, this sensorial figuration of
politics is an assertion of presence and an acknowledgment of its potential
for disturbing the spatial coordinates of center and periphery. Such a politics stages presences and confounds spatial consolidations that mark the
distinction between normalcy and deviancy. The politics of indifference furthers an answer to Étienne Balibar's interrogative "We, the People of Europe?"
(2003) by "staging the people" (Rancière 2011c) through "scenes" (Rancière 2003)
constructed by the disseminatory logic of fragments that germinate counter-
intuitively across bodies, gender, sexualities and nations.[2] The film's politics is
thus both a refusal and an assertion.

Asked to think the relationship between politics and the poetry of Keats,
Rancière argues that what characterizes poets like Keats is "a double refusal:
a refusal to make the poem a mark of their identity and a refusal to give their
dream a character of affirmation" (2011b: 244). Transposing this rendering of
the power of poetry to the poetics of the film and the sensuous figurations of
its characters, I argue that the visual perceptions of the trajectories of their
shifting relations produce a poetics of embodiment. In other words, the politics of the film derives not from a narratively produced explicit message about
the value of those in the margins. Rather, it embodies through sensual figurations presences that give flesh to experiences whose locations call into question the value of legitimizing spaces through a center/periphery distinction.
The film refuses to stabilize these relations of fragments into an identity, while
whatever futurity their desires point to (dreams perhaps?) are contingently articulated, connections which spin out "a spider's web" by "starting from a small
number of points of contact" (Rancière 2011b: 243). The fragility of the web and
the possible directions the protagonists' contacts might engender, make their
lives and indeed the space of the "wild side" indeterminate – no center, for the

---

2   Balibar undermines a center-periphery model by rewriting the discourse of belonging *to*
    Europe by asserting the presence of cultures *in* Europe. Jacques Rancière turns the question
    of identifying the people into one of *staging* the people. This metaphor from the theater is
    marked through the term "scenes" in the title of the original French version of *Staging the
    People: The Proletarian and his Double*. See *Scènes du peuple: Les révoltes logiques, 1975–1985*.

wild side occupies no identifiable periphery. The neutral figures this fragility of a presence that persists without affirming any determined goal or definite identity.

Works Cited

Balibar, Étienne. *We, the People of Europe? Reflections on Transnational Citizenship.* Princeton: Princeton UP, 2003.

Barthes, Roland. "Literature and Discontinuity." *Salmagundi* 18 (1972): 82–93.

———. *The Neutral: Lecture Course at the Collège de France (1977–1978).* New York: Columbia UP, 2005.

———. *Roland Barthes by Roland Barthes.* New York: Hill and Wang, 2010.

Bartolovich, Crystal. "Figuring the (In)visible in an Imperial *Weltstadt*: The Case of Benjamin's Moor." *Cultural Critique* 52 (Autumn 2002): 167–208.

Berlant, Lauren. "Intimacy: A Special Issue." *Critical Inquiry* 24.2 (1998): 281–88.

Buck-Morss, Susan. "Aesthetics and Anaesthetics: Walter Benjamin's Artwork Essay Reconsidered." *October* 62 (1992): 3–41.

Düttman, Alexander García. *Between Cultures: Tensions in the Struggle for Recognition.* London and New York: Verso, 2000.

Rancière, Jacques. *Scènes du peuple*: *Les révoltes logiques, 1975–1985*. Paris: Les Éditions Horlieu, 2003.

———. *Mute Speech: Literature, Critical Theory and Politics.* New York: Columbia UP, 2011a.

———. "The Politics of the Spider." *Studies in Romanticism* 50.2 (2011b): 239–50.

———. *Staging the People: The Proletarian and his Double.* London: Verso, 2011c.

Spivak, Gayatri Charkravorty. "Learning from de Man: Looking Back." *boundary* 2 32.3 (2005): 21–35.

Wild Side. Dir. Sébastien Lifshitz. Ad Vitam Distribution, 2004.

CHAPTER 4

Peripheral Worldscapes in Circulation: Towards a Productive Understanding of Untranslatability

Doro Wiese

In this chapter, I want to firstly shift understandings of untranslatability so that it can include narrative forms and tropes, and secondly discuss the novels *Ceremony* and *Almanac of the Dead* by the American Indian author Leslie Marmon Silko, of Laguna Pueblo and German origin, as case studies. I place myself squarely within seminal debates currently in progress in several academic fields: first, the discussion on so-called world literature as a distinct theoretical and practical approach within Comparative Literature; second, the question of untranslatability that has emerged from the "world literature" debate; and third, the issue of indigenous sovereignty and cultural autonomy that is central to American Indian Studies. When framed in terms of the discussion on world literature, untranslatability is a term that indicates a philosophy of language and culture. David Damrosch postulates that literary works are subject to transformations when circulating in other cultures, enabled by, for instance, translations; Emily Apter and Barbara Cassin remind us that processes of cultural transfer entail incommensurabilities, untranslatabilities and mis- or non-translation. Taking these positions one step further, I posit that untranslatability can also be established through narrative forms and tropes in works by authors like Silko, and that this untranslatability is discernable to Euro-Western readers, who then are able to come into contact with the fraying of meaning that, according to Gayatri Chakravorty Spivak, is experienced when one is translating.

Through a close reading that focuses on the formation of secrecy and the destruction of character in Silko's works, I will show that her textual strategies allow for a multi-cultural semiotics in which the untranslatable and the translatable meet. The proposed notion of untranslatability disturbs the dichotomy between center and periphery, a dichotomy that fundamentally relies on the discursive nexus between Western hegemonic power and the centrality of its knowledge production. Understanding how indigenous notions are or are not "translatable" is essential to our understandings of globalization processes and indigenous cultural autonomy, and can shift global power relations. Silko's novels are traversing the global and, as such, claim an undeniable presence

© KONINKLIJKE BRILL NV, LEIDEN, 2016 | DOI 10.1163/9789004323056_006

within what is considered the center and the periphery, while also shifting their boundaries and relations.

Shifting Understandings of Untranslatability

According to the authors, editors and translators of the *Dictionary of Untranslatables*, untranslatability is a concept that indicates the fragility inherent in sense making. Sense making is a never completed process inevitably threatened by unintelligibility and failure, especially when we work across languages and cultures. Yet, as I want to argue, when reading fiction, readers need to understand much more than the meaning of words and concepts. As I have contended elsewhere, readers need to make sense of "the use of vocabulary, syntax, semantics, characters, narration, and plot – the whole configuration of the fictional text's chronotopical world" (Wiese 6). Sense making can fail on any of these levels, and therefore a fictional configuration can, similarly to words and concepts, evoke a confrontation with untranslatables. According to translation theorist Lawrence Venuti (1995; 1998; 2000), this confrontation with untranslatables is desirable if we want to overcome an ethnocentric violence foundational for many translations that circulate on the global literary market. According to Venuti, translations are nowadays evaluated highly if they give readers the illusion of reading an original rather than a translated work. If translators want to become successful, they need to succumb to a common practice that aims to create a translation's immediate intelligibility and accessibility. According to Venuti, this economy of violence – which is partial to the hegemonic values of the target culture – can be interrupted by a translation practice that asserts the cultural difference of the original work (1995). For Venuti, a good translation reminds readers of the heterogeneity of discourses and reveals the translation to be a translation (1998: 11). This ethics of translation is also highlighted by Gayatri Chakravorty Spivak in "The Politics of Translation." She stresses that translations facilitate "the experience of contained alterity in an unknown language spoken in a different cultural milieu" if the translator allows a text's logic and rhetoric to diverge (179). Untranslatability can thereby be understood, as I want to show, as a marker of cultural difference.

Building upon this discussion, I argue that Silko withholds or distorts crucial information in her texts and establishes layers of meaning only those familiar with indigenous belief systems and narrative traditions such as, for instance, oral storytelling can detect. The text thereby gives rise to different reader-responses. Narratively established untranslatability can therefore be defined as being recognizable and discernable. By this I mean that Western, non-indigenous readers, including myself, can be confronted with notions that are untranslatable and impinge on their Western ways of knowing and being. Readers that are, however, familiar with the indigenous world-views established in Silko's work might be able to fill in the gaps established in her work. I will show that it is possible to register and discern what kind of narrative strategies give rise to this differentiated form of (un-)translatability.

My suggestion to extend the notion of untranslatability to include narrative forms and tropes gives even greater weight to the intervention that this concept is meant to make. According to Emily Apter, world literature as a field of study needs to be highly aware of how it contributes to the marketing of differences. In many of Apter's texts, including her most recent monograph *Against World Literature*, she admonishes scholars, editors and readers for "zoom[ing] over the speed bumps of untranslatability to cover ground" (3). Untranslatability is a means to disturb processes of appropriation within the field of world literature, and such disturbance is, according to Apter, brought about because any meaning is language-specific and cannot be separated from its original context. Untranslatables – words and concepts that often remain untranslated in other languages – are for Apter just an extreme case that makes the general condition of sense making visible. Any translation is an approximation, and any idea of easy access to linguistic, philosophical or literary knowledge is an illusion that bypasses the unsolvable problem of language specificity.

Apter's understanding of untranslatability contributes to a lively debate in the discipline of Comparative Literature on power relations within its field. Many comparatists that study world literature are aware of the problems that come along with such an all-encompassing term. To study world literature seems to indicate a comprehensive approach that includes literature from all over the world, regardless of its place and time, its genre or its linguistic belonging. Such an approach conceals the Eurocentric history of the discipline of Comparative Literature, which is mirrored in the conceptualization of the field of world literature as well. For example, the first anthologies of world literature that appeared after World War II were based on Judeo-Christian and European literary texts, reflecting the prevalently European origin of comparatist scholars at that time, a geopolitical situatedness that changed when Comparative Literature became predominantly taught in the USA (see D'haen; Damrosch; Kadir).

By now, the influence of multiculturalism and postcolonialism has shifted this Western-centered approach of text selections in anthologies of world literature considerably. Nevertheless, Erich Auerbach's bleak outlook on the possible development of the study of world literature still haunts the field. In his famous essay "Philology and Weltliteratur," he apprehends homogenization as a possible danger for the notion of world literature, a vision in which globalization leads to "a single literary culture, only a few literary languages and perhaps even a single literary language" (129). If scholars who work in the field of world literature want to avoid this homogenization, they need to pay attention to untranslatability precisely because this concept brings inappropriable cultural differences to the fore.

In accordance with Auerbach's understandings of the dangers of homogenization through globalization, I want to posit that it is not merely the untranslatability of words and concepts that readers, editors and scholars need to pay attention to. To avoid homogenization of the literary field, it is equally important to take account of narrative forms and tropes that do not accord with the Western literary tradition and thereby add to the multiplicity of literature and the literary. Narrative forms and tropes can show as much as words and concepts the specificity of cultural difference. Thus, an extended notion of untranslatability that includes them adds another dimension to the project that the editors of the *Dictionary of Untranslatables* have in mind when they state that they intend to outline a "political theory of community," one that goes beyond "the limits of discrete national languages and traditions" and makes place for a view that languages can neither be owned nor claimed (xv). This "political theory of community" is guided by the idea that untranslatables point towards uncontainable differences, differences that we as readers, listeners, and speakers are made aware of in and through languages. Untranslatables point towards the possibility of being together in a world beyond the nation-state as subjects marked by unerasable, uncontainable, uncontrollable, irreducible difference.

My understanding of narrative forms in which untranslatables can be perceivably distinct, while their untranslatability poses riddles to readers unacquainted with their specificity, aims to extend this democratic project. Silko's works are excellent examples of this democratic aim, since her establishment and inclusion of untranslatable notions brings the unique achievements of American Indians to the fore without betraying the need to keep indigenous knowledge "untranslatable" to a mainstream Western audience in order to avoid those exoticizing appropriations that Anishinaabe writer and scholar Gerard Vizenor has called "portraitures of dominance" (1998: 152). Instead of supporting a view of American Indians as being relegates of the past, Silko makes readers aware of the undeniable presence of untranslatable, hence unappropriable, indigenous narrative traditions that are part of the US American literary canon. I will look in particular at two novels by Silko, *Ceremony* (1977) and *Almanac of the Dead* (1991), to show how her use of oral traditions of storytelling clashes with Western reading habits. The untranslatability resulting from this confronts Western audiences with worldscapes in dissonance with their own linguistic and conceptual frames of knowing and being. At the same time, it can be central to the production of indigenous histories, creating an essential space for the expression of alternative worldscapes that cannot be seen to belong exclusively to the periphery since they circulate within a hegemonic culture, too.

The Multi-Cultural Semiotics of Silko's *Ceremony*

Leslie Marmon Silko's *Ceremony* is doubtlessly one of the key texts of American literature. In 1996, an informal survey at the meeting of the Modern Language Association concluded that the novel is among the four most important American publications (see Roemer 9). As Kenneth M. Roemer explains in "Silko's Arroyos as Mainstream," there are a number of factors that made the novel accessible to a broader public. The Civil Rights Movement and the Women's Movement brought social injustices to the fore, with repercussions in academic fields like Literary Studies. For instance, in the 1970s, the formation of canons was increasingly criticized, and scholars began looking outside the box for emerging new talents on the literary market. *Ceremony* was praised in high circulation newspapers and journals like the *Library Journal*, *The Choice*, *Newsweek* and the *New York Times Book Review* (see Roemer 16–17). The novel successfully combines hegemonic narrative genres like the Euro-American *Bildungsroman* with traditional Laguna Pueblo and Navajo myths, stories and heroic figures, so that Western readers have a grasp on the narrative genre, while possibly being attracted to its being "different enough" from their normal frame of reference (Roemer 13). With its story of a traumatized World War II veteran returning home to his reservation, *Ceremony* furthermore connects well to the issue of post-traumatic stress disorder (PTSD) that emerged in the wake of the Vietnam War. Of the soldiers who came home, 15.2% suffered from the psychological damage of warfare, and members of minorities suffered in considerably higher numbers, possibly because old and new racisms were a further burden when reintegrating into society. Since the effects of racism constitute another topic that *Ceremony* explores, the novel can be seen to participate in the analysis of societal issues contemporary to its publication in 1977.

Specific to *Ceremony* is, however, the unique exploration of indigenous myths, stories and heroic figures in combination with narrative patterns of Western provenance like those of the Bildungsroman. I would like to discuss here specifically the charge that Paula Gunn Allen has brought forward against Silko's appropriation of traditional stories of Laguna Pueblo heritage. Allen finds *Ceremony* particularly troublesome to teach, because, according to

Laguna Pueblo tradition, some of the knowledge depicted in the story should not be told to outsiders. In the classroom, she has therefore chosen to focus on its narrative techniques, foregoing an approach encouraging an attitude she has encountered in many of her students, who are

> voraciously interested in the exotic aspects of Indian ways – they usually mean by that traditional spiritual practices, understandings and beliefs ... At every least opportunity, they vigorously wrest the discussion from theme, symbol, structure and plot to questions of "medicine," sacred language, rituals, and spiritual customs.
>
> ALLEN 382

Allen fears that outsiders to Navajo and Laguna Pueblo traditions might objectify, explain, detail and analyze their practices and beliefs "as though they were simply curios, artifacts, fetishes ... objects of interest and patronization" instead of powerful ways of conceiving the world (383). When discussing Allen's charge against Silko, David L. Moore, in "Rough Knowledge and Radical Understanding: Sacred Silence in American Indian Literatures," argues that their understandings of story-telling diverge from each other: while Allen brings the issues of cultural privacy and property to the fore, Silko highlights the context of storytelling, specifically when she discusses her mythopoetics. Because the context is always changing, the content and use of traditional stories and knowledges is for Silko constantly changing, too.

As someone who is not familiar with Laguna Pueblo customs and myths, it is impossible for me to assess either Allen's charge or Silko's affirmation of change: I lack the appropriate knowledge and do not want to be disrespectful to important interventions made by writers who simply know better than me. In the current context, when discussing the value of untranslatability, I see, however, a chance to bridge their positions. Allen, from my point of view, is in particular wary about the exoticizing and intrusive questions that non-Laguna Pueblo readers might have, which Silko's disclosure of some elements that pertain to traditional Laguna Pueblo myths could give rise to. Yet a close reading of *Ceremony* shows that Silko only exposes certain elements, while being careful not to disclose others. To give an example: *Ceremony* tells the story of the mixed-blood Pueblo Tayo, who returns, after the end of World War II, to the reservation in which he grew up. He suffers from a mysterious illness that leads to constant vomiting, constant unresolved grieving and the constant return of traumatic war images. Therefore, his family decides to send for a traditional medicine man. The encounter between Tayo and Old Ku'oosh contains three important elements. Firstly, Old Ku'oosh speaks in "the old dialect," that is Western Keres, "full of sentences that were involuted with explanations of their own origins, as if nothing the old man said were his own but all had been said before and he was only to repeat it" (34). Secondly, Old Ku'oosh tells Tayo about a location of which "people said back in the old days they took the scalps and threw them down there. Tayo knew what the old man had come for" (35). Thirdly, Old Ku'oosh talks about the fragility of the world, in which everything is connected. This story is rendered in the following way:

> It took a long time to explain the fragility and intricacy because no word exists alone, and the reason for choosing each word had to be explained with a story about why it must be said this certain way. That was the responsibility that went with being human, old Ku'oosh said, the story behind each word must be told so there could be no mistake in the meaning of what had been said; and this demanded great patience and love. More than an hour went by before Ku'oosh asked him.
>
> SILKO 35–36

In this example, Silko renders an experience of traditional wisdom rather than providing access to traditional sacred knowledge. She renders the story neither in Western Keres, which, according to the description, allows one to connect to age-old meaning, nor does she disclose the sacred location that might have been used for traditional rituals. She also does not provide readers with an extensive explanation of how the world is interconnected in the same careful way that Old Ku'oosh hands on his knowledge to Tayo. On the contrary, she establishes blanks in her text by withholding knowledge from the reader, thereby shaping a central disparity in which the intradiegetic characters are shown to have knowledge of languages, rituals, places and worldviews in which the non-indigenous readers do not partake. She thereby decenters non-indigenous forms of knowledge and privileges those that are able to fill in the narrative gaps, such as that belonging to the Laguna Pueblo people. As Roemer recounts, Silko told participants of a Flagstaff seminar in 1977 that a Laguna Pueblo audience would be able to understand a thirty-page-version of *Ceremony*: "brief references to particular family names and veterans and to specific events in Laguna, Grants, and Gallup, New Mexico, would open up networks of stories, memories, and meanings" (19). According to Roemer, Silko then said that outsiders to this narrative tradition on the contrary continued to face a gap of knowledge "wide enough to swallow hundreds and hundreds of pages" (20). The blanks in the text, the knowledge that remains undisclosed to those uninitiated in the encoded details, is thus substantial and remains a secret within the text. Silko might thereby be considered to curb the curiosity of Western readers to know more about the details that the text withholds – a curiosity, possibly a nosiness, and eventually the exoticizing disrespect that Allen describes. Still, I would like to suggest that Silko could also be seen as actively and feasibly outlining the limits of non-Laguna Pueblo readers' knowledges. The blanks make tangible that some knowledge has not been disclosed and is not available to non-Laguna Pueblo readers. They constitute a fundamental gap between author, characters and readers, and mark the creative failure of Western readers to fill them in with precise meaning. Simultaneously, the limitations imposed on Western readers are highlighted by showing that indigenous knowledge is not shared precisely because of its devaluation and depreciation in Euro-Western culture.

Still, Silko does make the outcome of indigenous knowledges available, and shows that they can be healing even when confronted with the massive changes on a global scale that, for instance, modern warfare has brought about. This is because Silko discloses, as already stated, the effects of undisclosed traditional knowledge, and arbitrates Tayo's experiences with it. She thereby points to the unique contributions of indigenous peoples, which she evaluates highly, as the development of the storyline shows. At the end of the novel, Tayo regains his health through a ceremony that connects his wellbeing with that of his entire environment, human and non-human actors alike. He is described as sharing the knowledge that he acquired during the ceremony with the elders of his nation. Again, forms of secrecy are enacted that leave those unfamiliar with Laguna Pueblo heritage in the dark. Yet the sharing of secret knowledge is also shown to constitute a community that coincides with the different reading publics of Silko's novel.

To conclude, I would therefore argue that, in *Ceremony*, Silko uses untranslatability as a tool to create different publics that are co-present to each other in a non-hegemonic, post-national community of readers. Those accustomed to traditional Laguna Pueblo stories are asked to activate their knowledge to participate in the storytelling. To others, the value of traditional knowledge is shown. The narrative thereby serves as an entry point into indigenous narratives, but also communicates the non-knowledge of the specific languages, events, places and histories to Euro-Western readers. The theory of untranslatable narrative forms and tropes takes this non-knowledge as its cue for a new reading practice. Stressing those forms and figures in the text that mark the limits of Western, centralized knowledge, reading for the untranslatable facilitates non-appropriative encounters with that which traverses the center. This traversing destroys a clear-cut divide between center and periphery by showing that untranslatable and uncontainable difference is present within cultural hegemony rather than being outside of it at its periphery.

The Destruction of Character in *Almanac of the Dead*

Grand in scope and vast in vision, *Almanac of the Dead* offers a complex analysis of internal colonialism in the American Southwest. Silko enfolds a vast panoramic history that spans five hundred years and establishes some seventy characters in this novel. Some of the characters are outright evil, disconnected from any feeling of compassion or connectedness with their compatriots. Others struggle to find their balance in a world that deals out loss and rootlessness. She depicts corrupt officials and businessmen, mafia gangsters and crime lords, drug pushers and addicts, weapon smugglers and human traffickers, eco warriors and a TV psychic. These almost flat characters are used to undermine the novel as a form that transmits bourgeois ambitions, social longings and legitimations. Silko uses character set-up, of central concern to narratology, to weaken the discursive genre of the novel. This has strong ideological effects, since it compromises the powerful link between the Western bourgeoisie and novel writing. The novel traditionally depicts bourgeois social authority, energy and experience through the portrayal of the bourgeoisie's ability to make history and to take over space (see Said). In contrast, Silko puts social conditions and their limitations at the center. Contemporaneous forms of economic and psychic exploitation are established as inseparable from the region's colonial past. This inseparability is stressed by Silko's use of temporalization in the novel, in which past and present, rather than succeeding one other, are co-present and co-constitutive. Frequently, narrative focalizers will be exchanged unannounced, so that readers have to jump involuntarily from one storyline to the next. Through this narrative device, neither the division between past and present nor the clear-cut differentiation between diverse narrative voices can be maintained. Rather, narrators stemming from different timeframes can share stories with each other and be affected by them. Through these narrative devices, Silko establishes temporally and spatially mobile events that characterize a time-span ("the reign of the Death-Eye Dog") that began with the colonizing of the Americas over five hundred years ago. This temporal depiction constitutes a central untranslatability in the *Almanac of the Dead*, remaining incommensurable with both Western notions of linear time and Western notions of subjectivity as independent of its (spatial, human and non-human) surroundings.

As in *Ceremony*, Silko employs American Indian forms of storytelling and conveys the sense that characters act according to their mythical belongings. Characters in myth are usually Gods and Goddesses, human beings and totemic animals, and supernatural heroes and heroines. In myth, characters are employed to teach people across generations how to live together. In *Almanac of the Dead*, it is taught how a particular reign, that of the Death-Eye Dog, can be overcome, an overcoming that calls for heroic action. Yet Silko defies characterological readings: she does not emphasize *who* defeats Death-Eye Dog's reign, but rather *how* Death-Eye Dog can be defeated, and what it means to succumb to its reign. Silko's characters are designed to make social conditions available, social conditions that are sharply criticized. In the epoch of the Death-Eye Dog, "human beings, especially the alien invaders, would become obsessed with hungers and impulses commonly seen in wild dogs" (251). These alien invaders are human beings "attracted to and excited by death and the sight of blood and suffering" (475, qtd. in Sol 36). And, while these alien invaders – or the colonizers of the Americas – are aligned to the mystical category of the destroyers, they are opposed by those who have somehow escaped being determined by the spirit of their age.

Almanac of the Dead begins with a "Five Hundred Year Map." Plots are represented through dotted lines, characters allocated to place names. As numerous scholars have pointed out, the map assumes that a place – the American Southwest – is peopled; it inscribes indigenous struggles into the representation of a geography (see Anderson; Brigham; Horvitz; Powers). A box (or "legend") announces that the Almanac tells "the future of all the Americas" through "the decipherment of ancient tribal texts" (n. pag.). However, the indigenous almanac within the *Almanac* remains only partly decipherable. Parts of it were lost in ancient times during the tribe's northward flight from Spanish invaders; the remaining parts are within the narrative, deciphered by the drug-abusing psychic Lecha. Lecha's visionary forces are considerably crippled, so her deciphering activity remains unreliable and partial. The box's announcement that historical events are represented by "arcane symbols and old narratives" needs to be read as ironic (n. pag.). As in all of Silko's novels and stories, the almanac's prophecy is incomplete and the "symbols and old narratives" are untranslatable, since their context is missing.

Lecha as a character illustrates well how *Almanac of the Dead* uses narrative conventions to establish a differentiated form of untranslatability that favors indigenous (peripheralized) epistemologies while making the limits of Western knowledge available. Lecha, like all characters, is influenced by the spirit of an age that limits her possibilities of action considerably. While, together with her twin sister Zeta, she is a keeper of the indigenous almanac, her visions are only connected to death and destruction: "They are all dead. The only ones you can locate are dead. Murder victims and suicides. You can't locate the living. If you find them, they will be dead. Those who have lost their loved ones only come to you to confirm their sorrow" (138–39). As Zeta suspects, these catastrophic visions are imposed on Lecha and she cannot control what she sees. Yet, while Lecha is a medium and a messenger for the dead, she does not kill the living nor does she delight in their death. On the contrary, witnessing their death causes Lecha to lose strength, and she has to constantly battle against the destructive voices inside her head by numbing them with Demerol. Lecha's gift of vision – strongly connected to the spiritual heritage that, like the almanac, she received from her grandmother Yoeme – is a painful burden that she has to carry. Only when she avoids giving in to its alluring forces can she escape becoming one of the destroyers, those characterized as feeding off "energies released by destruction" and "delight[ing] in blood" (336).

Ultimately, *Almanac of the Dead* records, too, the stories of those who have been warned about the destroyers and know how to read the signs of their arrival. Their agency is, however, brought about by the possibilities of communal consciousness. As the character Clinton points out, "African and other tribal people had shared food and wealth in common for thousands of years before the white man Marx came along and stole their ideas for his 'communes' and collective farms" (407). And, while Marxism is rejected as an alternative model for living together, indigenous models of being in the world are evaluated highly. As David L. Moore writes, "communitism" remains the ethical ground of *Almanac of the Dead*, a communitism not brought about by the deeds of heroic individuals, but through a radical interconnectedness of all beings belonging to the earth. "The earth is worth protecting, and humans are part of the earth" (2014: n. pag.), he writes, and this radical interdependency of all life is what needs to be affirmed. *Almanac of the Dead*'s neglect of character development in favor of interconnectedness (through time and space) makes available to its readers that indigenous spiritual understandings have been there all along. Equally, it asks Western readers to engage with worldviews unfamiliar to them that they might not fully understand. This form of untranslatability is enabling, as it might evoke a different form of relationality with the topics displayed in a novel. Rather than identifying with a character, readers might agree with its analysis of a fundamental interdependency of all beings, an interdependency that Silko expresses through the interconnectedness of different times and spaces. When that happens, the novel itself becomes a semiotic machine able to evoke imaginings that allows them to keep "words, phrases, and gestures of human solidarity" threatened with extinction by the relentless actions of destructive forces unleashed by an Integrated World Capitalism that in Félix Guattari's analysis impoverishes the ability of human beings to connect to their environment, since it singularizes individuals, and it standardizes and thereby disciplines and moulds behavior (20).

In *Almanac of the Dead*, the destroyers' opponents in the ending's grand showdown gather in a tacky congress center. They include the twin sisters Lecha and Zeta, the drug pusher Mosca, the revolutionary La Escapia and the Barefoot Hopi, who all meet at the International Holistic Healer Convention in Tucson to combine forces. While remaining vague about whether the opposing protagonists will be able to overthrow the destroyers, at this point Silko's narrative method is more than clear. As Meredith Tax comments, it is its "alternating currents of irony and crackpot occultism, pity and disgust, common sense and messianic vision" that show Silko's intention to suck readers "in only to tip them off balance, the purpose being not to make them identify but to make them think" (61). Silko invites readers to share in her analysis of an interconnectedness of different times, spaces, peoples and the environment, and she entices her readers to share the hope that Death-Eye Dog and his seven brothers can be overcome. The destroyers' deeds are paralleled by heroic events brought about by those who oppose them. To be affected by this hope is the novel's ultimate goal.

Conclusion: Traversing the Center

I have discussed two novels by the American Indian author Leslie Marmon Silko to show how forms of secrecy create a multi-cultural semiotics in which different (un)translatable notions exist next to each other. Silko's literary works arbitrate incommensurability; they incite Western readers to encounter indigenous knowledges and the possibilities for healing they entail, without allowing them to decipher all the gaps created in the text. When readers are confronted with (un)translatability, reading becomes a dialogue without the safety net of interpretative closure. And, while this refusal to offer a definite meaning might be understood as a failure, I want to posit that it incites readers to reflect upon their limits of knowing and being in the world. The "speed bumps of untranslatability" (Apter) are thus productive forms of interruption, since they allow, for instance in the case of indigenous authors, an acknowledgement of the possibilities inherent in knowledges from peripheralized, non-Western contexts.

Significantly, Silko's works have a reach far beyond their original context. They circulate on the global literary market – by being translated into numerous languages. This circulation exemplifies how indigenous notions that cannot be simply appropriated and subsumed under Euro-Western ways of knowing and being, and that show the limits of Euro-Western understanding are available worldwide, thereby disturbing simplifying notions of center and periphery. The chosen works make a definition of globalization available as proposed by James Clifford, namely as "the multidirectional, unrepresentable sum of material and cultural relationships linking places and people, distant and nearby" (6). Silko's works have an important role to play in shaping these global "cultural relationships." Readers' responses within and about incommensurability are evoked; the chosen works activate untranslatability and make it into a force that can withstand attempts to coerce their forms of transmitting knowledge under the denominator of the already known. In Silko's works, untranslatability is used to forge readerly encounters with uncontainable difference, a forging that suggest an ethical approach to alterity that seems necessary for any democratic proceedings (see Spivak 2013; Wiese).

To conclude, I would like to return to the "political theory of untranslatability" proposed by the editors of the *Dictionary of Untranslatables* (xv). According to this political notion, cultural expressions can remain different, are unappropriable and can add a distinct voice to the global, babylonic, expressive choir that persists in language – and, as I would like to add, in literary forms. I want to connect this political notion of untranslatability to the specific stumbling block that any thinking about the distinctiveness of indigenous peoples evokes and that disturbs any easy assumptions about centers and peripheries. Firstly, indigenous peoples posit a challenge to the contemporary thinking of the nation-state and its relation to colonialism, since they often act independently within and across national borders. This is the case because indigenous peoples can have an independent sovereign status within nation-states while simultaneously being oriented towards transindigeneity. Secondly, their historical and continuous presence on their native land undercuts national myths of conquest, namely that European settlers were setting foot on virgin land or, as it has been called in juridical terms, *terra nullius*. Thirdly, they challenge assumptions that relegate colonialism safely to the past: the ongoing dispossession of indigenous land and the grave human right violations against indigenous peoples show that colonial systems of domination are still in place on a worldwide scale. Fourthly, the self-determination of indigenous peoples destroys images of otherness. As Jody Byrd shows throughout *The Transit of Empire*, notions of Indians and Indianness need to be continuously constructed as "past tense presences," a logic that relies on the "derealization of the Other" (193, 179). In Judith Butler's terms, any hegemonic construction relies on its own iterability and is therefore fundamentally vulnerable to re-significations. This is also true of constructions of the settler colonial state. To rely on images of otherness ultimately means to be threatened by failure, especially if this "Other" manages to become visible as a political, autonomous subject in her or his own right, as has been the case recently, for instance, with the Idle No More movement in Canada.

For this re-signification of indigeneity, literary discourse is a powerful tool. The presence of disturbing elements in Silko's novels reminds readers of the survivance of American Indian nations in general and of their distinct storytelling traditions in particular. Untranslatable notions "overturn the static reduction of native identities" and disrupt hegemonic constructions of American Indians as remnants of the past relegated to a peripheral existence that does not warrant attention or care (Vizenor 1989: 142). The novels of indigenous peoples in general and of Leslie Marmon Silko in particular are traversing the global and, as such, claim an undeniable presence within what is considered the center and the periphery, while also shifting their boundaries and relation. When literary texts such as Leslie Marmon Silko's show that indigenous knowledges are present within society and do matter, they trouble homogenizing globalization processes and invest the perceived periphery with vision by showing indigenous persistence, resilience and creativity.

Works Cited

Allen, Paula Gunn. "Special Problems in Teaching Leslie Marmon Silko's Ceremony." *American Indian Quarterly* 14.4 (1990): 379–86.

Apter, Emily. *Against World Literature: On the Politics of Untranslatability.* New York: Verso, 2013.

Anderson, Eric Gary. *American Indian Literature and The Southwest.* Austin: U of Texas P, 1999.

Auerbach, Erich. "Philology and Weltliteratur." Trans. Marie and Edward Said. *The Centennial Review* 13.1 (1969): 1–17.

Brigham, Ann. "Productions of Geographic Scale and Capitalist-Colonialist Enterprise in Leslie Marmon Silko's *Almanac of the Dead.*" *MFS Modern Fiction Studies* 50.2 (2004): 303–31.

Butler, Judith. *Bodies that Matter: On the Discursive Limits of "Sex."* New York: Routledge, 1993.

Byrd, Jody A. *The Transit of Empire: Indigenous Critiques of Colonialism.* Minneapolis: U of Minnesota P, 2011.

Cassin, Barbara, Emily Apter, and Jacques Lezra. *Dictionary of Untranslatables: A Philosophical Lexicon.* Princeton: Princeton UP, 2014.

Clifford, James. *Returns: Becoming Indigenous in the Twenty First Century.* Cambridge, MA: Harvard UP, 2013.

Damrosch, David. *What is World Literature?* Princeton, NJ: Princeton UP, 2003.

D'haen, Theo, David Damrosch, and Djelal Kadir, eds. *The Routledge Companion to World Literature.* New York: Routledge, 2012.

Guattari, Félix. *The Three Ecologies.* London: Continuum, 2008.

Horvitz, Deborah. "Freud, Marx, and Chiapas in Leslie Marmon Silko's *Almanac of the Dead.*" *Studies in American Indian Literature* 10.3 (1998): 47–64.

Moore, David L. "Rough Knowledge and Radical Understanding: Sacred Silence in American Indian Literatures." *American Indian Quarterly* 21.4 (1997): 633–62.

———. "The Ground of Ethics: Arrowboy's Ecologic in Almanac." *Howling for Justice: New Perspectives on Leslie Marmon Silko's* Almanac of the Dead. Ed. Rebecca Tillett. Tucson: U of Arizona P, 2014. E-book.

Powers, Janet M. "Mapping the Prophetic Landscape in *Almanac of the Dead.*" *Leslie Marmon Silko: A Collection of Critical Essays.* Ed. Louise Barnett and James L. Thorson. Albuquerque: U of New Mexico P, 1999. 261–72.

Roemer, Kenneth M. "Silko's Arrayos as Mainstream: Processes and Implications of Canonical Identity." *MFS Modern Fiction Studies* 45.1 (1999): 10–37.

Said, Edward. *Culture and Imperialism.* London: Vintage, 1993.

Silko, Leslie Marmon. *Ceremony.* New York: Penguin, 1977.

———. *Almanac of the Dead.* New York: Simon & Schuster, 1991.

Sol, Adam. "The Story as It's Told: Prodigious Revisions in Leslie Marmon Silko's *Almanac of the Dead.*" *American Indian Quarterly* 23.3 (1999): 24–48.

Spivak, Gayatri Chakravorty. "The Politics of Translation." *Destabilizing Theory: Contemporary Feminist Debates.* Ed. Michele Barrett and Ann Phillips. Cambridge: Polity, 1992. 177–200.

———. *Death of a Discipline.* New York: Columbia UP, 2003.

Tax, Meredith. "Return of the Native Americans: Leslie Marmon Silko." *Voice Literary Supplement.* Nov. 1999. Web. 12 July 2015.

Venuti, Lawrence. *The Translator's Invisibility: A History of Translation.* New York: Routledge, 1995.

———. *The Scandals of Translation: Towards an Ethics of Difference.* London, New York: Routledge, 1998.

Venuti, Lawrence, ed. *The Translation Studies Reader.* London, New York: Routledge, 2000.

Vizenor, Gerard. *Manifest Manners: Narratives on Postindian Survivance.* Lincoln: U of Nebraska P, 1989.

———. "Fugitive Poses." *Fugitive Poses: Native American Indian Scenes of Absence and Presence.* Lincoln and London: U of Nebraska P, 1998. 145–67.

Wiese, Doro. *The Powers of the False: Reading, Writing, Thinking beyond Truth and Fiction.* Evanston: Northwestern UP, 2014.

PART 2

Peripheral Spaces

∴

The Center of All Concerns at the Periphery of the World: The Sahara Desert from a Nomadic Perspective

Luca Raineri

From the Margins of the World to the Center of the Stage

The community of men is divided by uninhabitable parts of the earth's surface such as oceans and deserts, but even then the ship or the camel (the ship of the desert) make it possible for them to approach their fellows over these ownerless tracts.

IMMANUEL KANT

The Sahara Desert and its regions have been consistently qualified as peripheral in every possible sense. Due to an extremely low population density, economic irrelevance and very poor productivity, the Sahara Desert has been traditionally portrayed as a vast expanse of emptiness and therefore placed at the margins of the world, irrespective of the vantage point taken. Herodotus contended that the Sahara represented the southern edge, the impassable limit of the civilized world.[1] A similar understanding still stands in the Arabic conception of the Sahara Desert, as well as in some Sahelian languages spoken in Mali and Senegal on the southern edge of the Sahara. In the Bambara cosmography,[2] the world is divided into the space of the whites (*Fara Djela*) and the space of the blacks (*Fara Fina*, i.e. Africa by extension). Significantly, the Bambara language does not know how to classify the Sahara Desert, which lies in-between the two as the place where nomadic peoples live and roam, and consequently equates it to a non-human wilderness lacking all the attributes of social life.

---

1 Interestingly, for Herodotus the Sahara (which he calls *an-oecumene*) is the antithesis of the civilized world (*oecumene*). Herodotus's view recalls Turner's classical triumphal definition of the American western frontier as the "hither edge of free land" (Turner).

2 The Bambara are a Mandé people living in West Africa and are the largest ethnic group of southern Mali. For an introduction to Bambara cosmology, see Pulgram; Kahera.

Mainstream geopolitical thinking has tended to adopt a perspective implicitly incorporating the traditional view of the Sahara as a *limes* (Kaplan), a threshold neatly separating two distinct civilizations like the boundaries of the Roman empire. A supposedly natural barrier, the Sahara has been deterministically attributed the "objective" geopolitical fate of a place of disconnection or a "buffer zone" of weak interaction separating two distinct security complexes, which is also how it has been governed historically (Buzan and Waever). Even UN regional groupings discriminate the Sub-Saharan Africa (SSA) region from the MENA (Middle East and North Africa) region, implicitly assuming the Sahara to work as a geopolitical insulator lying at the periphery of two distinct entities, namely two separate Africas: a sub-Saharan black, "proper" Africa and a white North Africa.[3] The stress put by the European Union and the United States on engaging in the strengthening of policed borders as well as anti-migration and anti-drug controls along the Saharan borderlines stems directly from this perspective.

There is little doubt then that the Saharan space has traditionally lingered at the periphery of riparian states' territories and concerns, both to the north (Algeria, Libya, Egypt) and to the south (Mauritania, Mali, Niger, Chad). Due to its perceived marginality, local authorities based in capital cities have largely neglected the Sahara, and consequently have proved ill prepared to cope with the new security threats emerging in it, such as climate stress, food insecurity, transnational organized crime and armed radical Islamism. The same is true at a regional level, given the limited attention given by numerous regional organizations to Saharan issues, whether related to security, development or humanitarian policies.[4] Significantly, very few of these organizations emphasize the dimension of "saharanness" as a common denominator. Helly and Galeazzi correctly note that, given the fragmentation produced by the lack of a comprehensive regional framework, it is particularly difficult to coordinate

---

3   It is interesting to note how North Africans are hardly perceived as "white" in Europe, thus suggesting the idea that "whiteness," rather than an objective attribute, is largely a social construct whose nature and power effects depend on one's perspective.

4   A list of the most relevant regional organisations includes the African Union (AU), the Economic Community of West African States (ECOWAS), the Economic Community of Central African States (ECCAS), the Arab-Maghreb Union (AMU), the Organisation Internationale de la Francophonie (OIF), the Organization of Islamic Cooperation (OIC), the Communauté des Etats Sahélo-Sahariens (CEN-SAD), the Comité Permanent Inter-Etats de Lutte contre la Sécheresse dans le Sahel (CILSS), the G5 Sahelian states, the Comité d'État-Major Opérationnel Conjoint (CEMOC). The most comprehensive of these regional organizations is the African Union. Noticeably, however, the exclusion of Morocco from the AU is due precisely to "Saharan" problems, i.e. the unresolved issue of the Western Sahara.

the efforts of regional actors and to address emerging security threats in a coherent manner. A high-ranking officer of the Malian Intelligence Service notes: "It is particularly hard to tackle the root causes of insecurity in such a hybrid security complex, because there are several regional groupings with different scope and purpose, but none of them deals with the Sahel or Sahara, as such."[5]

Yet, just as the romantic imaginary of sandy dunes does not stand empirical scrutiny because it fails to capture the diversity of Saharan landscapes (Roux), the widely abused metaphor of a "no man's land" is equally ill-suited to understanding the geopolitical dynamics taking place in the Sahara. Radical transformations affecting the whole region have had a tremendous impact on the way local communities engage with the space they live in (and, eventually, fight for), and have made the Sahara an area where high stakes are being disputed. The growing deterioration of security conditions, including enduring civil wars in Libya, Mali and Darfur, oppressive regimes in Mauritania and Algeria, persistent instability in Niger and Chad, have brought the Sahara to the forefront of world attention. Previously obscure small villages arising amidst the sun and the dust, like Agadez, Kidal or Sebha, have suddenly made it to the center of the scene and of the security discourses of major world powers. A similar fate befell local bandits, who turned into international drug traders, arm smugglers and human traffickers, and established profitable working relationships with the indigenous outgrowth of global jihadism (Julien; Lacher; Briscoe; Global Initiative).

Thus, the supposed marginality of a global periphery is challenged. Neoliberal discourse securitizes ungoverned spaces (Dowd and Raleigh) in as far as these supposedly provide "safe havens" to non-state actors who, despite being rooted locally, are allegedly capable of striking globally and of threatening international security (Fukuyama). The dramatic escalation of military deployment in the Sahara underlines the growing geopolitical centrality of the area in major powers' security equations. In 2005, the Bush administration launched the Trans-Saharan Counter-Terrorism Partnership (TSCTP), a 500 million USD plan of joint military trainings involving eleven African countries. In 2011, the European Union approved its own Security and Development Strategy for the Sahel, the first of its kind under the newly created external action service, in order to recast existing development programs into a clear counterinsurgency strategy backed by massive military and economic means. Finally, in 2014, *Operation Barkhane*, involving 3,000 soldiers, armored infantry, dozens

---

5   Interview with a former general of the Malian Armed Forces (Bamako, November 2014), translated by the author.

of helicopters, jet fighters and drones saw a redeployment of French military presence in Africa that focused precisely on the Saharan regions.

This renewed centrality of the Sahara as a global security concern, whether promoted by national, regional or international actors, has so far seemed to rely uniquely on a conventional positivist, realist and structuralist paradigm (Waltz), whereas the only relevant variables of international order are states' behaviors. The latter are viewed as unitary actors rationally aiming to maximize their power, expressed in military and economic terms, in order to face the challenges of an anarchic international system. In this chapter, I claim that the situation in the Saharan regions deserves to be addressed differently. I will argue that the very notion of the modern State, exerting (in Weberian terms) a legitimate monopoly of violence over a well-defined territory with clearly determined borders, is not suitable for the unique geographic conditions of the Sahara Desert. Yet, it is this notion that the securitization of ungoverned spaces relies directly upon. Just because it is unquestionably an "area of limited statehood" (Risse and Lehmkuhl) does not mean that the Sahara can be simplistically defined as a mere ungoverned territory. Fostering an alternative view of the Saharan space, its borders and the political actors in it will therefore be key to advancing an alternative understanding of the forms of political organization that the Sahara can host and support. National, regional and international security strategies seem to neglect the different, non-state security logic that is emerging from peripheral borderlands, namely the one forged and experienced locally by nomadic actors and indigenous peoples living at the state's margins.

By adopting the point of view of these local actors, I seek to resurrect their "subjugated knowledge" (Foucault), which has been relegated to the periphery both physically and theoretically. This perspective enables a radical critique of some of the most fundamental concepts of modern political thought. Taking a view from the periphery, I argue, is the best strategy to question its alleged and problematic universality. In what follows, I try to show the extent to which the notions of both sovereignty and private property, which lie at the foundation of modern political organizations, are construed upon the *dispositif* of an exclusive border. This idea, however, holds little meaning in the Saharan context, which is characterized by different priorities and alternative patterns of territorialization (whose supreme expression is the custom of the *droits de passage*). I will introduce the concept of the borderland in order to capture the fundamental connective nature of Saharan peripheral space. As the example of trafficking and organized crime in In-Khalil will demonstrate, the primacy of mobility and connections has the potential to upset the conventional hierarchies of normality and pathology in the legal and political realm.

In conclusion, I will propose a different interpretation of the Saharan space and of its place in contemporary geopolitical theory and practice.

Geopolitics of the Desert: A Radical Alternative to the *Nomos* of the Earth

Les islamistes disent que la frontière est pour Dieu. Mais en fait, c'est pour le diable![6]

MAHAMANE, TIMBUKTU

One does not need to subscribe to an outdated geopolitical naturalism to acknowledge that the desert space, and the Sahara in particular, is quintessentially unsuitable to support "the geometrical abstraction of exclusive territoriality and linear borders" (Mezzadra and Neilson). Despite the role of dividing *limes* traditionally attributed to it, in the Saharan space borderlines are in fact largely dysfunctional. The Organisation for Economic Cooperation and Development (OECD) observes that about 85% of the borders in the Sahara-Sahel follow purely geometric abstractions. Under these circumstances, border patrolling and border enforcement are obviously extremely hard, especially when considering that most of the states one can find in the region are among the poorest on earth. According to a senior UN officer in Dakar who is in charge of security policies in the Saharan area:

> These are borders by name only. Geography is the main risk factor, as unchecked frontiers stretch for thousands of kilometers and it is impossible to control them. Fencing borders here, just like in Ceuta or in Mexico, is simply not an option, as space is much bigger and virtually infinite.[7]

Local law enforcement agencies do not hesitate to admit the same: according to the national criminal police department, Mali has 189 border control posts unevenly scattered along 7,245 kilometers of land borderlines[8] that is, one every 38.3 kilometers. However, an independent survey found that the actual number of border posts in Mali is 119, that is, one every 60.8 kilometers, with

---

6 "Islamists say that the frontier belongs to God. But indeed it belongs to the Devil!" For a more accurate interpretation, see also note 12.

7 Interview conducted in Dakar, October 2014.

8 Interview conducted in Bamako, November 2014, with a senior officer of the criminal police department.

the majority located in the southern, "sahelian" part of the country (Strazzari). Recent field research revealed that, along the borderline between Burkina Faso, Mali and Western Niger, one could hardly find a border post for more than 300 kilometers, and suggested that more northern Saharan regions are likely to be in an even worse condition (Danish Demining Group).

According to Van der Pijl, the notion of linear and exclusive borders was originally introduced at the beginning of the industrial era, with reference to the phenomenon of the enclosures described by Locke, and Marx after him. These required establishing clear-cut and indisputable bounds of distinct territories in terms of linear borders, which were considerably different from the fading limits of the overlapping authorities and legacies of the feudal era. Private land ownership and sovereignty are thus considered as parallel political phenomena, inasmuch as they both establish exclusive rights and dominion over clearly defined territories, including the right to exclude outsiders. As Carl Schmitt (2003) correctly observes, however, unstable landscapes unsuitable for agriculture seem to be inherently unfit for sustaining the geometrical design of firmly established bounds. Thus, given its implicit reliance on the hypothesized abundance of productive land, the Lockean enclosures-based paradigm of the modern state seems utterly irrelevant from a Saharan perspective (and, one may legitimately argue, even more so in a context of global climate change).

In the desert, it is mobility, not the soil's productivity, which ensures survival. Scattered patterns of population and smooth landscapes in which no limit can be firmly traced allow for the full development of what McDougall and Scheele qualify as "connectivity," the "all-round and nearly frictionless potential of communication" (28). Anthropological scholarship focusing on Saharan communities confirms that the nomads' notion of frontier features

> elastic contours, constantly interacting with the geographical, ecological and human environment, which matches badly with the "square of fenced land" of fixed, immovable, intangible borders, corresponding to the territoriality of modern states. ... The territoriality of modern states is often felt by nomads as stifling, mutilating and destructive.
> CLAUDOT-HAWAD 2008: 51

This is also because the territory of the nomads has been broken up and relegated to the very margins of the states created by the (de)colonization process. The desert, both naturally and socially constructed, opposes the otherwise prevailing Western *nomos* of the Earth (Schmitt 2003) and rejects its interconnected fundamental pillars: private ownership of the land, clearly determined linear boundaries and mutually exclusive sovereignties.

Looking from the margins of mainstream modern political thought, as Foucault's methodology suggests, and bringing into the debate the point of view of the peripheralized nomadic people of the Saharan borderlands, allows us to radically question the alleged universality of the *nomos* of the Earth (Schmitt) and to unveil the biases this has normatively inscribed into our present. Field research conducted for this chapter demonstrates that, from an empirical and historical perspective, in the Sahara-Sahel, notions of what constitutes a "normal" state are likely to be overturned.

In North Mali, much more present than the ideal-type of state postulated by Locke (based on fixed borders, enclosures and printed money) is a nomadic economy based on boundary-less smooth spaces, social capital and barter (*le troc*). This means that social and geographical practices challenge the normative assumption that lies at the heart of the "normal" political organization, such as today's (best?) practices of state building, recommended by international donors.[9] Cross-border smuggling of all sorts has existed for centuries – its perceived legitimacy and its duration far exceeds that of the state's institution (Scheele 2011 and 2012). A Tuareg tribal leader and philosopher goes as far as to claim: "The notion of the modern state is a very partial solution to our problems. In fact, it is assassinating our culture!"[10]

Based on extensive field research, I would argue that Malians, especially those living in areas affected by conflict, consider cross-border smuggling and trafficking a resource more than a security threat (Danish Demining Group 19). Even when performed by criminal networks and involving illicit goods like weapons or drugs, only between 2% and 6% of interviewees places these activities among the top ten security concerns. In the same vein, semi-structured interviews I conducted in the field, albeit based on a statistically limited sample, revealed that 45.5% of respondents from different social groups in Mali spontaneously stressed their unwillingness to condemn trafficking in general as a criminal activity.[11] Even more strikingly, this figure climbs to 71% when one excludes law enforcement officers, whose responses might be biased or distorted because of their professional duties. Instead, it is noteworthy that the majority of Malians hold the state judicial system to be inequitable and/or ineffective overall, and therefore unable to address their claims (The Hague

---

9   For a critical discussion of the concept and practice of state-building, see, for instance, Batmanglich and Høyer.

10   Interview conducted in Bamako, November 2014, translated by the author.

11   These provisional data derive from semi-structured interviews with twenty-nine respondents from different backgrounds (law enforcement, civil society, journalists, former combatants, internally displaced persons), conducted in Bamako in November 2014.

Institute for the Internationalisation of Law). In other words, illegal or extra-legal activities, as well as actors that, under the law, ought to be confronted with political banishment (Agamben) in reality enjoy a far greater degree of social entrenchment and recognition than do the state apparatuses supposed to eradicate them. The discrepancy between (inter)national norm(ality) and local legitimacy could not be greater.

Under these circumstances, the labels of "normal" and "pathological" seem to reflect nothing but an arbitrary and externally imposed preference, if not a geopolitical power relation. Studying the spatial practices and representations (in Lefebvre's terms) of nomadic indigenous peoples roaming the Sahara, both ancestral and modern, provides a unique opportunity to explore the dialectical relationships unfolding between centers and peripheries, and to analyze how these relationships are mobilized to frame identities, normative registers and contestations.

The Saharan Borderlands as a Space of Connection

> If you want to take the temperature of what is going on between two countries, you have to go to the border. Here anything goes on, all sorts of traffic. Everyone is there for the same reason: money. The border is like a mine: it attracts both men and women, in search of gold.
>
> MOUHAMADOU, Malian of Gao, ex-migrant in Libya

If the border*line* can be defined as a neat edge, performing in principle a clear-cut separation, then the notion of border*land* (McDougall and Scheele 78) seems better suited to meaningfully describing the social possibilities of demarcation available in the Saharan geography. Borderlands are defined as transitional zones of indetermination between inside and outside, belonging and non-belonging, where any dividing line between two distinct discrete units, as those encompassed by standard structuralist theories of international relations, is *a priori* untenable. This is close to what the French philosopher Étienne Balibar qualifies as e*space de partage*, playing on the double meaning of the French word *partage* as divide/split and allocation/communion. In this view, the Sahara is more aptly interpreted as a space of connection, rather than one of insulation, a busy crossroads and a central node of a communication network rather than a periphery laying in a spatial and temporal rearguard.

Land "ownership" and territorial regulations in the Sahara, especially in the areas inhabited by the Tuareg communities scattered across Mali, Algeria and Niger, have been traditionally ruled according to the framework of *droits de passage* (rights of way). This framework assigns every social unit to a given area, where it enjoys a priority right to exploit its (very limited) natural resources, with some caveats: the usufruct over natural resources is compensated by a symmetrical duty to guarantee their reproduction:[12]

> Unlike the private land ownership which applies the concept of *usus* and *abusus* in most modern states, the soil itself is not subject to exclusive appropriation ... Once the resources of the lean season are consumed by the beneficiaries, the boundaries are blurred, prerogatives on territories are annihilated and the land becomes vacant: any group can cross or settle temporarily in these areas.
>
> CLAUDOT-HAWAD 2008: 57

Borders, then, are a dynamic concept, insofar as they are temporarily and spatially shifting. "'My place' is always contemporaneously one point in space, as well as a route, a bundle, the wider roaming spaces," commented a Tuareg tribal leader, inadvertently suggesting a parallel with Heisenberg's uncertainty principle.[13]

From this perspective, it is unsurprising that the *droits de passage*, unlike land ownership, do not include the right to exclude outsiders: "trespassing does not exist because of the absence of land that has been divided up and legally distributed" (Lecocq 113). A former Tuareg rebel now integrated into Malian administration puts it like this:

> In our culture, the land is given in common to the whole community to share. None has the right to keep me out, nor the right to deny me the authorization to graze my cattle. Nevertheless, it is my duty to ask the permission to do so. It is the same with the right of way, which is a tribute paid to the locals so that they grant your protection on their territory. In fact, it is not a right; it is a matter of respect and recognition. It is about acknowledging local leaderships.[14]

---

12   French scholar Marceline Breton correctly points out that in many local languages the attribution of land is expressed with the indirect object rather than with the complement of specification. Because there is no such thing as the complement of specification in English grammar, I would rephrase her idea as follows: many local languages use the indirect object rather than the genitive or a complement stating ownership to express a property relation. Land is not said to be somebody's, but rather "for someone," highlighting a different relation to property.

13   Interview conducted in Bamako, November 2014, translated by the author.

14   Interview conducted in Bamako, November 2013, translated by the author.

The fee that is demanded is indeed symbolic, and its amount negotiable. Weak patterns of territorialization correspond to weak political allegiances. Instead of enjoying specific ownership on a well-defined area of "tenure," the *améno-kal* (the title of the Tuareg's traditional leader) exerts some form of authority over a much bigger and symbolic "estate." Whereas the former is grounded in the concept of private property and includes the right of exclusion, the latter refers to the medieval ancestor of the modern notion of sovereignty (whence the derivation of "state" from "estate"), although with a much weaker sense of political obligation.

Tuareg political organization is therefore deeply interwoven with Tuareg spatial practices. The foundations of the social bonds lie in circulation, rather than in territorial rooting. As a result, social and spatial hierarchies are overturned. The territorially rooted natives, in Tuareg semantics, are only the poor and marginalized ones, while those living in the peripheral margins are the interfaces of an outward-looking attitude. Social exchanges and articulations with outsiders are indeed perceived as signs of social advancement (Claudot-Hawad 1996). Unlike in traditional state organizations, therefore, the core of power is situated at the peripheries, not in the secrecy of the inner control room.

From this perspective, significant patterns of more or less unauthorized and repressed flows of trade, smuggling and trafficking across the Sahara are less an anomaly deserving explanation than the rule. The connective nature of the Saharan borderlands is perfectly illustrated by the thriving criminal(ized) economy that has developed around In-Khalil, a village in the middle of the Sahara along the borderline dividing Algeria from Mali. Local people define In-Khalil as "the capital of *al-frud*," which refers to the illegal smuggling that has been the cornerstone of the nomadic economy for ages. The first fixed house in In-Khalil was built in 1993, when a massive flow of internally displaced persons, fleeing the 1990s Tuareg-led insurrection, settled in the nomad camp established there. Since then, In-Khalil has remained beyond the reach of any formal state structure. Reportedly, the people living in In-Khalil insist on their statelessness, which they value as a matter of personal pride (Scheele 2012). The remoteness of the location and its proximity to an international border – or, in other words, its status as a borderland – represent the most significant assets of the local political economy.

Indeed, In-Khalil has been consistently seen as the fundamental cornerstone of all illicit trading in the region.[15] Subsidized goods, such as foodstuffs

---

15   Although empirical evidence on these matters is hard to collect, many reports citing credible sources have been published. See Lacher; Musilli and Smith; Scheele 2011, 2012; Shaw and Tinti; Briscoe; Shaw et al.; UNODC 2008, 2011; Global Initiative.

and oil, come from Algeria and are sold on the black market of Gao, north Mali's biggest town. Migrants and human smuggling proceed via the opposite route: coming from all the countries bordering the gulf of Guinea, they are gathered in Gao, where fake Malian passports can be bought cheaply, allowing them visa-free entry into Algeria and Morocco. They are then packed into 4x4 vehicles, leaving daily to In-Khalil via the desert Tilemsi valley. From In-Khalil, further *passeurs* facilitate their way towards Ceuta, the Spanish enclave in Morocco, or Sebha, in southern Libya. The international smuggling of cigarettes is another lucrative business, which follows more or less the same path: from the seaports of the Gulf of Guinea towards Algeria and Libya. In-Khalil, with its *garaji* (garages) and infrastructures, can satisfy all sorts of needs drivers may have, including repairs, water refill, entertainment and women, making it a mandatory stop. In-Khalil is also reportedly an important trading post for narcotics: hashish resins come from Morocco, via Mauritania; South-American cocaine is allegedly unloaded in Guinea-Bissau's, Guinea-Conakry's and Mauritania's seaports, and flows to In-Khalil along the relatively unpatrolled borderlands that lie in-between Guinea, Senegal, Gambia, Mauritania and Algeria. According to local investigative journalists and interviews conducted with former member of drug cartels, one kilogram of cocaine can be valued at up to 30,000 euros.[16] Narcotics proceed northeast to Egypt before being diverted to the Balkans or to Arab countries. As an actual global trading epicenter, In-Khalil is also an infamous site for money laundering operations.

Representing the very opposite of the traditional bounded village community, In-Khalil can therefore be best described, in the same way as many other Saharan cities (Pliez), as a crossroads or a node that thrives on external inputs and makes outer worlds live. Here, all the fundamental concepts of modern political thought, such as citizenship, power and legitimacy, undergo a twist. Power relations are not based on territorial control, but on access to the resources of a deterritorialized network, organized in terms of protection and social capital. Transnational networks based on family and kinship often fade into those devoted to organized crime.

New cross-border identities, grafted onto these existing commercial networks, arise and more or less overtly challenge the legitimacy of state-based identifications. It is not by chance that, among the armed groups that thrive in the Saharan region, the most resilient are precisely those who have adopted names and brands boasting their regional coverage and boundary-straddling roots. These include the MOJWA (English acronym for the "Movement for Oneness of Jihad in West Africa"), and Al-Qaeda in Islamic Maghreb (AQIM, whose name stresses the common features between the northern and the southern

---

16   Interviews conducted in Bamako, November 2014.

shores of the Sahara). Significantly, in August 2013, the MUJAO merged with an AQMI *katibah* (a military unit the size of a brigade) in order to form a united organization called *Al-Mourabitoune* (the Almoravides), an explicit reference to the Moor dynasty that ruled the Western Sahara, from Marrakesh to Timbuktu, in the twelfth century. Significantly, *Al-Mourabitoune* was led by splinter AQIM's emir Mokhtar Belmokhtar, a former cigarette smuggler (hence his nickname, *Monsieur Marlboro*) who allegedly converted to the trans-Saharan trafficking of cocaine and weapons (Lacher; Shaw and Tinti). Recent research conducted in the region has found that one of the reasons for their success is precisely the propagation and practical implementation of the ideology of without-borderism present in both *sharia* law and the free trade economy of trafficking (Strazzari).

Thus, it may be argued that, instead of being a buffer zone, as postulated (rather than demonstrated) by the standard geopolitical view, the Saharan borderlands are the epicenter of significant political interactions precisely because of their peripherality, as the example of In-Khalil demonstrates. In other words, "marginality" can be viewed as an asset, provided that one is able to disentangle its pristine, descriptive and positional meaning, from its normative, evaluative, metaphorical abuse.

Conclusion: A Bid for Barbarization from the Saharan Peripheries

> In Europe, once you are master of two or three large cities, the entire country is yours. But in Africa, how do you act against a population whose only link to the land is the pegs of their tents?
>
> MARECHAL DE CASTELLANE

What kind of alternative security thinking could the observations sketched above possibly suggest? Nietzsche prophetically recognized that "the idea of uprooting, liquidity, restlessness, desire to be wanderers and nomads, is a principle of inevitable new *Barbarie* generating a new mixed race, ready to leave, and lover of short habits," against which blind decision-makers belatedly insist on fostering "an artificial nationalism, a state of emergency and siege that keeps credit only with cunning and violence" (Nietzsche sec. 475, emphasis added).[17] These words seem to apply to our case, too, as they propose a critique

---

17   There is a noteworthy proximity, both etymological and conceptual, between the notion of *Barbarie* and the reference to the berbers, to which the Tuareg and other nomad desert tribes are directly related.

of conventional security strategies adopted in the Sahara. Despite evidence that conflicts across the Sahara are interconnected, regional organizations and security approaches have been designed to address domestic or international rather than cross-border threats, and have adhered to the fiction of functional borders delimiting areas of homogeneous sovereignty. Carl Schmitt aptly recalls that Hobbes's *Leviathan*, perhaps the most successful and long-standing paradigm of modern statehood, refers to a biblical monster rising from the moving waters in order to provide indisputable rule over their otherwise uncontrolled flows and infinite space, as well as to hinder pirates and firmly establish the bounds of the community (1997: 97). Since their beginning, one may contend, state apparatuses have been designed to capture and constrain the "all-round, almost frictionless communication (McDougall and Scheele 28) expressed by the spatial practices of people living in the periphery. The very dichotomy opposing centers and peripheries, just as much as the normative threshold dividing accepted and banned forms of conduct, may arguably be said to be nothing but a state effect.

Stressing the common features between the smooth spaces of the desert and the steppes, as well as between Saharan nomadic people and the Cossacks, some scholars have suggested that the Sahara might be equaled to Russia's role of "heartland" in global geopolitics (Lacoste; Van der Pijl). In classical geopolitical thought (Spykman), the latter in fact represents the epicenter of all potential threats and concerns, in as much as it is isolated from the oceans and inaccessible to sea powers like the UK or the US. The imperial doctrine of containment is inferred on these premises, pointing out the need not only to prevent the consolidation of a strong and unitary state-actor in the heartland, but also to obstruct the latter's access to the oceans by exercising constant diplomatic and military pressure on the surrounding coastal states, described by Spykman as the "rimland."

I argue, however, that this hypothesis needs to be overturned. The Sahara is unlikely to harbor successful nationalisms and imperialist enterprises, or modern states rooted in the Weberian model. In other words, Saharan shaky sands are unlikely to provide the necessary ground for the emergence of the Leviathan. To be consistent with Saharan natural and human geography, an alternative geopolitical understanding should draw from the maritime paradigm of space management, favoring freedom of access over domination, connection over clear-cut separation, and surveillance over ruling (Spykman). It is only by emphasizing the centrality of the Sahara as a node of connections that one can return the notion of *Sahel* – which means "shore" in Arabic – to its original meaningfulness. Adopting the point of view of the peripheries would then allow a conceptualization of Saharan moving frontiers, the Sahel southward and the North African shores to the north, as "a new rimland," to paraphrase Spykman and Lacoste in one fell swoop. Based on the theoretical framework sketched above it is here, then, that forthcoming frictions and tensions are more likely to emerge. A quick look at the actual sites where violence is exercised in the Sahara Desert region nowadays seems to provide encouraging support for such a conjecture. A more accurate study focusing on the geography of conflicts therefore seems to provide a promising avenue for further research, and is likely to empirically sustain a critical review of the assumptions upon which the standard geopolitical understanding of the Sahara is based. Facing the worrying and endemic instability that affects the Saharan region today, this seems to be a fundamental premise in order to come up with policy recommendations that are epistemologically sound and politically sustainable.

Acknowledgments

I am grateful to Alessandra Russo and Francesco Strazzari, with whom I had the opportunity to discuss many of the ideas found in the present chapter. I am also indebted to all those people who agreed to be interviewed and shared their time and knowledge in order to help me understand, without expecting anything in return.

Works Cited

Agamben, Giorgio. *Homo Sacer: Sovereign Power and Bare Life*. Stanford: Stanford UP, 1998.

Balibar, Étienne. "Qu'est-ce qu'une 'frontière'?" *La crainte des masses. Politique et philosophie avant et après Marx*. Paris: Galilée, 1997.

Batmanglich, Sara, and Kathrine Høyer. *The New Deal's Peacebuilding and Statebuilding Goals and Organised Crime*. London: International Alert, 2013.

Briscoe, Ivan. *Crime after Jihad: Armed Groups, the State, and Illicit Business in Post-Conflict Mali*. The Hague: Clingendael Netherlands Institute of International Relations, 2014.

Buzan, Barry, and Oliver Waever. *Regions and Power: The Structure of International Security*. Cambridge: Cambridge UP, 2003.

Claudot-Hawad, Hélène. *Touaregs et autres Sahariens entre plusieurs mondes. Définitions et redéfinitions de soi et des autres*. Paris: Cahiers de l'IREMAM, 1996.

———. "Un territoire bati comme une tente nomade." *Réfractions* 21 (2008): 51–60.

Danish Demining Group. "Évaluation des risques sécuritaires aux frontières, régions du Liptako-Gourma." Copenhagen: Danish Demining Group, 2014.

Foucault, Michel. *Society Must Be Defended: Lectures at the Collège de France, 1975–76.* London: Penguin, 2004

Fukuyama, Francis. *State-Building: Governance and World Order in the 21st Century.* Ithaca: Cornell UP, 2004.

Global Initiative against Transnational Organised Crime. *Libya: A Growing Hub for Criminal Economies and Terrorist Financing in the Trans-Sahara.* Geneva: Global Initiative against Transnational Organized Crime, 2015.

Helly, Damien, and Greta Galeazzi. "The Alphabet Soup of Coordination in the Sahel: In Search of Collective Leadership." Maastricht: ECDPM, 2014.

Julien, Simon. "Le Sahel comme espace de transit des stupéfiants. Acteurs et conséquences politiques." *Hérodote* 142.3 (2011): 125–42.

Kahera, Akel Ismail. "Cosmographies: West African Aesthetics." *Dippost.com.* Diplomacy Post, 27 Dec. 2013. Web. 1 Dec. 2015.

Kaplan, Robert D. "The Coming Anarchy." *Atlantic.com.* Atlantic Magazine, February 1994. Web. 1 Dec. 2015.

Lacher, Wolfram. "Organized Crime and Conflict in the Sahel-Sahara Region." *The Carnegie Papers.* Washington: Carnegie Endowment for International Peace, 2012.

Lacoste, Yves. "Sahara, perspectives et illusions géopolitiques." *Hérodote* 142.3 (2011): 12–41.

Lecocq, Baz. *Disputed Desert: Decolonisation, Competing Nationalism and Tuareg Rebellions in Northern Mali.* Leiden: Brill, 2010.

Lefebvre, Henri. *La production de l'espace.* Paris: Anthropos, 1974.

McDougall, James, and Judith Scheele. *Saharan Frontiers: Space and Mobility in Northwest Africa.* Bloomington: Indiana UP, 2012.

Mezzadra, Sandro, and Brett Neilson. *Border as Method, or, the Multiplication of Labor.* Durham: Duke UP, 2013.

Musilli, Pietro, and Patrick Smith. "The Lawless Roads: An Overview of Turbulence across the Sahel." Oslo: NOREF, 2013.

Nietzsche, Friedrich. *Human, All Too Human.* New York: Prometheus Book, 2008.

OECD. *An Atlas of the Sahara-Sahel: Geography, Economics and Security.* Paris: OECD, 2014.

Pliez, Olivier. *Les cités du désert: des villes sahariennes aux saharatowns.* Marseille: Presses Universitaires Marseille, 2011.

Pulgram, Ernst. *Writing without Letters.* Ed. Haas William. Manchester UP, 1976.

Raleigh, Clinoadh, and Caitriona Dowd. "Governance and Conflicts in the Sahel's 'Ungoverned Space.'" *Stability: International Journal of Security & Development* 2.2 (2013): Art-32.

Risse, Thomas, and Ursula Lehmkuhl. *Governance in Areas of Limited Statehood: New Modes of Governance?* Berlin: Collaborative Research Center (SFB), 2006.

Roux, Michel. "Sahara: géographie de l'imaginaire." *Mappemonde* 2 (1991): n. pag.

Scheele, Judith. "Circulations marchandes au Sahara, entre licite et illicite." *Hérodote* 142.3 (2011): 143–62.

———. *Smugglers and Saints of the Sahara: Regional Connectivity in the Twentieth Century.* Cambridge: Cambridge UP, 2012.

Schmitt, Carl. *Land and Sea.* London: Plutarch Press, 1997.

———. *The Nomos of the Earth in the International Law of the Jus Publicum Europaeum.* New York: Telos Press, 2003.

Shaw, Mark, and Peter Tinti. *Organized Crime and Illicit Trafficking in Northern Mali.* Geneva: Global Initiative against Transnational Organized Crime, 2014.

Shaw, Mark, Reitano Tuesday, and Hunter Marcena. *Comprehensive Assessment of Drug Trafficking and Organized Crime in West and Central Africa.* Report to the African Union, 2014.

Spykman, Nicholas. *The Geography of the Peace.* New York: Brace and Company, 1944.

Strazzari, Francesco. *Azawad and the Rights of Passage: The Role of Illicit Trade in the Logic of Armed Group Formation in Northern Mali.* Oslo and The Hague: NOREF/Clingendael, 2015.

Turner, Frederick Jackson. *The Significance of the Frontier in American History.* New York: Norton, 1921.

UNODC. *Drug Trafficking as a Security Threat in West Africa.* Vienna: UNODC, 2008.

———. *The Transatlantic Cocaine Market.* Vienna: UNODC, 2011.

Van der Pijl, Kees. *Nomads, Empires, States: Modes of Foreign Relations and Political Economy.* London: Pluto Press, 2007.

Waltz, Kenneth. *The Theory of International Politics.* New York: Addison-Wesley, 1979.

CHAPTER 6

Cast(e)ing Life: The Experience of Living in Peripheral Caste Quarters

Durgesh Solanki

Introduction

"The salvation of the whole of India lies in greater urbanization," said B.R. Ambedkar in 1939 while addressing the constituent assembly. Ambedkar, the architect of the Indian Constitution and the founder of the Dalit[1] movement, saw the Indian "village [as] a cesspool, a den of ignorance, narrow-mindedness, and communalism" (62). For him and for other Dalit scholars, cities were beacons of hope for migrants, helping them break feudal ties that were marked by "graded hierarchical"[2] (Ambedkar 101–102) caste structures and gender oppression. They saw cities as spaces that would generate new identities, erasing centuries of discrimination and violence. Accordingly, after Independence in 1947, the Indian state passed laws to abolish the caste system and provide support to Dalits and backward castes through affirmative action.

Today, India is emerging as a globalizing capitalist state with the world's largest democracy. Despite this rapid urbanization, the caste system has not vanished like Ambedkar hoped. Instead it is emerging in newer avatars and geographies, interwoven with processes of urbanization, globalization, and liberalization. In cities, the overt, horrific acts of violence that occur in rural India have been replaced by structural violence manifested in spatial segregation, normalized exclusion, discrimination and peripheralization. The peripheralization of Dalits on the basis of caste is inherently linked to the notion of the untouchable body. This notion of untouchability arises from the Hindu varna system, which marks lower caste bodies, linking them to certain "polluting" occupations such as leatherwork or manual scavenging. Mobility in caste is almost impossible. In cities, the polluting bodies of Dalit are controlled by insidious processes with planning emerging as a violent tool to relocate and

---

1 "Dalit" is a term coined by Ambedkar to refer to the untouchable caste.

2 The defining feature of caste for Ambedkar is graded inequality. He uses the concept "graded" to distinguish caste from a social system based on inequality which is not capable of self-replication. In the case of the caste system, even low castes have power when compared to a lower caste and hence each caste has an interest in maintaining the system.

© KONINKLIJKE BRILL NV, LEIDEN, 2016 | DOI 10.1163/9789004323056_008

marginalize certain communities. Caste is perhaps the most enduring feature of Indian society, a crucial marker of identity, a determinant of opportunities and a hierarchy informing varied citizenship in the city. Caste and modernity, rather than clashing, have "animated each other and learned to endure each other" (Shaikh 491).

This chapter seeks to argue that the BMC (Brihanmumbai Municipal Corporation) conservancy workers' quarters, which are located all over the city, represent the use of spatial segregation by the state as a tool to control the bodies of scheduled caste groups. I will use the concept of "dirt" (Guru) to explain the ways in which the state and caste elites segregate scheduled caste groups by subscribing to Brahmanical notions of purity and pollution.[3] This segregation of people based on caste can be understood in terms of center and periphery, as Dalits are marginalized socially, economically, politically and physically, resulting in their being deprived of opportunities and resources (Ram). Further, I attempt to understand the experience of the people staying in such peripheral quarters. What is it like to live in an area that is marked by caste? How has the community life of these neighborhoods changed? Why, even after a hundred years of conservancy work, has this community not been able to move out of their jobs? And finally, how is caste discrimination different in the urban context? Using the lens of segregated housing, I explore the ways in which caste is manifested and perpetuated within the space of the city.

I employ native/self-ethnography as a method to understand the experience of people from the Meghwal community who work in the BMC as conservancy workers and who live in the caste ghetto (Wolcott). Self-ethnography is defined as a form of self-narrative that places the self within a social context. It can refer either to the ethnographic study of one's own group(s) or to autobiographical reflections that include ethnographic observations and analysis (Reed-Danahay). I am familiar with the area and the people, and belong to the same caste group. In turn, they are familiar with me and my family, given that my mother's natal family resides in these quarters. Alvesson asserts that in self-ethnography the researcher is not a stranger in the research area and thus needs to break out of the group that is being researched (Alvesson). This breaking out involves "making the transition from insider to insider researcher" (Hodkinson). In order to make this transition, I used reflective ethnographic methods – going back to my notes and audio files, and examining them vis-à-vis my own position. As an insider, the researcher is able to negotiate the

---

3   Brahmans are the elite or knowledge producing caste. They maintain the caste hierarchy and
    inequality through a discourse of purity and pollution.

power hierarchy that exists between researcher and researched, which other-wise inhibits rapport (Oakley).

In short, this was research conducted in my own cultural backyard, where I was accepted as part of the social environment, so that my presence would not greatly disrupt the life of the community. This enabled my movement within the area and my access to information through formal and informal meet-ings. The study was conducted over a period of eight months in 2014–2015 by means of formal and informal in-depth conversations with individuals from the community.

This chapter can also be understood in terms of the larger debates in India around reservation (a form of affirmative action). Reservation, formalized after Independence in 1947, provides a certain percentage of positions in higher edu-cation and government employment to the erstwhile lower-caste and minority groups. Many civil society groups, like Youth for Equality, vehemently oppose reservation on the grounds that the "unreasonable inclusion and continuation of castes with 'backward' status [amounts to] reverse discrimination" (Youth for Equality). In the case of conservancy work, there is an unstated 100 percent reservation for those belonging to scheduled and backward caste groups. This raises the important question of why reservation in certain sectors is seen as a problem, while policies like PT, which ensure the endurance of caste-based work, are not considered contentious.

Historical Context

In the rapidly changing city of Mumbai, the Class IV BMC quarters, where the conservancy workers[4] live today, represent the scheduled caste[5] and for-mer untouchable caste settlements. Out of the 40,000 conservancy workers employed by the BMC, approximately twenty percent live in conservancy quarters, which are separate and spread all across the city, extending from the island city to the suburban areas.[6] Most of these settlements have colonial

---

4   "Conservancy worker" is an official term describing sweepers and sewage drain cleaners working in urban municipalities.

5   All the ex-untouchable castes, which were known as depressed castes in the colonial era, are grouped under the scheduled caste category. The population of the scheduled caste is 16.6% of the total Indian population.

6   Those who have not been allocated state housing, who make up the majority, live in slums and on the outskirts of slums.

roots and, in contemporary times, have become increasingly rundown due to the negligence of the BMC.

The twentieth century played a significant role in the shaping of contemporary Bombay.[7] It was marked by an increase and then a sudden and rapid decrease in population, a detailed census, the expansion of the cotton mills, multiple plague epidemics, the first Hindu-Muslim riots and the migration of Hindu Meghwals[8] and other communities from Gujarat. Gujarat experienced a major drought at the start of the twentieth century and many communities migrated to Bombay in search of jobs and better opportunities (Masselos). Others migrated to break away from the grip of the feudal ties and caste nexus in rural areas.

By 1900, the swamp-ridden seven islands of Bombay were connected and combined into one contiguous island. At this time, the city had undergone rapid industrialization under British colonial rule and had become an important trading hub. The rapid expansion of the cotton mills from 1870 onwards had a major impact on the political economy of Bombay (Kidambi). The city witnessed a huge influx of migrants from different parts of the country, who were employed in these cotton mills. It became known as "Urbs Prima in Indis," the biggest urban center in Asia and second in the world, after London (Kosambi; Bhide). The population of Bombay increased from approximately 500,000 in 1849 to 821,764 in 1890 (Edwardes).

The lack of housing facilities in Bombay to accommodate the increasing population forced working-class migrants to live on the streets or in overcrowded localities in poor conditions, creating pressure on the urban and social fabric of the city (Kidambi; Chandavarkar). As a result, a plague broke out in 1896, spreading rapidly across working- class localities and creating such fear amongst the migrant populations that many fled Bombay. This resulted in a decrease in population. Bombay also witnessed the huge out migration of mill workers (Arnold). At the same time, there was a major drought in the Saurashtra region of Gujarat, which resulted in the migration of a huge population

---

7   Bombay was renamed Mumbai in 1994 when a right-wing government came into power in
    the state of Maharashtra. Here, Bombay is used for the period before 1994.
8   Hindu Meghwals are also known as Vankars. After repeated droughts in Gujarat, many
    Vankars, Bhangis, Barot and other communities migrated to Bombay. They were all categorized as "Dhed" by the colonial government, a slang term which derives from the Gujarati
    word *dhayadavan* meaning "to drag." The term itself refers to people who would drag the
    dead carcasses of animals. Post-Independence, in 1947, there was a demand for a change in
    terminology and Dhed was replaced with Meghwals. Here, Meghwals, Dhed and Vankar are
    used interchangeably, depending on the context.

to Bombay (Virani). It was a paradoxical situation in which communities from Gujarat were migrating to Bombay while mill laborers were migrating out.

Migration to the city was not independent of caste, kinship, region and village connections (Chandavarkar; Mhaskar). Many different jobbers existed whose responsibility ranged from the recruitment of people for the textile mills to obtaining contracts to clean various localities and drains (Chandavarkar). Jobbers played an essential role in the labor market and they relied on caste, kinship and social ties (Mhaskar). However, Dalit workers were not allowed to work in the weaving sheds by the Maratha[9] weavers. Chandavarkar explains this phenomenon as "an expression of caste consciousness which extended beyond the workplace" (227). The notions of caste and religion were reinforced in the city by both the division of work and the segregation of working-class houses on the basis of caste (Mhaskar). Even the colonial administration worked within this framework. As Hansen writes: "The paramount aims of colonial bio-politics were to maintain stability and order, whereas the grooming of colonial quasi citizens was highly selective and always circumscribed by class, caste and race" (177–78).

At the time of the influx of migrants to the city, the Mahar[10] community was employed by the BMC for conservancy work. When they went on strike in the 1920s, they were removed from these positions and Hindu Meghwals and Matangs[11] were given these jobs on the condition that they signed stringent contracts (Shaikh). To incentivize this work, the municipal corporation provided them with housing and the possibility of transferring their jobs to their children when they retired or if they died while still in service. This system emerged when there was a major housing shortage in the city. The Preferential Treatment Policy, instituted by the colonial administration, was formalized by the Indian government after Independence through caste-based reservation in government employment and education.[12] Through housing, the colonial state thus created a ghetto of conservancy workers often belonging to the same caste, subcaste and region.

---

9   The Maratha are a caste group from Maharashtra, comprised of warriors, landowning classes and peasant cultivators.

10   The Mahar community is a historically untouchable caste in India, living largely within Maharashtra. Ambedkar, the famous social reformer, was born into the Mahar caste and later in his life converted to Buddhism. The community has the largest population among scheduled castes in Maharashtra.

11   Matangs are a historically untouchable caste in Maharashtra. They are the most exploited of the three scheduled caste groups in Maharashtra, i.e. Mahar, Matang and Chamars.

12   Through one of the tenets of this policy, which is only applicable to conservancy workers, conservancy employment can be inherited by and bequeathed to next of kin.

The strategy that underscores the Preferential Treatment[13] policy is that it simultaneously provides benefits to scheduled castes and is an attempt at paternalistic and tokenistic social justice. Since the lower-caste body is considered to be a "sociological danger" that needs to be quarantined (Guru), in providing this treatment, the government is both regulating and controlling the social life of the conservancy worker. For Guru, the underlying notion of this control is "dirt,"[14] based on caste identity and on separating the body that embodies dirt from the rest of the population, to be contained in the periphery. It is significant that the very same body that has to clear the dirt of the city is segregated and ghettoized because of it. As Guru articulates, the "untouchable is dirt and that dirt is the untouchable, both completely indistinguishable from each other. Yet, ironically this shit is not disposable, as it is required to dispose the emitted shit" (13). In this context, humiliation becomes a felt experience of being a conservancy worker (Geetha). Through this experience of humiliation, Dalit aspirations are moderated and Dalits are taught to blame themselves for their own exclusion (Guru). Preferential Treatment works as a tool to replicate the experience of humiliation and keep Dalits confined to a whirlpool of dirt.

The Conservancy Quarters

The area of study for this chapter is located in the island city of Mumbai in a neighborhood called Chinchpokli, which derives its name from two Marathi words: *chinch*, meaning tamarind, and *pokli*, meaning betel nut. Historically, it was a hilly area covered with tamarind and betel nut trees. During the colonial era, the trees were cut down and Chinchpokli became a hub for millworkers, dominated by Marathas and people from Other Backward Castes (OBC) with a segregated scheduled caste population that lived in one settlement. While originally several cotton mills surrounded Chinchpokli, today most of these are defunct and the mill lands are now slated for redevelopment. As a result, the area around Chinchpokli has witnessed dramatic spatial changes, with high-rise structures replacing the original warehouses. This has resulted in a

---

13   The Preferential Treatment policy was adopted during Independence to improve the status of lower-caste groups. During interviews and conversations, the PT case was frequently used by respondents to refer to Preferential Treatment in BMC class IV jobs.

14   Mary Douglas, in her book *Purity and Danger*, defines dirt as "matter out of place" (36). For her, dirt becomes a spatial problem. She further argues that dirt is a "by-product of systemic ordering and classification of matter [that] involves rejecting inappropriate elements" (36).

skyrocketing of land prices and in Chinchpokli emerging as a residential hub for people who work as domestic helpers and chauffeurs to those in the high-rises. Nonetheless, it still remains a lower middle-class neighborhood dotted by chawls[15] and low-rise tenements. It also continues to have a segregated Dalit population, which mainly lives in municipal housing.

The BMC quarters themselves are tucked between the Arthur Road Prison and the Ambulance Garage. Arthur Road Prison, one of the oldest prisons in Maharashtra, was strategically constructed in 1926 by the colonial adminis-tration, as it was easier to construct a prison next to a Dalit settlement than near an upper-caste/class settlement. As mentioned before, during that era, Chinchpokli was on the periphery of the city and was also a hub of working-class activity. The city has since expanded and Chinchpokli now lies in the cen-ter of the city; indeed, it is a rare sight to see a prison surrounded by residential and commercial establishments. In many ways, this reflects a spatial geogra-phy of deviance and control in the city during colonial times; the bodies of both criminals and Dalits had to be controlled and confined to the periphery to maintain the urban status quo.

Two distinct features of Dalit settlements, a Buddhavihar[16] and a seekh ka-bab[17] stall, mark the entrance of the quarters. The Buddhavihar, which was constructed in 1970 by Bhagwan Rathod, one of the few Meghwal followers of Ambedkar,[18] is known among the community as the Dalit Panthers' office. The Dalit Panther movement is the Dalit movement that was founded in the 1970s by Namdeo Dhasal and others, inspired by the revolutionary Black Panther Movement in America. Most Meghwals, however, do not identify as Dalits – for them, Dalits are followers of Ambedkar who have converted to Buddhism. In terms of nomenclature, they identify more with Gandhi's framing of the com-munity as Harijan (meaning "people of god"), since they see this as more in line with their practice of Hinduism.

As shown in figure 6.1, the settlement itself is divided into two sections based on the type of physical structures: three five-storied buildings (vertical)

---

15   A chawl is a housing or residential structure commonly found in working-class localities in Mumbai. Chawls can be single-storied or two- or three-storied, consisting of rows of houses with a common toilet and in some cases even a bathroom. They were built by the colonial government to provide housing to low-wage earning migrants working in the city.

16   A Buddhavihar is a Buddhist place of worship.

17   A seekh kabab is a food item made from beef or mutton that is similar to a hot dog in shape. In this case, it is made from beef, which is culturally taboo for Hindus.

18   As noted above, Ambedkar was a revolutionary and canonical figure of the Dalit movement.

FIGURE 6.1   *Map of the research area.*
SOURCE: GOOGLE EARTH IMAGERY, 2014.

and nineteen chawls (horizontal). The vertical part consists of three buildings, which have a mix of Meghwals and Buddhists (Mahars), and a single row
of houses that are only occupied by Meghwals. These three buildings were
originally three-storied cement-colored chawls, which were redeveloped into
buildings by the BMC in the late 1980s because of the dilapidation of the old
structures. Unlike the current closely spaced buildings constructed under the
Slum Rehabilitation Scheme in other parts of the city, there is abundant space
between them. Every building has 48 houses, which are about 180 square feet
each. One of the buildings has been declared a dangerous structure and the
residents of this building have been given houses in a different location in
Mumbai.

There are nineteen chawls, marked from D to V, and each chawl has nine
houses, except E, which has five houses, and I, which has four houses. These
chawls also have a row of common toilets. Historically, when the chawls were
built they consisted of a single 100-square-foot room attached to a spacious
veranda or common space with a large window at the back of the house. The
veranda was a multipurpose space where people would sleep in the summers,
do most of their cooking on a chula,[19] and also a place where most marriages
and other social functions would occur (see figure 6.2). There was no system of
having marriages in private banquet halls; besides, most could not afford the

---

19   A chula is a wood-fired cooking stove.

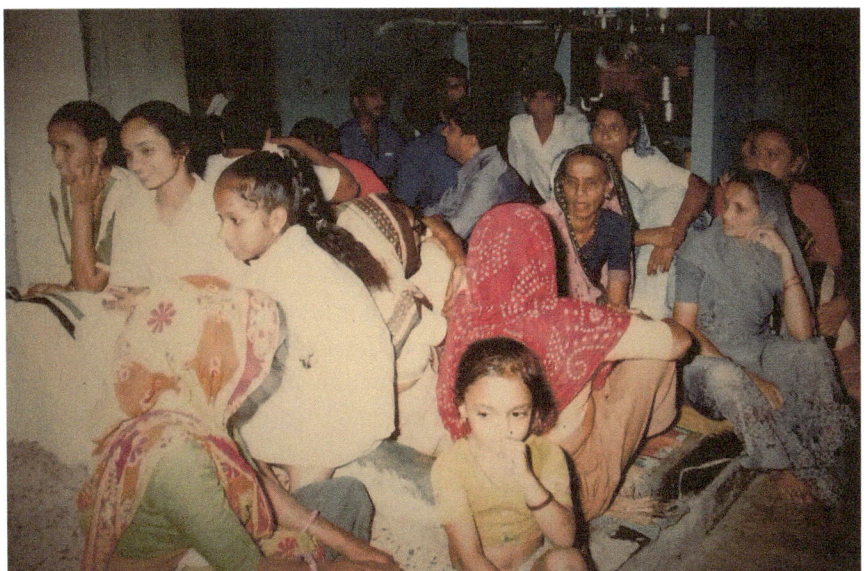

FIGURE 6.2 *People gathering for the engagement of Rashmi Wagh. They are sitting in the open*
space outside the house. The open kitchen and raised veranda are also visible. This
image was taken approximately twenty-five years ago.
SOURCE: FAMILY ALBUM OF RAMESH SOSA.

costs. While the spatial layout of these houses was the same as in the villages,
the materials used to construct them were not. Since they were constructed by
the BMC, they consisted of concrete walls protected by a Mangalore tile roof.
This was in stark contrast to the rural houses, as well as to some of the urban
houses that were still constructed out of natural materials like grass (Shaikh).
Thus, acquiring a conservancy job and housing in the city was a sign of upward
mobility.

As liquid petroleum gas became easily available, it became more popular,
and people started buying gas stoves to replace chulas. With the use of gas
stoves, people slowly started increasing the height of the walls. Subsequently,
the height of the space in front of their homes was extended and semi-enclosed,
because gas stoves needed a platform for safe and easy cooking. This is how the
concept of a kitchen arose in the community, marking a transition from public
to private space. The veranda was now seen as an extension of the house rather
than as a public space. A common structure of the house during this phase was
an inner room and a roofed kitchen outside without any doors. A drum filled
with water was kept outside on a raised platform for washing utensils.

A further distinction between public and private spaces was made in the
mid-1990s when families started constructing additional stories. This marked a

change in the structure of the house, in the space around it and in community life. The kitchen space, which was open before, became fortified with walls and doors. Windows with transparent glass were replaced with translucent or colored ones, preventing those on the outside from seeing inside. Additional floors were also built – today, all the chawls are two-storied structures. Typically, in these structures the outside rooms on the first floor are used as a kitchen and bathroom, while the inside room is used as a living room and bedroom for parents and elderly people. Generally, the second floor of the house is occupied by the younger couple. If there are more couples, the space is divided into two rooms. Before the construction of the floor above, there was no need for tube lights during the daytime, but now the structure has changed and sunlight hardly enters the houses. Houses allocated to conservancy workers in the buildings are in bad shape due to a lack of maintenance. In 2013, one of these buildings collapsed, killing 61 people. Using this dilapidation as a reason, the BMC has also stated its intention to move all conservancy quarters to the Mahul area of M-east ward.[20] Such a move would further peripheralize this population.

The common space, which was outside the house, has disappeared, so that the interactions that used to take place between the women while they cooked have also ceased (see figure 6.3). This was also a space where small children would play with their neighbors, in a way providing a childcare support system where mothers would leave their children and someone would be there to take care of them.

The change in housing structure has occurred as a result of various social and political factors. The new structure provides more private space and the size of the house has increased. One of the narratives that has emerged is how bigger houses are essential for grooms to find a bride. Nobody wants to have their daughter married to a groom from a family with a smaller house, as a bigger house is a marker of improved class position or mobility. On the whole, the transition that has occurred is in tune with that of the city's spatial politics in that it has produced a decline of public space and an increase in private space.

In the official BMC records, the houses still measure a hundred square feet, with provision for an extra floor above. The extensions into the space outside are not legally recognized, making these illegal structures. In fact, in 2002, when G.R. Khainar[21] was the Deputy Commissioner of the BMC, several

---

20   M-east ward has the lowest human development index in the city. It contains the city's garbage dumping ground, a large number of informal settlements and many resettlement colonies.

21   G.R. Khainar was known in popular culture as the "one man demolition army."

FIGURE 6.3 *Contemporary image of a chawl in the* BMC *quarters. The common space is now a narrow lane.*
SOURCE: TAKEN BY THE AUTHOR DURING FIELD WORK IN 2015.

families were given notice that the illegal portions of their houses would be demolished. When Khainar retired soon after, however, no further action was taken.

Having explained the history and development of the conservancy quarters, in the next section, I will examine stories from three different generations to understand the experience of living in a state of inherited peripherality.

Inherited Peripherality

Sachin's parents are third-generation conservancy workers in the BMC. He is 22 years old and has just finished college. His mother, who took up the job when his father succumbed to tuberculosis, still works in the BMC and has ten years left before she retires. Sachin aspires to work in banking or insurance. When I asked him what will happen to the house if he does not take up the job, he replied: "I will give it to my wife when I get married."

This reply resonates with the life of Laxmi Rathod, who is in her 70s and who has lived in Chinchpokli her whole life. Laxmi was born in the recently demolished chawl to conservancy workers. Laxmi's grandfather migrated to Bombay during the drought of 1900 from Saurashtra, joined the BMC as a conservancy worker and was allotted the house where the family currently lives. After a few years, her grandfather returned to Saurashtra and convinced his brothers to move to Bombay as well, because the BMC was providing both employment and housing. Eventually, the entire family moved to Bombay and began working in the BMC as conservancy workers. Laxmi studied until the second grade in the local Gujarati medium school and got married at the age of sixteen to Palji Rathod, who also lived in the area. Palji's father was a conservancy worker, but Palji did not take up the job and instead gave the PT case to his wife. He was one of the first people in the community to complete high school. Once he graduated, he began work in the Central Government Labour Institute as a clerk, a job he had until he retired years later. Palji was never promoted to cashier because of his caste; he was often told: "A dalit can't handle money." Before taking up her father-in-law's PT case, Laxmi worked as domestic help in a Muslim household. When Palji's father retired, she took up the PT case but also simultaneously continued working as domestic help. Laxmi worked for twenty-four years; when she retired, the work was taken up by her son and the legacy continues. Though there is a difference of almost 40 years between their stories, Sachin's aspirations and Laxmi's life bear testament to the unchanging nature of the caste system, particularly the ways in which it is gendered and inherited. This is the case for most households in the peripheral caste quarters, which have passed down the same peripheral (conservancy) work for generations.

Rakesh Parmar is a commerce graduate in his late 20s who is doing conservancy work. "I am doing it because I don't have any other job to do. At least this is a permanent job and a salary with which I can sustain myself," he says. As a conservancy worker Rakesh would earn a starting salary of Rs. 15,000–16,000, earning an increment of Rs. 2,000 after a year. "It is very difficult to get a good paying and sustainable job in the private sector without any additional skills. With a graduate degree I was getting jobs which were paying from 8,000 to 10,000 per month," says Rakesh. As he notes himself, Rakesh is not an exception; there are many others who have graduated from college and continue doing conservancy work. A lack of social and cultural capital among young people is one of the reasons for this. When they enter into the competitive job market with just an undergraduate degree, they struggle to find a job. Conservancy work is always a viable option because of their caste. As Rakesh says, "This situation has disheartened many youth and even parents. There is apathy towards their education and their situation."

The Preferential Treatment Policy, which was instituted by the colonial administration and formalized by the BMC after Independence, plays an important role in molding the lives of Laxmi, Sachin, Rakesh and many others who live in the conservancy quarters. Through this policy, which is only applicable to conservancy workers, the job is transferred to the closest next of kin. In this way, the state creates a link between occupation and inheritance, an important and enduring feature of the caste system. Many well-qualified young people are still forced to take up conservancy work in order to maintain their housing status. In this way, the policy shapes or decides the future of many of the people living in the quarters. For those living in the BMC quarters, it is neither merely a transfer of a job nor merely a transfer of a house. Housing is thus used as a tool to ensure a supply of conservancy workers belonging to the same historical caste, doing the same job for generations. The status quo of caste hierarchy is efficiently managed and maintained by the state by ensuring that housing, the most expensive commodity[22] in Mumbai, is not an assurance. This lack of ownership and the inability to transfer houses to other persons has become a state policy of caste oppression.

In cases where there is more than one child, the job is transferred to one child and the fund service[23] and other financial assistance is given to the other child to buy a house or another PT case. In most instances, people prefer to buy a PT case over investing the fund service elsewhere, as it will provide them with a house and a job. Even BMC officers are involved in the trading of PT cases. It is important to note here that there is fierce competition for conservancy jobs both within the family and within the community. According to Rakesh, the current price of a PT case with a house is Rs. 1,200,000 and without a house Rs. 600,000. This has impacted the domestic sphere of life and created many disputes within families over who inherits the PT case.

It is important to note that the amount that each individual family has paid over the years as Housing Rent Allowance (HRA) is more than equivalent to the cost of the house. Currently, the HRA for a house in the chawl is approximately Rs. 3,000. People staying in the area have been paying HRA for the last three generations, roughly seventy-five years. There is a movement of conservancy workers, then, who demand that home ownership be transferred to them, as this will help them in moving out of the profession.

---

22   According to Praja's report on affordable housing in Mumbai, the average price of a 269 square feet house is 28 lakhs. The stark inequality further shows from the fact that 50% of the population stays on a mere 6% of the total land.

23   Fund service is the same as provident fund. Respondents kept referring to it as fund service.

Cast(e)ing the City

From the above narratives from the peripheral caste quarters it is clear that the urban metropolitan area remains a site of anxiety for upper caste groups (Guru); anxiety that is resolved by different technologies of power, including the institution of the PT policy. Through this, the state ensures a constant supply of scheduled caste conservancy workers who all stay in one location (or, if they do not have access to state housing, will not be able to afford houses in prime locations in the city). Moreover, housing in most urban metros is informally regulated by housing societies and colonies. Muslims and scheduled caste and tribe groups, for instance, are not permitted to buy or rent houses here, even if they can afford to do so, on the basis that they consume meat. These restrictions are clearly based on an idea of ritual purity in which certain bodies and occupations are seen as polluting. As Geetha writes, the "complicated norms of tactility mandate that the low-born alone should labor at difficult and hazardous tasks, since their bodies, being constitutively impure, are held to be suited to these and not other vocations" (97). Through policies like the PT case, the state is able to control the labor of the scheduled caste and employ them in hazardous tasks. In fact, every year at least 250 conservancy workers die in Mumbai because of various diseases. Even though the state provides housing security while they are working, this is a constant reminder of their caste realities.

The socio-spatial transformations of the city have followed the colonial path of spatial segregation. While the forms and tools may have changed, the results have been more or less similar: spatially segregated neighborhoods on the basis of class, caste, and religion. In the contemporary neo-liberal scenario, it seems like the state has receded and the market has taken precedence. This is, however, only partially true, as the state and the market together play an active role in policy making and planning, shaping a "world-class" city that excludes the already marginalized and vulnerable. The Slum Rehabilitation Authority (SRA), created by the Maharashtra government to amend the Maharashtra Slum Areas Act in order to oversee the redevelopment of informal settlements in the city, is one such instance where state and market are colluding with each other to marginalize the poor. It is based on public-private partnership but "in reality, the private builders use their economic power to influence the resettlement plans" (Ghadge). This privatization of slum redevelopment in the name of public-private partnership reveals the SRA as a neo-liberal solution for housing the urban poor (Anand and Rademacher). The SRA is designed to benefit private developers by enabling them to build spacious luxury apartments on slum land, while assigning the plot's original occupants only a small portion of the land (Bharucha).

Conclusion

Through an ethnographic study of the BMC quarters, I have tried to highlight how caste operates in the urban sphere and how the state reinforces the caste system. Urban spaces, marked by the processes of liberalization and globalization, bear remnants of the caste system. From a distance, Mumbai looks like a chaotic city, but a close analysis reveals how housing and occupation play a major role as tools of the state through which the population is controlled, disciplined and divided across locations conceived as central and peripheral. The circulation of discourses of dirt is used to legitimate this spatial segregation and engenders a sense of humiliation that further marginalizes Dalits. This spatial segregation occurs at the multiple levels of labor, livelihood and housing to create peripheralized caste bodies, reducing the chance of intergenerational mobility and of moving away from a caste-based livelihood. This makes it possible to maintain the Hindu social order[24] in urban space. Rather than annihilating caste, institutions like the BMC maintain and replicate the caste system, perpetuating an order in which Dalits remain at the periphery of Indian society.

Works Cited

Alvesson, Mats. "Methodology for Close Up Studies Struggling with Closeness and Closure." *Higher Education* 46.2 (2003): 167–93.

Ambedkar, Bhimrao. "Dr. Babasaheb Ambedkar Writings and Speeches." Vol. 3, Vol. 5, Vol. 13. Dr. Ambedkar Foundation, Ministry of Social Justice and Empowerment, Government of India, 2014.

Anand, Nikhil, and Anna Rademacher. "Housing in the Urban Age: Inequality and Aspiration in Mumbai." *Antipode* 43.5 (2011): 1748–72.

---

24   Ambedkar coined the term Hindu Social Order to describe a society that is not based on the principles of equality and fraternity. The three distinct features of the Hindu social order are: (1) it is based on graded inequality; (2) it demonstrates a hereditary fixation on occupation and its continuance; (3) it fixes people within their caste (Ambedkar 106–13).

Arnold, Caroline E. "The Bombay Improvement Trust, Bombay Mill Owners and the Debate over Housing Bombay's Mill Workers, 1896–1918." *Essays in Economic & Business History* 30.2 (2012): 105–23.

Bharucha, Nauzer. "229 Mumbai Flats Meant for Slumdwellers' Rehab Sold." *Times of India*. Times of India, 3 March 2014. Web. 1 Dec. 2015.

Bhide, Amita. *The City Produced: Urban Development, Violence and Spatial Justice in Mumbai*. Mumbai: Tata Institute of Social Sciences, 2014.

Chandavarkar, Rajnarayan. *The Origins of Industrial Capitalism in India: Business Strategies and the Working Classes in Bombay, 1900–1940*. Cambridge: Cambridge UP, 1994.

Douglas, Mary. *Purity and Danger: An Analysis of Concepts of Pollution and Taboo*. London: Routledge, 2003.

Edwardes, S.M. *The Gazetteer of Bombay City and Island*. Bombay: Government Central, 1909.

Geetha, V. "Bereft of Being: The Humiliation of Untouchability." *Humiliation: Claims and Context*. New Delhi: Oxford UP, 2011. 95–107.

Ghadge, Ravi. "Globalizing Marginality: Spatial Politics of 21st Century Mumbai." *unitcrit.blogspot.ch*. 22 Apr. 2008. Web. 10 Sept. 2015.

Guru, Gopal. *Humiliation: Claims and Context*. New Delhi: Oxford UP, 2011.

Hansen, Thomas Blom. *Sovereign Bodies: Citizens, Migrants, and States in the Postcolonial World*. Princeton: Princeton UP, 2009.

Hodkinson, Paul. "'Insider Research' in the Study of Youth Cultures." *Journal of Youth Studies* 8.2 (2005): 131–49.

Kidambi, Prashant. "'The Ultimate Masters of the City': Police, Public Order and the Poor in Colonial Bombay, c. 1893–1914." *Crime, Histoire & Sociétés / Crime, History & Societies* 8.1 (2004): 27–47.

Kosambi, Meera. "Commerce, Conquest and the Colonial City: Role of Locational Factors in Rise of Bombay." *Economic & Political Weekly* 20.1 (1985): 32–37.

Masselos, Jim. "Migration and Urban Identity." *Bombay: Mosaic of Modern Culture*. Bombay: Oxford UP, 1995.

Mhaskar, Sumeet. "Locating Caste in a Globalising Indian City: A Study of Dalit Ex-Millworkers' Occupational Choices in Post-Industrial Mumbai." *Dalits in Neoliberal India: Mobility or Marginalisation?* Ed. Clarinda Still. New Delhi: Routledge, 2014. 107–32.

Oakley, Anna. "Interviewing Women: A Contradiction in Terms." *Doing Feminist Research*. Ed. Helen Roberts. London: Routledge & Kegan Paul, 1981. 30–61.

Ram, Nandu. *"Beyond Ambedkar: Essays on Dalits in India."* Revised ed. New Delhi: Har-Anand, 2009.

Reed-Danahay, Deborah. *Auto/ethnography: Rewriting the Self and the Social*. Oxford: Berg, 1997.

Shaikh, Juned. "Imaging Caste: Photography, the Housing Question and the Making of Sociology in Colonial Bombay, 1900–1939." *South Asia: Journal of South Asian Studies* 37.3 (2014): 491–514.

Virani, Pinki. *Once Was Bombay*. 2nd ed. New Delhi: Viking, 2001.

Wolcott, Harry F. *Ethnography: A Way of Seeing*. Walnut Creek: AltaMira, 1999.

Youth for Equality. "Why We Are against Caste Based Reservation." *Youth for Equality*. Youth for Equality, 2006–2007. Web. 10 Mar. 2015.

CHAPTER 7

The South African Backyard as a Very Local Peripheral Space

Ena Jansen

In October 1938, J.D. Rheinhalt Jones, a liberal pragmatist in Johannesburg, realized it was impossible to prevent rural black people from migrating to South African cities when he said: "We may today pass a hundred Urban Areas Acts, but not even steel fences and police guards will keep the Bantu from our cities" (qtd. in Eales 143). The dichotomy us/them was clearly demarcated, even though white people were recent newcomers to the newly formed cities themselves. Largely as a result of the continued undermining of black people's ability to sustain themselves and their pastoral lifestyle in rural areas, many flocked to the cities, entering a space that both needed and resented them. Rheinhalt Jones's observation was made fifty years after the discovery of gold on the Witwatersrand in 1886, which, within a few dramatic years, resulted in the booming city of Johannesburg. Black people's labor was desperately in demand, though initially only that of men, on whose strength the so-called Randlords relied to dig for gold in the deep mines.

Besides miners, black men were also the first domestic workers on the Rand. The powers that be, however, soon realized that their labor was wasted making beds and doing dishes above ground. The few white women who started arriving in the rough and tumble mining city feared the attraction black women domestic workers might have for their men, but the so-called "Black Peril" scare, during which a few "kitchen boys" were found guilty of raping their madams,[1] provided the final leverage to get black men out of the kitchens and into the mines. Whilst cooks and domestic workers to this day often still are men in countries such as Zimbabwe, Tanzania and Kenya, male house workers have for decades now been a rarity in South Africa. The presence of black women in white kitchens has become a familiar and distinct feature of the South African lifestyle. Fear and even loathing were overcome to make way for often close relationships between white families and their domestic workers. Despite many tensions, these relationships are also often idealized and nostalgically recalled.

---

1   In his study of the Witwatersrand, Van Onselen describes the Black Peril as a collective sexual hysteria that, in the period from 1890 to 1914, embittered race relations in the Johannesburg area.

© KONINKLIJKE BRILL NV, LEIDEN, 2016 | DOI 10.1163/9789004323056_009

The lives of practically all South Africans have been touched by the institution of paid domestic work: either because of the presence of domestics who are always on hand as carers and cleaners, and even as a second mother or sister, or because of the absence of a mother who does paid housework or cares for the children of white people. White people seem to take it for granted that black people will be thankful for the chance to work and will always be available to clean up after them. Oral history interviews and research by sociologists such as Jacklyn Cock and Shireen Ally, however, stress the fact that black people are often angry, disgusted and saddened by the restrictions and discrimination resulting from racism and limited work opportunities (Cock; Alley). Although the political scene in South Africa changed completely when the African National Congress Party came to power in 1994, not much has changed with regards to private domestic arrangements: most white neighborhoods have retained the demographic character they had during the twentieth century. Black people entering these neighborhoods still do so mostly in their capacity as servants, gardeners and cleaners, while black nannies pushing white toddlers around in prams on city sidewalks remain a familiar sight.

Part of the Family

As Melissa Steyn demonstrates in *Whiteness Just Isn't What It Used To Be: White Identity in a Changing South Africa* (2001), many white people construct their memories of apartheid around the figure of a domestic worker; the learning of white dominance is understood by many as hinging upon their contact with black women in the home. White people became conscious of "difference" and of the fact that color determines power relations precisely because of the presence of servants. Tamara Shefer, in "Fraught Tenderness: Narratives on Domestic Workers in Memories of Apartheid" (2012), notes that, however unequal the relationships were, these memories are steeped in emotion, especially love and guilt: "The nanny is remembered nostalgically as a source of comfort and care" (311). Based on white people's memories collected in the Apartheid Archive Project, Shefer concludes that domestic workers play a major role in white people's experience of and memories of apartheid.[2]

---

2 The Apartheid Archive Project is an international research initiative that aims to examine the nature of the experiences of racism of (particularly "ordinary") South Africans under the old apartheid order and their continuing effects on individual and group functioning in contemporary South Africa. See: http://www.apartheidarchive.org.

All over the world, but in any case very often in apartheid and post-apartheid South Africa, female domestic workers were and still are described as "part of the family." These black women are without a doubt the most important contact figures in South Africa between white and black, urban and rural, rich and poor. Although kitchens and backyards in white homes can therefore most certainly be described as "contact zones" in the sense meant by Mary Louise Pratt when she coined the term to refer to the "meet, clash and grapple" contacts between people from hugely different cultural backgrounds (4), my contention is that her term is ultimately too "neutral," and can sound too positive when used to refer to the space where the center meets the peripheral, particularly in the very confined space of backyards. The ambivalence of the relationship between "maids and madams," especially where nannies and children are concerned, *always* makes for intricate negotiations. After researching a large part of South African history and exploring the literature archive for the purpose of writing my book *Soos familie. Stedelike huiswerkers in Suid-Afrikaanse tekste* (*Like Family: Domestic Workers in South African City Texts*, 2015), I came to the conclusion that the ongoing negotiations between domestic workers and their employers invite comparisons to a frontier or border zone rather than a contact zone. Whilst black people for decades were officially prohibited from living in white neighborhoods and kept out by way of laws such as the Group Areas Act, their labor was needed so that exceptions were always made for domestic workers. They were therefore tolerated and, as a result, often lived in close and intimate proximity to white people. The South African backyard is, therefore, an extremely local and upfront peripheral space.

On a frontier, the one who wants to enter an area needs the right documents and the right attitude, especially if she wants to stay there. For thirty years between 1955 and 1985 a black woman literally had to present her pass book when she applied for work in cities and went knocking at the back doors in white neighborhoods. Once she had a job, not laws but convention prescribed *accoutrements* signifying her low status inside the house, such as having to use an enamel plate and mug.

Conversations between employer and domestic worker to this day usually take place in a neutral zone: standing in the kitchen or seated at the kitchen or veranda table. The black woman is only welcome for as long as she does the work required of her. There is often tension and the possibility of conflict. Clear but often also vague borderlines determine codes of conduct and behavior. The suburban house, then, is the site of intercultural contact, but at the same time the scene of huge discrepancies and negotiations. There are certain "no go" areas in and around the house, and certain foods the servant should know are not meant for her. Separate toilets and cutlery used to be and still often are important instruments of division.

Codes of conduct are a minefield because of the subtlety of the borderlines. In her recent article "Buying the Maid Ricoffy: Domestic Workers, Employers and Food," Sarah Archer, for example, establishes that domestic borders still clearly exist in post-apartheid South Africa, even though they are being articulated more subtly than during previous decades. Madams would now *say* that their maids could eat anything in the fridge, but they actually expect, based on their own perceptions of black people's "traditional" tastes and on what they presume to be the internalized knowledge of domestic workers, that the latter would just *know* the smoked salmon, strawberries and white wine in the fridge are not meant for them.

After framing the peripheral nature of the backyard, I discuss childhood memories about the backyard as articulated in diverse (semi-)autobiographical texts by both black and white authors, whilst the last part of this essay concentrates on the anguish described by two white authors who use the huge divide in their own backyards as settings for analyses in fictional form of the economically unequal situation South Africa was in during the 1980s and still is in during the 2010s.

The Backyard as a Peripheral Space

The typical backyard of a South African suburban house can be compared to the pre-interbellum spatial and societal divide in British society, which is still kept very much alive in modern-day literature, soaps and period films: that of the divide between upstairs and downstairs.[3] The South African backyard is, however, not an indoor but an outdoor space, usually within direct sight from the kitchen door of the main house. In relation to the home, a typical backyard is a peripheral tract of paved ground enclosed or set apart, usually small, but sometimes quite large, encompassing the space between the kitchen and the back and side fences or walls of the property. It is often enclosed on one side by the wall of the garage and the maid's room. Someone standing at the kitchen window or on the threshold of the kitchen door can usually survey most of the yard. Some potted plants, the garbage can, a dog kennel and the washing line are typical attributes of the backyard. In the yard, in very close proximity to the main house, black people were and often still are only welcome in so far as their labor can be put to use.

---

3   See Esther Peeren's analyses in Chapter 2 of *The Spectral Metaphor* (76–109).

The word "backyard," in Afrikaans "*agterplaas*," stresses its most distinct feature: that it is *at the back*, *agter*, out of sight from the front where civil appearances and decorum are important middle-class values. In the backyard, home owners can do pretty much what they wish, especially to a person rendered vulnerable by her dependency on work and on the living space on offer in the servants' quarters.[4] The backyard brings to mind Jeremy Bentham's panopticon because of the isolation and "captivity" of domestic workers it enforces and the constant possibility of surveillance and inspection by their employers.[5]

For centuries, the backyards of white South African homes have, to my mind, been the most important but largely unrecognized peripheral spaces in the country. In contrast to distant rural areas or even black townships on the outskirts of cities, which are obvious peripheral spaces in the minds of white South Africans, backyards in the core of white towns and cities are not abstract, faraway spaces. Consequently, the periphery of the backyard cannot be ignored. It is a space of exclusion, but also a meeting place, a potential positive space where people who might otherwise never have contact can get to know each other. The backyard therefore is often a dramatic and complex space where employer and employee, upstairs and downstairs, meet in caring but also often denigrating ways. As artist William Kentridge maintains: "For a white suburban house the journey through Africa began across the yard in the servant's room" (qtd. in Cameron et al. 109). But this journey was seldom undertaken wholeheartedly, especially not during the apartheid years when both black and white people were paranoid because of the many laws regulating contact between them.

The black woman was acceptable on the premises thanks only to her position as the servant. The minute she took off her maid's uniform, she was in danger of being essentialized as "the other." Because of the strict Immorality Act prohibiting sexual relations between black and white, her sexuality was feared and therefore ignored, although this taboo at the same time heightened the attraction she embodied. The door of her stuffy little room was always closed, so that the chance of seeing her in any state of undress was eliminated. Her employers would seldom knock on the door, but would rather call her from the safe distance of the main house whilst standing framed by the kitchen door, even though they were responsible for the "hospitality" they were offering to the occupant of the maid's room. Children did, however, spend time there,

---

4   Such maid's rooms used to be a fixture of white neighborhood planning, but have in recent times often been transformed into so-called granny flats or a second garage.

5   "Disciplinary power inverted the scenic principle of sovereignty, for its functioning demanded not the visibility of itself but of its target, and that target was the individual body which became at the same time both object and effect of the disciplinary gaze" (Butchart 27).

mostly whilst their parents presumed that the nanny was looking after them in the main house.

Judging by childhood recollections described in novels as diverse as Etienne Leroux's *Die eerste lewe van Colet* (1955) and John van de Ruit's *Spud* (2005), many children who grew up during especially the second half of the twentieth century, after the apartheid laws caused South African society to become even more schizophrenic than it already had been since the seventeenth century, intensely remember the comforting smells of soap and porridge in such a room. Usually, it was very small with a tiny window high-up, had a concrete floor and steel door, perhaps a light bulb, a cold tap and a toilet outside. A tactile memory found in many childhood recollections is of the maid's single bed covered by white sheets embroidered in colorful flower patterns. The bed was lifted as high as possible from the ground by placing bricks under the legs, reportedly so that the mythical horny little *tokoloshe* man with his huge penis could not reach the woman on the bed and sexually assault her.

Mysterious and Unknowable

One of the earliest descriptions in South African literature of the backyard is told from the perspective of Ezekiel Mphahlele (1919–2008) in his autobiography *Down Second Avenue* (1959). As a small black boy, he usually saw his mother only once every two weeks when she had a Sunday afternoon off to come to the township Marabastad, where he and his siblings lived with their grandmother and aunt during the 1920s and 1930s. Mphahlele describes two situations when he entered the backyards of white homes where his mother was a "live-in" domestic worker:

> She worked for a Dr. Broderick once. His children often came to me or called, "John, you want Eva?" Eva was my mother, John was not my name, Or, "Eva, here's your son." Then they looked me up and down, faces screwed up, eyes squinted. Sometimes they tossed me an orange. I never got used to being examined like that. I resented it but at the same time feared that any moment the children might decide to tell their parents that I was undesirable. Apparently they didn't. But after a time I just went straight to lean against the side wall of my mother's little room and waited until she should come out of the big house.
>
> MPHAHLELE 102

In another recollection, Mphahlele returns a bundle of washing to a house and enters another backyard:

> The Afrikaans people for whom Aunt Dora washed made no bones about
> the fact that they didn't want me to get into their kitchen. Their children
> merely peeped through a window. Otherwise I didn't seem to exist. It felt
> easier that way. If a child wanted to let the mother know I was about, it
> said, "Ma, die wasgoedkaffir is hier – Mummy, the washing Kaffier has
> come." And the child took no more notice of me.
>
> MPHAHLELE 102

These descriptions of both the English and Afrikaans children's behavior at the
back door emphasize the estrangement and compulsive distancing between
black and white city children. The backyard is a traumatic space. Mphahlele
tries to escape from his objectified position by going to stand out of sight
against a wall. The white children stay away from him, most probably warned
by their parents that strange black people are dangerous. Thus, both do their
best to evade the set-up in which they find themselves. These observations are
written down by Mphahlele with little comment: "I came to learn the hard
way that one had to keep out of the white man's way" (102). Thus, even in the
already peripheral backyard, a further peripheralization is enforced so that the
white man (or woman or child) does not have to be confronted with a black
body, even if only that of a child.

Rian Malan, born in 1954, recalls in his highly acclaimed autobiographical
book *My Traitor's Heart: A South African Exile Returns To Face His Country, His
Tribe and His Conscience* (1990) that despite the "*swart gevaar*" ("black danger")
which the government was continuously warning white people against, servants were always considered an exception to black people in general: "I loved
them all, indiscriminately," the white grown-up Malan remembers (34). But the
apartheid socialization was so strong that even the smallest white child was
raised to become a member of the "master race," to not realize how absurd it
was that grown-up black people were doomed to a life of servitude, to always
being the other on the periphery of his own world. In Malan's case, these black
people lived only meters away from the house he grew up in:

> In my childhood, there were always Africans in our backyard. We called
> them natives. They lived in cold, dark rooms with tiny windows ... The na-
> tives quarters smelled of Lifebuoy soap, red floor polish, and *putu* ... Natives
> cooked my meals, polished my shoes, made my bed, mowed the lawn ... They
> ate on enamel plates and drunk out of chipped cups with no handles, which
> were known as the boy's cup or girl's cup and kept separate from our china.
> They spoke broken English or Afrikaans, wore old clothes, had no money
> and no last names. That was all it was really necessary to know about them.
>
> MALAN 30

His first sexual encounter was with such a servant woman, who came to listen to him and his school band friends practicing in a garage on Thursday nights, traditionally the "maids' night off" in Johannesburg. She fancied him and, dared by his friends, Rian crept to her room behind the large white house: "The room smelled of all the things I associated with servants – red floor polish, *putu* and Lifebuoy soap" (44). The bed was on bricks. He could not stand the thought of kissing her, but he had to, "because I was a social democrat, and I did not want to insult her." All was quickly over: "she was very kind" (44). For years, Malan pretended that this incident proved his anti-apartheid credentials, but later he admitted how scared he had been and also that he always prayed no one would ever ask what the woman's name was because he did not know. A year or so after the incident, not wanting to be conscripted into the army, he left the country: "I ran away because I hated Afrikaners and loved blacks. I ran away because I was an Afrikaner and feared blacks. You could say, I suppose, that I ran away from the paradox" (73). Reflecting on his childhood memories, Malan is filled with amazement and regret, realizing how astonishing it was that his family never realized how amazing the woman was who lived in their backyard. Instead of getting to know her, she was kept at much more than arm's length.

Thinking back on her South African childhood at roughly the same time, Griselda Pollock writes from a white woman's perspective and confirms in "Territories of Desire: Reconsideration of an African Childhood" (1994) that "the child, however innocent, [was] being formed as a bearer of the dominant order of whiteness through an Oedipalization which is profoundly historical, social and ... racial" (78):

> As the little white girl I was, born and formed in this socio-psychic space, I know the twin forces that conflict between identification with the white mother and its possible freedoms for a woman in a still bourgeois world, and the lost fantastic identification with a black woman, who, whatever her own pain and desperate sense of exploitation and loss, generously gave me her care and nurtured me at the cost of her own daughter's need for her mothering.
> POLLOCK 83

Mark Gevisser (born 1964) gives a graphic description of a similar socio-psychic space in *Lost and Found in Johannesburg* (2014). As a boy, he was fascinated by maps and stared for hours at his Holmden's Register of Johannesburg, not realizing how different the world of his own affluent neighborhood Sandton was from the township Alexandra just across the Sand River. Hope, the fourteen-year-old daughter of his nanny Bettinah, sometimes came to visit her mother after school. "Hopey and I were contemporaries. We eyed each other across the frontier of the backyard" (304). Whilst she regularly "crossed that boundary between pages 75 and 77 [of the city map of Johannesburg] many times" (306), he had no clue about the black township. There was very little contact between him and Hope even in the enclosed and "safe" space of the backyard: "I see the expanse of paving between the kitchen door and the servants' quarters ... I see a borderland, a place that is part of my world but also inexplicably beyond it, a passage from the known certitudes of my childhood to something mysterious and unknowable" (81). Yet they had to make do with the backyard, which was their only possible meeting place in apartheid South Africa:

> The yard was the place where my brothers and I, as children, heard other languages and played with the words of these languages ourselves, and where our aural landscape expanded to include the jaunty squash-box melodies and fusillade of tongue-clicks of the Radio Bantu stations; where we played, too, even if fleetingly, with the servants' children when they came to spend their school holidays ... I intuited, from an early age, the ways that the winds of the outside world blew across the yard, bringing the danger or the thrill of a broader urbanity into the very confines of the white suburban laager.
>
> GEVISSER 82–3

White South African families have for generations been physically very close to black women living in their backyards. Much too late, the white man Gevisser realizes how easy it could have been to build meaningful relations with black people, especially with children visiting their mother. The system of apartheid, however, was so rigid that even the children were brainwashed to such an extent that no spontaneous interaction occurred.

From "Agterplaas" to Courtyard

In this section, two texts are considered, both presented as works of fiction but both having a strong autobiographical ring to them. At the time of publication of their texts, both Elsa Joubert and Antjie Krog were living in the affluent suburb Oranjezicht, high against the slopes of Table Mountain in Cape Town. Both of the protagonists in their texts are tormented by the discrepancy between their own lives and those of their domestic workers. As noted, employers meet their workers mainly in the frontier areas of kitchen and backyard, and both white women are very conscious of their inability to communicate with the black women. One of the workers is a live-in servant; the other commutes to her work from a township outside Cape Town. Both women have strong ties with the poor rural Eastern Cape, an area where the previous so-called "home-lands" of apartheid times are situated: the Transkei and the Ciskei. In spite of monumental political changes in South Africa due to the official ending of apartheid in 1994, the problems the workers face are still huge. Both texts in-terrogate "the figure of the servant [who] takes us into history but also into ourselves" (Light 314).

In the short story "Agterplaas" (Backyard, 1980) by Elsa Joubert (born 1922), a new domestic worker moves into the servant's room. The first-person nar-rator realizes that the black woman could be a bridge to a world unknown to her, but she finds it impossible to bridge the gap, describing herself as literally "living on the periphery" of a world she will never know. Joubert is famous for her international bestseller novel *Die swerfjare van Poppie Nongena* (1978), in which she gives a heart-rending account of the effects of pass laws on the life of one woman. In "Agterplaas" she is fascinated by the people and what goes on in the maid's room, but at the same time, because of convention and laws prohibiting social interaction between races, she does not dare to enter the room. It is a taboo space. In the story, the backroom "throbs and stirs" ("*bult en roer*") with life, but the employer never enters. She hovers in the back part of the garden close to the room, often watering the plants there, trying to catch an impression of what goes on in the room, but she never ventures closer. Often, five or more people visit Flora and the sounds of desperate conversa-tions emanate from the room. Flora's life is described as "multiple," related to that of many others: "an amorphous body which invades my own" (80). The "missus" evades contact, but the people that visit Flora nevertheless "enter my life and say 'help me'" (81). One man's work permit has expired and when Jou-bert looks at his pass book she realizes that he cannot read. A grandchild of someone else who was born in Cape Town but had been sent to the Eastern Cape wants to come back to the city. This is legally impossible because of com-plicated laws but she nevertheless returns when she is pregnant and comes to stay with Flora. Joubert's maternalistic protagonist intends to help and to chase the inspectors who might come to enquire from her property, but both Flora and the young mother have already disappeared from the room when she returns from a week's holiday. Rather than wait for mercy in the periph-eral space of the backyard, over which they have no control, they have chosen the anonymity of the township wilderness, which is peripheral in many ways, but inside which they are marginally "safer" from inspection, prosecution and banishment to the "outermost" peripheral zone of South African spaces, the desperately poor so-called "homelands."

In "bediendepraatjies" (servants' talk, 2014), a series of poems by Antjie Krog (born 1952) published 35 years after Joubert's story, Krog unflinchingly explores the entangled relationship between a white Cape Town couple and their Xhosa domestic worker Victoria in post-apartheid South Africa. The backyard is now called a "courtyard," but it is still an ambivalent border zone where desperate negotiations take place. In keeping with a long tradition of works in which domestic worker characters feature (J.M. Coetzee's *Age of Iron* is an important intertext), the organization of the South African world in which whites are still at the economic center but have moved to the political periphery is interrogated. The moral dilemma of "radical alterity" and the ways in which the gap between you and the other might be imagined and perhaps bridged are questioned.

Twelve of the fourteen "bediendepraatjies" have the same structure. The first part consists of snippets of dialogue between a couple discussing their servant Victoria – in Afrikaans (or English; in the English translation of *Mede-wete*, *Synapse*). The middle section of each poem consists of Victoria's words in isiXhosa, making it incomprehensible for the majority of the probable readers of the poems. The short last section of each poem, introduced by a question mark, is a mangled translation of the Xhosa section. Victoria relies on the guilty feelings of her employers and uses her knowledge of their shame about apartheid to continuously "just shake the white people tree and watch the money falling" (Krog 68). The network of her extended family, who live in the Eastern Cape, survives thanks to what she can wrangle out of her employers to supplement their pension funds and child support grants.

Krog convincingly gives a postcolonial, postmodern and post-apartheid voice to Victoria. The "praatjies" are *about* servants, but also *by* servants. Krog feels just as powerless as Joubert in her efforts to alleviate the needs of her domestic worker and resents the fact that Victoria needs her help. Compared to Joubert, Krog, however, not only establishes the *fact* of her impotence. The *form* of the series of poems is a "form of listening" and brings about a sense of equality, in spite of the still seemingly insurmountable economic problems in post-apartheid South Africa.

Frontier of the Backyard

In South Africa, multiracial and intercultural relations have, for centuries, depended upon and been based on backyard situations. The archive of literature reveals how close black and white people came to meeting each other. If white employers had gone to the trouble of exploring a little further than the backyard, important discoveries of the other's humanity could have been made. However, the racial divide in the context of domestic work was too harsh to allow more than some soul searching. To this day, the homes and backyards of white employers are disconcerting spaces where the brunt of the violence and degradation stemming from apartheid took its course and often continues unabated. During apartheid, few people questioned the "self-evident fact" that black people should be servants and even now the patterns of dependence and domination continue: due to massive unemployment figures and bad education for black people, and because of the historical advantages of whites, the latter's feelings of responsibility and caring still often go hand in hand with a patronizing attitude. The complexity of this relationship can be brought into focus by bringing to the fore the seemingly mundane space of the backyard from as many perspectives as possible.

As Achille Mbembe reminds us in *On the Postcolony* (2001), it is exactly the simultaneity of intimate care and destructive violence that delineates the psychic field of domination, most specifically in colonial subjectivation. Although Mary Louis Pratt's term "contact zone" (1992) is certainly useful as a description for the backyard where both the more neutral "meet" and the often violent "clash and grapple" contacts take place, I argue that this term in the South African domain of domestic work can too easily be endowed with a sense of nostalgia in which the domestic worker becomes the psychic repository of the encounter of whiteness with its "other." Although the relationship between employers and domestic workers often consists of attentive forms of care and affection, it is important to acknowledge that the relationship, which in its core is troubled, should also be represented as troubling in literature rather than this trouble being glossed over, as happens, for example, in songs such as Koos Kombuis's "Kytie jy's nie net 'n meid nie" and "I Miss" by Jack Parow. The term "border zone" is therefore considered more applicable than "contact zone," in line with the author Mark Gevisser's description (2014) of the "frontier of the backyard," where "the winds of the outside world blew across the yard, bringing the danger or the thrill of a broader urbanity into the very confines of the white suburban laager."

Works Cited

Ally, Shireen. *From Servants to Workers: South African Domestic Workers and the Democratic State*. 2009. Scottsville: U of KwaZulu-Natal P, 2010.

Archer, Sarah. "Buying the Maid Ricoffy: Domestic Workers, Employers and Food." *South African Review of Sociology* 40.2 (2011): 66–82.

Butchart, Alexander. *The Anatomy of Power: European Constructions of the African Body*. London and New York: Zed Books, 1998.

Cameron, Dan, Carolyn Christov-Bakargiev, and J.M. Coetzee. *William Kentridge*. London and New York: Phaidon, 1999.

Cock, Jacklyn. *Maids and Madams: A Study in the Politics of Exploitation*. Johannesburg: Ravan Press, 1980.

Coetzee, J.M. *Age of Iron*. 1990. New York: Penguin Books, 1998.

Eales, K.A. "Gender Politics and the Administration of African Women in Johannesburg 1903–1939." MA thesis. University of the Witwatersrand, 1991.

Gevisser Mark. *Lost and Found in Johannesburg*. Johannesburg and Cape Town: Jonathan Ball, 2014.

Jansen, Ena. *Soos Familie. Stedelike Huiswerkers in Suid-Afrikaanse Tekste*. Pretoria: Protea Boekhuis, 2015.

Joubert, Elsa. "Agterplaas." *Melk*. 1980. Cape Town: Tafelberg, 2011.

Krog, Antjie. "bediendepraatjies." *Mede-wete*. Cape Town: Human & Rousseau, 2014.

Leroux, Etienne. *Die Eerste Lewe van Colet*. Cape Town: Culemborg, 1960.

Light, Alison. *Mrs Woolf & The Servants: The Hidden Heart of Domestic Service*. London: Fig Tree, 2007.

Malan, Rian. *My Traitor's Heart: A South African Exile Returns to Face His Country, His Tribe and His Conscience*. New York: Atlantic Monthly Press, 1990.

Mbembe, Achille. *On the Postcolony*. Berkeley, Los Angeles, London: U of California P, 2001.

Mphahlele, Ezekiel. *Down Second Avenue*. London: Faber & Faber, 1959.

Peeren, Esther. *The Spectral Metaphor: Living Ghosts and the Agency of Invisibility*. Basingstoke: Palgrave Macmillan, 2014.

Pollock, Griselda. "Territories of Desire: Reconsideration of an African Childhood." *Travellers Tales, Narratives of Home and Displacement*. Ed. George Robertson et al. London and New York: Routledge, 1994. 63–89.

Pratt, Mary Louise. *Imperial Eyes: Travel Writing and Transculturation*. London and New York: Routledge, 1992.

Shefer, Tamara. "Fraught Tenderness: Narratives on Domestic Workers in Memories of Apartheid." *Peace and Conflict: Journal of Peace Psychology* 18.3 (2012): 307–17.

Steyn, Melissa. *Whiteness Just Isn't What It Used To Be: White Identity in a Changing South Africa*. New York: SUNY Press, 2001.

Van de Ruit, John. *Spud*. Johannesburg: Penguin, 2005.

Van Onselen, Charles. *Studies in the Social and Economic History of the Witwatersrand 1886–1914*. Vol. 1 and Vol. 2. Johannesburg: Ravan Press, 1982.

PART 3

Peripheral Mobilities

∵

Mobile Peripheries? Contesting and Negotiating Peripheries in the Global Era of Mobility

Magdalena Ślusarczyk and Paula Pustułka

Introduction

> To my friends from work I am not an immigrant. To them an immigrant
> is someone poor, from Africa or Asia. Even with the "Polish Tsunami,"
> I still do not qualify: I am white, highly educated and from a capital city
> [Warsaw] – I am somehow more cosmopolitan than some of the girls
> from the industrial North-West [of England]. So I have trouble associat-
> ing myself with migrants – Polish or others.[1]
>
> BOGUSIA, Corporate Accountant, UK[2]

There is a growing confusion regarding the labels that scholars who deal with
migration and mobility use to signify people participating in the contemporary, globalized cross-border flows of people, especially within the context of
the free movement policy implemented in the intra-European landscape. This
chapter seeks to investigate the conceptual boundaries between the often polarized categories of, on the one hand, the economically framed labor migrants
and guest workers, and, on the other, the often well-educated cosmopolitan
expats equipped with high human (as well as cultural and educational) capital.
The latter transgress the neatly demarcated boundary between what is considered "the center" and what remains "the periphery." Overall, the growing
scholarship on the interconnectedness of periphery and center in the global
era is useful for looking at people on the move and at whether they are seen

---

1 "Polish Tsunami" was a headline used by the British press to describe a mass-migration wave
   from Poland following its EU accession in 2004. It is estimated that 200,000 Polish citizens
   entered the UK in 2004–2005, and that a further 160,000 arrived the following year, according
   to the Workers Registration Scheme. The increase is further illuminated by the National Census Data, which show just over 60,000 Poles registered in the UK in 2001 compared to 580,000
   in England and Wales alone in 2011. The Office for National Statistics issued an estimate of
   853,000 Polish inhabitants of the UK in 2015.
2 When using narratives of people interviewed, we use brackets to provide a coded name
   (pseudonym), profession and destination country, the latter abbreviated to UK for United
   Kingdom, DE for Germany and NOR for Norway.

(and see themselves) as "migrants" or as belonging to their new surroundings. This distinction still practically impacts migrant identities, as people are often classified through polarized categories (migrant/native/ethnic minority/local majority), subjected to processes of othering (white/non-white, us/them) and affected by peripheralization, not only in a geographic, but also in an economic and cultural sense. It is crucial, however, to see these processes as having potentially different meanings and consequences for individual biographies and trajectories of migrants. The growing heterogeneity of the Polish mobile population evidences the pitfalls of applying universal characteristics to a group that is not necessarily bound by any collective spirit and shape.

The value of conceptualizing a "periphery" lies in its potential to shed light on what it means *not* to be in the center. In the context of intensified human mobility, it is more specifically able to challenge the labor-centered paradigm, which continues to foreground economic issues and categorizes migrants from certain global regions, such as Central America and Southeast Asia, as *mobile peripherals*. Similarly, in the context of Poland as a periphery of Europe that is discussed here, migrating peripherals signify lower-educated employees who often take on the non-desirable "3D-type" (dirty, difficult, dangerous) jobs in the destination country (Anderson). In the receiving states' discourses, migrant populations in general are almost exclusively portrayed as temporary, regardless of the number of decades they have been there and of the many signs of successful integration. In addition, they are problematized as causing social unrest and as abusing the local welfare and benefit systems. This occurs despite growing evidence attesting to long-term settlement, non-economic migration motivations, high levels of professional achievement and traits of a cosmopolitan (rather than simply transnational) disposition (see Ignatowicz; Trevena; Favell; Ciupijus; White).

This chapter deals with the tensions between the strategic employment of the notion of "periphery" in public discourse and nation-state-representing institutions on the one hand, and the notions, conceptions or visions that migrants themselves have about how their peripheral origin may or may not be framed through "backwardness." We argue that the ways in which people express and handle their standing in terms of peripheral vision can result either in empowerment or, conversely, in a restrengthening of a peripheral position. In a manner similar to the reservations gender and migration scholarship now expresses about the way "the arrow of progress" assumes that mobility to the center (i.e. to a gender equal country) unequivocally results in empowerment (see, for example, Szczepanikova; Hondagneu-Sotelo; Morokvasic 2007), we also demonstrate a more nuanced perspective on outcomes of periphery-to-center mobilities. Overall, we argue that some migrants can indeed overcome the discourse of exclusion and move towards globally recognized central positions in various dimensions of their lives (place of residence, position in the labor market, political power), while others experience a worsened status as peripherals who cannot escape their position and are pushed away further from the center.

The empirical material used for the analyses presented here stems from two distinct yet thematically connected research projects. The data subset pertaining to the cases of migrant families in the UK and Germany originates from Pustułka's doctoral research, the findings of which are presented in more detail in the thesis "Polish Mothers on the Move – Gendering Migratory Experiences of Polish Women Parenting in Germany and the United Kingdom."[3] This data subset comprises a total of 37 biographic/semi-structured interviews conducted between 2011 and 2013 with Polish women parenting abroad.[4] The second dataset belongs to the TRANSFAM Project "Doing Family in a Transnational Context: Demographic Choices, Welfare Adaptations, School Integration and Every-day Life of Polish Families Living in Polish-Norwegian Transnationality."[5] Specifically, it consists of the interviews with Polish migrant families in Norway conducted in 2014 for Work Package 2 – "Migrant Families in Norway: Structure of Power Relations and Negotiating Values and Norms in Transnational Families." The respondent pool contains 40 members of 30 households (cases), and covers individual mothers (18) and fathers (2), as well as migrant parenting couples interviewed together (10).[6]

---

3 The PhD study was funded by the 125th Anniversary Research Scholarship awarded by Bangor University for the 2010–2013 period. Supplementary funding for fieldwork was obtained from the DAAD grant (2011) and the PON UJ London short-term summer grant (2013).

4 All study participants were female, married, between the ages of 23 and 64 (avg. = 37.9), having arrived in their destination countries between 1980 and 2010 (with an average length of stay amounting to just below 9 years) and residing outside of the metropolitan urban centers (in villages, small towns and city outskirts/suburbs). The women mostly led middle-class lives but represented an array of educational and professional backgrounds, as well as diverse migratory characteristics.

5 The research leading to these results has received funding from the Polish-Norwegian Research Programme operated by the National Centre for Research and Development under the Norwegian Financial Mechanism 2009–2014 in the frame of Project Contract No. Pol-Nor/197905/4/2013. Magdalena Ślusarczyk is the WP 2 Leader.

6 Coincidentally, the socio-demographic portrait of this group determines an age average similar to that for Germany and the UK at 37.5 years old and a slightly shifted 29–54 age range. The migrants settled in Norway between 1990 and 2013, which yields a corresponding average of just below 8.5 years spent abroad. In Norway, the respondents also represented diverse educational and professional backgrounds, yet their residence was concentrated in the capital of Oslo and its surrounding area within a 200-kilometer radius.

This cumulative approach to data analysis was dictated by the goal of broadening the geographical scope and increasing the internal validity of the data by means of observing saturation, meaning that a robust analytical framework could be built through coding procedures applied to the substantial and rich material. As the number of the surveyed household was rather high for a qualitative study, the similarities and discrepancies in the narratives collected across the three countries could be noted, compared and analyzed.[7] Therefore, this chapter largely relies on both comparative and case-by-case analysis of the interviews and of the biographical accounts of the migration history of a respondent and his or her family. It also presents extensive details gathered from questions about the meaning of migration in the respondents' lives and about their evaluation of the decision to migrate and live abroad.

Situating Mobile Peripheries

The ideologies involved in demarcating peripheries have been problematized and challenged since the long nineteenth century, especially with regard to Central and Eastern Europe, often deemed a zone of violence where a clash of civilizations occurs. Intellectuals looked at this sensitive borderland or in-between land situated between the generally established (Western) centers and the presumably (economically, sometimes also culturally) "underdeveloped" lands in the East, inventing and mapping them from the position of central power (Wolff 1–16; Petrakos 5–7). Toponymic ideas include the "continental centrality" label assigned to the region by prominent writers (Kundera, Konrad, Stasiuk) and recent historians' underlining of its conflicted positionality as "the lands between" (Prusin), which endured a detour but essentially moved "from the periphery to the periphery" (Berend 1996; see also

---

7   The destination countries of the migrants that we focus on are not accidental, but rather crucial in the broader landscape of Polish post-EU accession mobility in the past decade (Burrell 9; Iglicka and Gmaj). While Germany was always listed among the main destinations of migrant Poles – likely due to its geographic proximity – it was earlier accompanied by the United States and the Benelux countries. It was primarily the order in which EU countries opened their labor market to Poles that determined the key statistical (and later also socio-cultural) significance of the UK and Ireland. Similarly, as a consequence of macro-economic conditions, primarily the 2008 financial collapse, Norway joined the list of Polish destinations as relatively less affected by the crisis. At the same time, the transatlantic direction of flows has been losing importance.

Berend 2005), confirming the relatively stable global order of liminality and core (Bordo; Flandreau 418). Scholars have also tackled the applicability of critical postcolonial notions, such as Said's "adjacency," to the region (Sandru; Wolff).

Not only economic ideologies that analyze Central Eastern Europe (CEE) as a European periphery (Karasavvoglou et al.) are anchored by these notions, but sociological and anthropological scholarship too. Appadurai, for instance, has long propagated the contextualization of central-peripheral dynamics in qualitative and ethnographic approaches to places, regions, and world geographies more broadly (1986; 1990). In his world system analysis, Wallerstein also details the core-periphery antinomy on the macro-level of the nation-state, concurring that the set ways of capitalist modes of production defy the relational potentiality for change in the world orders. In global economic, political and social theory, CEE, including Poland, has consistently been ranked or described as a global semi-periphery.

Importantly, certain strategies can be employed by people in these systemically constructed global peripheries to overcome this disadvantageous position. Concentrating on global reference points (economic globalization, global culture) rather than national identity provides such a competence – and a capital-based option for contemporary cosmopolitan and mobile elites (Hannerz; Bauman; Skrbiš et al.; Beck 2006, 2007; Vertovec and Cohen). Indeed, examining migration shows how national and ethnic identities are arguably becoming (to a degree) replaceable by different identifications (such as pan-European, global, transnational, cosmopolitan or Western; see Castells; Temple 2011a, 2011b; Cinpoes; Wagner). However, this framing has only tentatively been applied to Polish migrants, who continue to be positioned as peripheral. It is also common for even skilled Polish migrants in the post-EU accession context to be normatively split into the categories of "winners" and "losers" (Kaczmarczyk; Tyrowicz). These labels are assigned on the basis of the so-called objective variables of the labor market (e.g. income levels, types of contracts, job sector, match between education and work position) rather than on the basis of – in our opinion more relevant – subjective evaluations (e.g. expressed degree of well-being, satisfaction with family life or work/life balance, being able to spend quality time with one's family). This fission of migrant experiences makes it rather typical for Polish migrants to end up in the periphery, especially in the eyes of policy-makers, scholars and politicians.

The 2001 edited volume *People on a Swing: Migrations between the Peripheries of Poland and the West* (edited by Jaźwińska-Motylska and Okólski) marks the closure of a certain era of migration scholarship by summing up the trends in the spatial movements of Poles in the twentieth century, which largely encompassed pendular and temporary migration. In addition, the collection highlights and forecasts certain new trends, such as the increase of family reunifications abroad and of settlement-oriented mobility, that have emerged since the start of the new millennium, particularly as a result of Poland's European Union accession in May 2004, and that are our focus here. Poland's post-1989 "fast-tracked" neo-liberal politics emphasized labor market privatization and the flexibility of workers in the context of global competition, leading to a race to embrace more and more cuts and worsening working conditions (Kurian 200; see also Płomień; Shields). The domestic sphere in Poland continues to be "invisible" and fosters a rebirth of what Sassen calls a class of servants (262) and Ehrenreich terms a servant economy (103; see also Cox), which is permanently confined to the periphery. Those who are said to have lost in this transformation, especially laborers formerly employed in the state-industry, have been similarly excluded and marginalized (Mrozowicki; Dunn; Petrakos).

At the same time, Polish migration debates rarely move away from economy- and periphery-focused framings, and oftentimes include *all* migrants in the category of "in trouble" or "entrapped" economically "redundant" citizens affected by hardship, seeking opportunities through (somewhat forced and unavoidable) mobility. This "washes out" the most underprivileged and peripheral categories (Anacka and Fihel; Kaczmarczyk; Dyczewski; Korczyńska). Within this context, we focus on how the notion of "periphery" has changed (or retained) its meaning, shape and place in the Polish migratory research landscape, as well as on how it functions in the stories of contemporary Polish migrants in Norway, Germany and the United Kingdom.

Examining Migrant Narratives: Who Can Escape the Periphery?

The stories of migrants arriving to countries perceived as central from what is considered the periphery take the shape of either a scenario of perceived success or one of perceived failure. Determining the distinction in the general pattern of "periphery-to-center" migration are differences in skill and education levels. These features are seen to define the individual's peripheral (low capital) or central (high capital) position, both in the country of origin and the country of residence.

Echoing the opening quotation from Bogusia (UK), the stories heard from Adam (NOR), Lena (UK), Kaja (DE) and Sławek (NOR), which are presented below, depict how migratory identity narratives are constructed by underscoring success and, concurrently, by distancing oneself from how one *might be* perceived or labeled more broadly. These are all stories of rather high-skilled, well-educated global or transnational professionals (Wagner). A snapshot comparison is presented in the Table below. The columns show (1) the respondents' biographical details; (2) the respondents' education trajectory and their motivations for emigrating; (3) interview quotations highlighting the respondents' self-perceived position with regard to peripherality; (4) the way in which the respondents would have been categorized in the terms of the Polish migration discourse.

Name, age, profession/occupation destination country	Migration/Life path nexus	"Distancing" and self-perception, visions of peripherality	"Statistical"/ Discursive portrait
Bogusia, 34, HR Consultant, UK	Raised and educated (Psychology & Business) in Warsaw; wanted an "adventure," found prestigious job and received multiple promotions, has a British upper-class husband.	"I am not an immigrant" – class, status, education-driven explanations (see the opening quotation). "I don't understand Polish women anymore." Self-proclaimed exit from the national group; perceiving oneself as "different," also due to inter-ethnic marriage.	Labor migrant – "young and educated" representative of the EU accession wave.
Adam, 38, Engineer, NOR	Well educated, had a good job in Poland, then was offered a better one in Norway – transfer within a company.	"This was a kind of attempt, it was not like we were coming and had to stay, exactly that, because when I started working in 2001 at a Polish company which closely cooperated with a Norwegian one, so I have known all that and indeed we had it easy because we were going but also had a place to go back to, since I continued to be employed in Poland, despite working in Norway." "That was the best time for me because I was earning really good money ... and, most importantly, had opportunities to return."	Expat mobility, often not at all seen as "migration," assumed to be temporary.

Name, age, profession/occupation destination country	Migration/Life path nexus	"Distancing" and self-perception, visions of peripherality	"Statistical"/ Discursive portrait
Lena, 35, Doctor, UK	Post-graduation "traveling" with then-boyfriend (now husband), both have prestigious education (M.D. & Therapist), raised in Warsaw, elite family.	"Migrant is such a derogatory term. Especially in Britain – multicultural means you have different cultural baggage, but can learn from one another, ... we have friends from all over – Africa, Middle East, I don't really think it's morally acceptable to differentiate between us, them and the posh British locals." Equality and inclusion ideology, denying the existence of peripheries/ centers; somewhat naïve in refuting the existing differences.	Medical personnel migration; treated as "temporary assignment."
Kaja, 34, Retail Manager, DE	Followed her mother to Germany (family migration) prior to EU accession (in 1999), brought her future husband along; has a dual-degree (PL/DE) in Management.	"It might sound strange but I feel very European, like I have developed this extra-special term to describe that I feel at home here in Germany, but Poland is also my home. And I do not feel like a stranger in France or The Netherlands, when we go [there]." "I'm a migrant. So what? Who isn't one here? It's really not a big deal, I made something of myself here." Empowered pan-national identification.	Family/economic migrant, young and educated post-EU mobility.
Sławek, 46, Engineer, NOR	Sees his own decisions as "career mobility" rather than migration. A migrant is somebody forced to leave his/her country not by choice but by "fate"/war/ persecution.	"Well, first and foremost, I am NOT a migrant, I have never thought of myself as an emigrant." "It is like, I was even getting annoyed when someone was categorizing me as emigrant, because emigration is a kind of word that has a negative meaning."	Global mobility paths for well-educated individuals – "specialists."

The presented narratives are stories of people who migrated despite having a relatively good position in their country of origin. For them, life in the perceived periphery of Poland did not include many struggles; they were well-educated, economically established people with a professional network, located in what could be seen as the centers of the periphery. In their case, mobility confirmed their high status, which generally translated to even better (prestige- or income-wise) positions abroad. The narratives ascertain what is known about the mobility of those in high demand, such as sought-after medical specialists or other so-called "expats" (see Plüss; Favell). However, the way in which the respondents "distance" themselves from other Polish migrants demonstrates how coming from a central position in a peripheral country affects one's actions in the destination country. Even these well-off migrants from CEE may be seen as oscillating in a permanent state of competition for rank and order (Wallerstein 79–83), as they need to reassure their status as desired and welcome members of an ethnic minority group.

Slightly different in character, but nevertheless similar in their implications, are the stories of migrants who struggled in the perceived European periphery, but possessed qualifications or skills that could be transferred and advantageously used abroad. This was the case for the family of Sabina (35, Office Worker, NOR). In Poland, her husband could be classified as a discarded skilled laborer, an exemplary "loser of the post-communist transformation period" (Mrozowicki; Jarosz; Kaczmarczyk). In Norway, however, he acquired a lucrative job at a garage as a car mechanic specialized in painting and panel beating, earning more money than the family could have ever imagined. Their disappointment in Poland translated into narratives of integration, limited transnationality and full satisfaction with becoming Norwegian. Though they see Poland as a "periphery," they address it as something in their past, no longer a part of who they are "in the world," or, more precisely, in Norway.

The biography of Alina (57, Dentist, DE) reveals a similar perspective. Her husband also became a car mechanic, in this case in Germany in the 1980s, when political engagement prevented him from finding employment in his original profession in Poland. As a dentist, Alina struggled initially, especially since the couple had small children, no language competency, and the husband's employer had them living in a completely rural and secluded village. Learning to navigate the "local periphery" of Germany on the basis of her experiences in the small-town "Polish periphery," Alina eventually managed to acquire knowledge that allowed for successful integration and "centrally" global educational pathways for her children, who were sent to live and study in the United States and Canada during high school, attended language and culture summer programs in Italy and France, and then obtained degrees in the sciences and arts from top-ranked universities in Germany. Alina also returned to her profession as a dentist and now insists that migration actually enabled her to be in the center of progress in the field, performing cutting-edge treatments with top-notch equipment. Though the couple still plans to return to Poland "someday," their vision of themselves and their positionalities has changed. Alina explains:

> Initially I was a "nobody" here, came from somewhere no one knew, I was invisible ... But times changed, and I guess we changed. And my children are very global – traveling all over the world, having all the opportunities that we did not have growing up in Poland. ... Germany is a global power, it is not the worst place to be a citizen of, opens many doors – back in Poland, in America, almost everywhere ... I also think that small towns are somewhat alike, so growing up in one in Poland actually made me aware of how to handle the mentality of the villages and tiny towns here.

As demonstrated, the line between "peripheral" and "central" social, professional and spatial locations becomes blurred in Alina's narrative. Though she clearly identifies as someone "from the (European and Polish spatial) periphery," she uses her knowledge and pairs it with an "in demand" medical qualification to move herself towards the "center," bettering her position in many ways. While she could be simply viewed as a politically and economically motivated 1980s migrant, her self-identification proclaims complexity and challenges the simplifications common within dominant discursive framings of migration.

A distinctly different scenario is the search for a new life from a peripheral position in "peripheral" Poland. Interestingly, these migrants oftentimes choose to follow a path of periphery-to-periphery (or rural-to-rural) migration, moving to socially and geographically underprivileged sectors and areas in Norway, Germany and the UK. The migrants following this path are not at all prepared for migration, lacking language skills, education, and labor-market translatable/desirable qualifications and/or experience:

> Had my husband prepared for his migration? No, he did not. He came here with no language knowledge, and just when he was awaiting all the documents for family reunification, then I taught him a little bit, we studied together and only then he went to classes.
>
> JULIA, 41, Nurse, NOR

A similar "all over the place" narrative of life and employment is presented by Sonia, whose upbringing took place in the Polish periphery and who, in spite of her efforts, was only marginally successful in terms of her education (part-time studies at the local and little respected school, dropping out and restarting) and her position in the labor market (part-time employment, rotation, changing jobs, sectors, using networks):

> I graduated ... well I actually started to study for a B.A. in Sociology, psycho-social studies for advising others. Sometime later I finished this B.A., then I worked contract hours, part-time. But it was, well, thanks to the fact that a friend started her own fitness center and I was a receptionist there.
>
> SONIA, 36, Bakery Assistant, NOR

Following migration to Norway, Sonia still does not hold the most prestigious position as a bakery employee, but she nevertheless lives in Oslo and has upgraded the social status of her family. This is typical for migrants who use niches in the destination country's labor market and take on jobs that many local inhabitants do not find attractive enough; as noted, these are often low-paid 3D jobs (dirty, difficult, dangerous):

> Looking back at Poland now, we compare it and think that in Poland one does not live, one just vegetates. This is our opinion ... In Poland we thought it was okay but we did not know the reality here and could not fathom how one can actually live. So we really aren't God knows who in Norway – we have common professions.
>
> ILONA and ADRIAN, both 41, Office Worker and Carpenter, NOR

Helena (63, Nanny, UK) followed a similar path. As another person affected by the post-communist transformation, she lost her income source and was left to her own devices with a vocational training (as a mining employee) that was no longer usable in the new Polish labor market. Although Helena had never left her Polish town in the Silesia region, she was suddenly forced to explore the option of labor migration, eventually following her son to the UK and becoming a nanny for Polish children in the suburban area near Liverpool. She can be seen as consistently confined to the periphery, from which she has little chance to escape. Yet Helena has accepted that she is now in a space that, if still peripheral, is perhaps less so in terms of the income she earns and her proximity to family members who have managed to secure better social positions in the global center. She says:

> I never had much, and never expected much ... I was born in the wrong period, probably also in the wrong place, so I don't think I could do things differently. You could not just pick up and leave in my youth – government,

poverty, family obligations. We did not know that there was a world out there because we mostly had what we needed ... In the end I am glad my son and grandson live here in Britain, this means chances.

Helena's story foregrounds the importance of the historical dimension of peripherality/centrality dilemmas, which can be embedded in distinct understandings of one's position in relation to what the surroundings provide or deny. It cannot be said that Helena significantly altered her own peripheral vision and trajectory, but she seems to assume that a more "centralized" position and life experience will be beneficial for the next generations of her family. This is especially evident as she repeatedly mentions in the interview that her grandson has plans to study law in London – a dream that could never have been a part of Helena's own life story.

Finally, Zosia (41) and Maciek (43) constitute a family with a plethora of migratory experience gathered over several decades. They both were (at different times) working seasonally in Germany, and then moved back and forth between Poland and Norway between 2003 and 2007. In 2007, they settled in Oslo, both starting out by doing seasonal agriculture jobs (fruit picking) and then moving on to construction work (Maciek, 43, NOR) and hospital work (Zosia, 41, NOR). For them, migration became a way of life, not because they could not find work in Poland, but because the wages they could have counted on there were not satisfactory and their employment conditions there persistently precarious. This provided them with little opportunity to become an economically independent young family:

> Everything was just to get by, to survive, the income was really only for that, it was difficult to start something, to become independent, have one's own flat. ... We were then ... highly relying on our parents all the time.

Their first trips abroad were largely chaotic and strictly temporary, regardless of the potential they offered to earn more money:

> There were perspectives [to stay in Germany], but as I went our child had just been born. My wife stayed behind, so I was really eager to go home; at present there is Skype and all sorts of other communication tools, but then [in the 1980s], it was almost impossible to call from a payphone, the cost was enormous. During the entire time I am not sure if we even spoke once.

Accepting an old house as part of an inheritance turned out to be a catalyst for further mobility, as costs incurred by renovations required Zosia and Maciek to expand their migratory pathways. The couple made rotational arrangements during this time, and the wife went to Germany as a cleaner (substituting for her friend for a year). Finally, the couple decided to try Norway, which was presented to them as a country of unbelievably high basic wages. By then, they had fallen into debt. They got to know a farmer in Norway who spoke some German and who was a lifeline at a time when they were struggling to make ends meet. They admit: "We caught the bug – we realized that you could earn more money elsewhere." After a period of some turbulence, in which only one of the spouses was able to go abroad, they followed the advice of the local priest to reunite their family for the sake of their marriage.

Drawing on the migrants' narratives, it can be stated that the basic predictor for leaving the peripheries behind is one's original position in the country of origin, making it that much more important to look at the complexity of migrant trajectories. Arriving at the center does not magically revoke the former status, nor does it allow the migrants to simply "start afresh." On the one hand, those migrating with high capital usually acquire central positions in the social hierarchy of their destination countries, though they do need to periodically ascertain their desirability and belonging with the locals. On the other hand, low capital that translates into a low social position in the periphery of the center may be fully accepted by some migrants, who subjectively experience a positive improvement of their status as a result of their mobility.

Patterns of Peripherality

The relationships between perceived centers and peripheries should be analyzed in a holistic manner that takes macro-, meso- and microsocial contexts into account. The macro-level is strongly present in theoretical conceptualizations and tied to discursive framings, primarily pinpointing the inequalities and uneven development between emigration and immigration countries in international, mobility-focused scenarios (Wallerstein). The belief in a symbiotic relation between center and periphery obscures the fact that the character of exchange actually heightens and increases the existing global differentiation and distribution of resources. It is also important to note that the center/periphery relation has long ceased to be seen as a dichotomy adequate for describing nation-states' positionalities, which should instead be seen as lying along a continuum, as evidenced by the post-socialist countries, for example.

The establishment of global spatial and economic centrality translates to other dimensions of social relations and exemplifies how global power struggles affect everyday lives. The micro-social individual identifications and self-labeling processes analyzed here shift the focus from the level of international, geopolitical and macroeconomic relations to that of migrants' places of residence and their economic and social worlds. Looking at the labor market and at the social meaning of positions occupied by migrants in what can be seen as "central" societies, we can delineate two patterns of how mobile individuals from the "periphery" function.

First, "expats" or highly-skilled migrants seem to execute an "exit" from Poland as a "peripheral" nation. Importantly, their journey is considerably eased by the fact that many of them already occupy privileged "central" positions in Poland. Often, they originate from the capital city, have lived in major towns, have worked at prestigious international companies and have studied at top universities in Poland and abroad. Their trajectories, then, could be summed up as a move from the "periphery's center" to the "center's center," as they change geographic location and benefit from this modification's positive consequences. Second, the pathway of those who similarly originate from the periphery, but from less privileged positions within it, and who then move to a more advantageous but not locally privileged position in a central location, is deemed a movement from the "periphery's periphery" to the "center's periphery." Those Polish nationals with limited qualifications and skills seem substantially more peripheral in the "periphery" than their highly-skilled counterparts. As a result, they are unable to leave the peripheral space even when moving abroad, ending up in second-tier employment and substandard residential areas in the "center's peripheries."

The two patterns can also be distinguished in terms of the degree of "agency" migrants have, an approach well-described in gender and migration scholarship (see Hondagneu-Sotelo; Morokvasic 2004; Lutz 2010, 2011; Palenga; Dunn; Coyle; Ehrenreich and Hochschild). Though there is clearly a relationship between mobility, gender and social class, migration can have similarly intersectional consequences, as recalling the distinction between "migration as a system-determined fate" versus "migration as a system-determined choice" (Slany) demonstrates. Evidently, the first group of privileged migrants falls into the latter category, while the former covers low-skilled individuals with less valued capacities.

It is especially noteworthy that the low-skilled group of migrants, in general, does not benefit much from the centrality of their destination country and tends to become marginalized, separated in peripheral social, geographic and citizenship-related locations:

In Stavanger all city bus drivers are Polish, I also sometimes talk to them and hear very interesting stories, like, people coming without their families, so one may also imagine that this is a type of emigration, that it is all nice and pretty, but it is all based on chaos, on the concerns of people who have no money in Poland and have to do something to get it, families are falling apart and so on.

KALINA, 38, Teacher, NOR

The narratives of these migrants show that their satisfaction with their improved living standards and considerably higher income does not mean that they feel like locals, citizens or even inhabitants. Administratively, Polish migrants, sometimes also those from the more privileged group, can remain confined to the second-class categories of "temporary resident" or "temporary worker," experiencing their peripheral status and the bad treatment that results from this in their daily lives. Such experiences may be independent from their actual social status:

When I called the police, they simply did not listen to me, told me to bugger off.

ADRIAN, 41, Carpenter, NOR

He could not communicate, he spoke Norwegian but he did not have the confidence that he'd understand everything and he did not really jump at [the police] with information, calling their attention or arguing his stance. They first said they do not have time, then this and that, they had to do something in the city center. And now it is completely different, knowing the language well changes everything, it gives a confidence boost.

ILONA, 41, Office Worker, NOR

It was like this: a friend of my boss came as a substitute for a while and then suddenly it turned out that they didn't need me anymore. After a month they told me goodbye and this lady took my place. Yes, these things really happen, that's the truth.

MALWINA, 43, Unemployed, NOR

Feeling unwelcome or at least experiencing a greater distance from society is often due, migrants explain, to being associated with a particular country of origin:

I am extremely careful at work. I mean now not so much anymore, because now the people know me there, at least a little bit, because I have worked there for some time already. But in the beginning, because in my bakery there is also a French girl, she works there like me. So the Norwegians can tell from the accent and ask her where she's from and she says she is from Paris and they are fully blown away, in awe. They sing "oh my Jesus, Paris! Wow!" And the compliments and all begin. And when I'd say I come from Poland, then a surprise followed, shock or something different even – appalment.

SONIA, 36, Bakery Assistant, NOR

Even when the migrants do not directly state that they feel unwelcome, their experiences showcase the existence of institutional and individual discriminatory practices touching the lives of certain national or ethnic groups:

Earlier on here when we were not in the EU, the regulations and restrictions really were a bother. For example, being Polish meant that I had to exchange my driving license to have a Norwegian document, that was a law then. I had to pass an exam, take lessons to show that I can drive, had to take ten hours of driving lessons in order to be even allowed to take a driving test, even though I had my driving license for over ten years then. [Conversely, a] friend from Australia who has been driving on the left side for all his life ..., who has never seen snow, he was given a new driving license just like that, because he was on this "green list," and I was on a list together with Africa ... such examples. Later on, however, it was when I was planting some flowers in front of the house, we were not married yet, and a neighbor just came over to me and said: "So, three months have passed now, so you have to go back to Poland, right?" – this is how much they were checking whether I did not stay for too long.

SŁAWEK, 46, Engineer, NOR

Some migrants seem to be able to create their own strategies for handling their position of peripherality. This is less of a challenge for the highly skilled group, in which people often choose to reject their origin and engage in citizenship practices that orient them towards centrality. They often unsubscribe from their national belonging, cease to engage in transnational practices and confirm their status through a legal process of obtaining a citizenship status in their destination country (see Bogusia). Others, however, transgress the normative and conceptual boundaries of the central/non-central dichotomy and follow a path of pan-national and beyond-border identifications that disregards inequalities and differences (Lena, Kaja). Though this might eventually become a trap, as Polish framings of migrants' non-negotiable roles of loyal family caretakers and guarantors of family heritage have come to argue over the years, this strategy is facilitated by the marketable skills possessed by these migrants. Such skills allow them to participate in social worlds on terms they have partially negotiated and partially received on the basis of their systemic privilege (in terms of their education, skills, whiteness).

Another strategy that deserves further discussion pertains to a conscious pro-periphery choice, meaning a wish to operate on the peripheries of both destination and sending societies. This might not fully mirror the classic "migration as a system-determined choice" (Slany 2008), but can be linked to a phenomenon we call translocal peripherals. Expanding on White's discussion of translocalism in the Polish case, we see a possibility for people who engage in translocal lives to escape the center-periphery discourse, particularly when they realize they will never achieve centrality. Just as nations and economies have been described in terms of avoiding confrontation and resisting change due to their "fear of floating" (Bordo; Flandreau 418), the biographies of Polish migrants suggest that gambling everything on a shot for a central position may not seem unambiguously worthwhile to all. Unlike that of the transnationals and global professionals described above, the existence of translocals is split between two local peripheries (of home and destination countries) and their daily and broader self-identification practices are grounded in their connections with particular locations (for example in Poland and Germany). Even how these translocal migrants travel foregrounds locality and peripheral embeddedness, with anchors in provincial airports, bus stops and no visits to capital cities ever (White). Essentially, their behaviors can be called "home oriented" (Lutz; Palenga), lacking much engagement in broader public life, both prior to migration and following it, as Sonia's case, discussed in detail above, illustrates:

> I have really been on cloud nine here, so to speak. I am extremely happy with my job, I work full-time, my boss is happy with me thus far, I would never have found a similarly good job elsewhere ... with my Norwegian, because my language skills are very basic, very poor, only those terms I need for work ... I know I would not have managed elsewhere, not right now.
>
> SONIA, 36, Bakery Assistant, NOR

A conscious decision to situate oneself on the perceived peripheries of home country and destination country facilitates something of an escape from instability:

> I go to work and I know I will get my salary. I know what I can buy with this salary. I know I will be able to pay the bills, I will be able to afford an extravagant purchase once in a while, yes ... We can afford a normal life here ... I really appreciate this tranquility, I really like the calm of it all.
>
> SONIA, 36, Bakery Assistant, NOR & PAWEŁ, 37, Unemployed, NOR

When honing in on migrants making a choice to remain in the peripheries, it must be said that acceptance and decision do not necessarily exclude contestations. It remains a fact that while migrants may perceive their country of origin as a "periphery," they rarely see themselves as people living on the social periphery. A majority of the recounted narratives demonstrate that migrants prefer to see themselves not as forced into a particular position but as taking advantage of the opportunities presented by the contemporary globalized world, and as doing so with ease:

> After those couple of years here I believe that going to Norway is no different than moving from Cracow to Warsaw, I am telling you – no difference whatsoever.
>
> KALINA, 38, Teacher, NOR

> Truthfully, it is sometimes quicker to go to Gdańsk [from Norway] than to go to Hel from Gdańsk [two not too distant Polish cities].
>
> ILONA & ADRIAN

Conclusions

The narrative evidence presented in this chapter demonstrates that there is a range of discrepancies between people's accounts of their positionalities/ identities and the labels that scholars who deal with mobility use to describe the participants in globalized cross-border migration flows. The center-periphery dichotomy in particular may no longer be sufficient to explain how migrants view their own paths. Empirical data from several research projects focusing on recent migration between Poland and the West (UK, Germany, Norway) were used to illustrate how the categories of rural/urban, peripheral/ central and local/global were destabilized in the migrants' narratives. Building on the example of the transitional society of Poland as an aspiring (semi?)- periphery, we have attempted to show nuances of experiences that neither signify inescapable exclusion and marginality nor are fully explained by the "world-system" development lens. Our approach to peripherality and centrality follows the path created by migration scholarship, in which the exclusivity of countries of origin and destination is abandoned. Instead, it is necessary to underscore the multiplicity of sites around the world where migrants can be active because of their feelings of familiarity and connectedness to home, regardless of their "central" or "peripheral" status. We put forward the argument that, while macro-level categories may aid group-centered analysis, they are less relevant for understanding individual migration narratives. The divisions that stem from social and educational capital, as well as from migrants' original position in the specific country of origin, are mitigated by the modern landscape of "global" access facilitated through new technologies of communication and transportation, as well as by new discourses that, to a certain extent, redefine the meaning of peripherality. This redefinition is due to the interplay of peripheral social locations (e.g. deskilled employment, social marginality) with concurrent spatial centrality (e.g. living in Western Europe, benefitting from the destination country's welfare regime). In such situations, individuals may be inclined to disregard their peripheral standing in the latter realm.

Zooming in on the "periphery" concept, we have tackled questions about whether it can still be used in its objective or generic sense, and about which categories we need to explore in times of globally intensified movements of people that represent diverse and intersected social localities. In order to show the different possible meanings of periphery on social, cultural and economic, as well as intertwined micro-, meso- and macro-levels, we examined framings of peripherality expressed by people migrating from both the centers and the peripheries of their own country to the centers and peripheries of the destination society. The stark differences among those who left "global" (Poland) and "local" (rural Poland) peripheries behind (spatially and metaphorically) calls for less universalism in social research. This is especially urgent where the preemptive situatedness of the "neither-nor" Polish context is concerned. Some Polish spaces (e.g. urban metropolises) and groups (highly-skilled internationally educated young generations) can clearly be considered more centralized and European than others (those from certain regions – e.g. Southeastern Poland, losers of the Polish transformation, the uneducated), who remain bound to their position on the fringes.

On the basis of this, we have contextualized how migrants frame their own positionality with regard to being "from the peripheries" through negotiating their place to live, investing in their social, cultural and economic capital, and contesting the rooted dichotomies of East/West, Europe/non-Europe, minority/majority and, last but not least, high-skilled/low-skilled laborer.

Works Cited

Anacka, Marta, and Fihel Agnieszka. "Selektywność emigracji i migracji powrotnych Polaków – o procesie >wypłukiwania<." *Central and Eastern European Migration Review* 1 (2012): 57–67.

Anderson, Bridget. *Doing the Dirty Work? The Global Politics of Domestic Labour*. Basingstoke: Palgrave Macmillan, 2000.

Appadurai, Arjun. "Theory in Anthropology: Center and Periphery." *Comparative Studies in Society and History* 28.2 (1986): 356–74.

———. "Disjuncture and Difference in the Global Cultural Economy." *Theory, Culture and Society* 7.2 (1990): 295–310.

Bauman, Zygmunt. *Wasted Lives: Modernity and Its Outcasts*. Cambridge: Polity Press, 2004.

Beck, Ulrich. *Cosmopolitan Vision*. Cambridge: Polity Press, 2006.

———. "Beyond Class and Nation: Reframing Social Inequalities in a Globalizing World." *British Journal of Sociology* 58.4 (2007): 679–705.

Berend, Ivan T. *Central and Eastern Europe, 1944–1993: Detour from the Periphery to the Periphery*. Vol. 1. Cambridge: Cambridge UP, 1996.

———. "What is Central and Eastern Europe?" *European Journal of Social Theory* 8.4 (2005): 401–16.

Bordo, Michael D., and Marc Flandreau. "Core, Periphery, Exchange Rate Regimes, and Globalization." *Globalization in Historical Perspective*. Ed. Bordo Michael et al. Chicago: U of Chicago P, 2003. 417–72.

Burrell, Kathy. "Scaling Polish Migration: Overview and Observations." *Post-Accession Migration in Europe: A Polish Case Study*. Ed. Alison Stenning and Aneta Słowik. Cracow: Impuls, 2011. 9–14.

Castells, Manuel. *Siła tożsamości*. Warszawa: Wydawnictwo Naukowe PWN, 2008.

Cinpoes, Radu. "From National Identity to European Identity." *Journal of Identity and Migration Studies* 2.1 (2008): 3–14.

Ciupijus, Zinovijus. "Mobile Central Eastern Europeans in Britain: Successful European Union Citizens and Disadvantaged Labour Migrants?" *Work, Employment & Society* 25.3 (2011): 540–50.

Cox, Rosie. *The Servant Problem: Paid Domestic Work in a Global Economy*. London: I.B. Tauris, 2006.

Coyle, Angela. "Resistance, Regulation and Rights: The Changing Status of Polish Women's Migration and Work in the 'New' Europe." *European Journal of Women's Studies* 14.1 (2006): 37–50.

Dunn, Elisabeth. *Privatizing Poland: Baby Food, Big Business, and the Remaking of Labor*. Ithaca: Cornell UP, 2004.

Dyczewski, Leon. *Polacy w Bawarii*. Lublin: Redakcja Wydawnictwa Katolickiego Uniwersytetu Lubelskiego, 1993.

Ehrenreich, B., and A.R. Hochschild, eds. *Global Woman: Nannies, Maids, and Sex Workers in the New Economy*. New York: Henry Holt, 2003.

Favell, Adrian. "The New Face of East–west Migration in Europe." *Journal of Ethnic and Migration Studies* 34.5 (2008): 701–16.

Hannerz, Ulf. "Cosmopolitans and Locals in World Culture." *Theory, Culture and Society* 7.2 (1990): 237–51.

Hondagneu-Sotelo, Pierrette, ed. *Gender and U.S. Immigration: Contemporary Trends*. Berkeley: U of California P, 2003.

Iglicka, Krystyna, and Katarzyna Gmaj. *Poland – Past and Current Migration Outflows with the Special Emphasis on Norway*. CSM, 2014. Web. 22 May 2015.

Ignatowicz, Agnieszka. "Travelling Home: Personal Mobility and 'New' Polish Migrants in England." *Przeglad Polonijny – Studia Migracyjne* 1 (2011): 33–46.

Jarosz, Maria, ed. *Wygrani i Przegrani Polskiej Transformacji*. Warsaw: Oficyna Naukowa, 2005.

Jaźwińska-Motylska, Ewa, and Marek Okólski, eds. *Ludzie na huśtawce. Migracje między peryferiami Polski i Zachodu*. Warsaw: Scholar, 2001.

Kaczmarczyk, Paweł. "Poakcesyjne migracje Polaków – próba bilansu." *Studia Migracyjne – Przegląd Polonijny* 4 (2010): 5–36.

Kaczmarczyk, Paweł, and Joanna Tyrowicz. *Winners and Losers among Skilled Migrants: The Case of Post-Accession Polish Migrants to the UK* (No. 9057). Institute for the Study of Labor (IZA), 2015. Web. 22 May 2015.

Karasavvoglou, Anastasios, Ongan Serdar, and Persefoni Polychronidou, eds. *EU Crisis and the Role of the Periphery*. Cham: Springer International Publishing, 2015.

Korczyńska, Joanna. *Sezonowe wyjazdy zarobkowe Polaków do Niemiec*. Warsaw: Scholar, 2003.

Kurian, Rachel. "Globalizacja pracy domowej i uslug opiekuńczych." *Gender i ekonomia opieki*. Ed. Elżbieta Charkiewicz and Anna Zachorowska-Mazurkiewicz. Warsaw: Fundacja Tomka Byry "Ekologia i Sztuka," 2009.

Lutz, Helma. *The New Maids: Transnational Women and the Care Economy*. London and New York: Zed Books, 2011.

Lutz, Helma, and Ewa Palenga-Möllenbeck. "Care Work Migration in Germany: Semi-Compliance and Complicity." *Social Policy & Society* 9.3 (2010): 419–30.

Morokvasic, Mirjana. "'Settled in Mobility': Engendering Post-wall Migration in Europe." *Feminist Review* 77 (2004): 7–25.

———. "Migration, Gender, Empowerment." *Gender Orders Unbound: Globalisation, Restructuring and Reciprocity*. Opladen: Barbara Budrich Publishers, 2007.

Mrozowicki, Adam. *Coping with Social Change: Life Strategies of Workers in Poland's New Capitalism*. Leuven: UP Leuven, 2011.

Petrakos, George C. "The Regional Dimension of Transition in Central and East European Countries: An Assessment." *Eastern European Economics* 34.2 (1996): 5–38.

Płomień, Ania. "Welfare State, Gender, and Reconciliation of Work and Family in Poland: Policy Developments and Practice in a New EU Member." *Social Policy & Administration*. 43.2 (2009): 136–51.

Plüss, Caroline. "Migrants' Social Positioning and Inequalities: The Intersections of Capital, Locations, and Aspirations." *International Sociology* 28.1 (2013): 4–11.

Prusin, Alexander V. *The Lands Between: Conflict in the East European Borderlands, 1870–1992*. Oxford: Oxford UP, 2010.

Roudometof, Victor. "Transnationalism, Cosmopolitanism and Glocalisation." *Current Sociology* 53.1 (2005): 113–35.

Sandru, Cristina. *Worlds Apart? A Postcolonial Reading of post-1945 East-Central European Culture*. Cambridge: Cambridge Scholars Publishing, 2013.

Sassen, Saskia. "Global Cities and Survival Circuits." *Global Woman: Nannies, Maids, and Sex Workers in the New Economy*. Ed. B. Ehrenreich and A.R. Hochschild. New York: Henry Holt, 2003. 254–74.

Shields, Stuart. "From Socialist Solidarity to Neo-populist Neoliberalisation? The Paradoxes of Poland's Post-communist Transition." *Capital & Class* 31.3 (2007): 159–78.

Skrbiš, Zlatko, Gavin Kendall, and Ian Woodward. "Locating Cosmopolitanism: Between Humanist Ideal and Grounded Social Category." *Theory, Culture & Society* 21 (2004): 115–36.

Slany, Krystyna, ed. *Migracje kobiet, Perspektywa Wielowymiarowa*. Cracow: Jagiellonian UP, 2008.

Szczepanikova, Alice. "Becoming More Conservative? Contrasting Gender Practices of Two Generations of Chechen Women in Europe." *European Journal of Women's Studies* 19.4 (2012): 475–89.

Temple, Bogusia. "Influences on Integration: Exploring Polish People's Views of Other Ethnic Communities." *Studia Migracyjne – Przegląd Polonijny* 1 (2011a): 97–110.

———. "Polish Migrants' Narratives of 'Us' and 'Them,' Language and Integration." *Post-Accession Migration in Europe – A Polish Case Study*. Ed. Alison Stenning and Aneta Słowik. Cracow: Impuls, 2011b. 39–54.

Trevena, Paulina. "Divided by Class, Connected by Work: Class Divisions among the New Wave of Polish Migrants in the UK." *Studia Migracyjne-Przegląd Polonijny* 1 (2011): 71–96.

Vertovec, S., and R. Cohen. "Introduction." *Conceiving Cosmopolitanism: Theory, Context and Practice*. Ed. S. Vertovec and R. Cohen. Oxford: Oxford UP, 2002.

Wagner, Izabela. *Becoming Transnational Professional. Kariery i mobilność polskich elit naukowych*. Warsaw: Scholar, 2011.

Wallerstein, Immanuel. "The Construction of Peoplehood." *Race, Nation, Class: Ambiguous Identities*. Ed. Étienne Balibar and Immanuel Wallerstein. London and New York: Verso, 1991.

White, Anne. *Polish Families and Migration since EU Accession*. Bristol: The Policy Press, 2011.

Wolff, Larry. *Inventing Eastern Europe: The Map of Civilization on the Mind of the Enlightenment*. Stanford: Stanford UP, 1994.

CHAPTER 9

"Repairing Europe": A Critical Reading of Storytelling in European Cultural Projects

Astrid Van Weyenberg

While European integration was long considered to be primarily about economic and political cooperation, since the 1992 Maastricht Treaty it is increasingly approached from a cultural angle. Culture has become a key instrument in trying to shift people's national sentiments to a loyalty to the European community and in seeking agreement on how Europeans collectively remember their past and envision their future. In what follows, I look at two cultural projects that reflect this ambition of European political and cultural bodies to strengthen the European Union's legitimacy by anchoring "Europe" in a shared narrative. The first project is the future House of European History, initiated by former President of the European Parliament Hans-Gert Pöttering in 2007 and scheduled to open in Brussels in 2016. The second is the Via Regia, one of the touristic trajectories promoted by the European Institute of Cultural Routes, an organization launched by the Council of Europe in 1987. My focus is not so much on the projects themselves, as the museum is yet to be built and the route yet to be travelled (at least by me), but rather on how they are presented online and, more specifically, on the European narratives these online presentations imply. These are narratives of "Europeanization," understood here, following Kaiser, Krankenhagen and Poehls, as a cultural practice that seeks to produce a "specific European culture and history" and to contribute to the creation of "new forms of individual and social identification in Europe" (4).

My primary aim, then, is to critically examine the role and function of narrative in both cultural projects. Within the broader context of this volume, I additionally wish to shed light on the relation between narrative and the notion of peripherality. The House of European History's proclaimed "leitmotiv" of "centre and periphery" is significant in this respect. While it promises a productive and critical thematic focus, the museum's plans ultimately fail to give room to those stories considered "peripheral" to the central narrative of Europe on display. This means that despite its proclaimed attention to the historically shifting dynamic between center and periphery, and to the altering power relations that such shifts entail, the museum actually builds on a problematically static center-periphery model, so as to keep the European story on display intact. With regard to the Via Regia route, which runs from Santiago

© KONINKLIJKE BRILL NV, LEIDEN, 2016 | DOI 10.1163/9789004323056_011

de Compostela in Spain to Kiev in Ukraine, it is significant that the conceptualization of locations on the route as either "peripheral" or "central" entirely
depends on the different narrative functions they are intended to perform
within various (regional, national or supranational) narrative frames. Both the
House of European History and the Via Regia cultural route, then, reveal centrality and peripherality as narrative constructions. Before delving further into
these two projects, however, let me first introduce my preliminary questions by
looking at "Narratives for Europe," the European Cultural Foundation's guiding
principle between 2010 and 2012.

"Narratives for Europe"

With "Narratives for Europe" the European Cultural Foundation (ECF) invited
"thinkers, artists, writers and activists from Europe and beyond" to "share their
thoughts and observations," to "juxtapose, compare, dare, contemplate, open
new perspectives and to provide food for thought" and to "build Narratives
for Europe."[1] The result was an online collage of contributions from Europe
and beyond, among them an exchange between the Dutch writers Abdelkader
Benali and Jan Brokken on "the sadness of the discourse on Europe," pieces by
the Belgian cultural historian and writer David Van Reybrouck and the Egyp-
tian playwright Laila Soliman on "Flirting with Stereotypes," and contributions
by the Belarusian journalist Iryna Videnava and the Tunisian activist Lina Ben
Mhenni on "Historical Taboos." This kaleidoscope of voices was intended to
"form a showcase against generalisations and populist streamlining," because
"only a subtle, nuanced and determined approach can help us find the answers
for today's world." These answers, it is suggested, come in the form of stories,
which is also the message conveyed in the contribution by Indian writer Ami-
tav Gosh: "The new Europe has yet to find its story – and politicians and leaders
will never be able to give it that story. This story can only come from writers,
dreamers, and thinkers – and it has yet to be told."[2]

Despite the ECF's emphasis on providing a forum for reflection and debate, the overarching framework is clear from the start: "building Narratives
for Europe." As the choice of the preposition "for" indicates, these narratives
should first and foremost be beneficiary to Europe. Europe, it is suggested, is
in dire need of new stories. But why this desire for new stories and what does

---

1   http://www.narratives.eu/.

2   This is part of Gosh's keynote lecture for the ECF's "Imagining Europe" event in 2012, pre-
    sented in PDF form on the "Narratives for Europe" website.

it tell us about the current state of Europe? It seems primarily a symptom of what ails Europe. While, as Martin Kohli observes, Europe was still the political and geographical center of the world at the beginning of the twentieth century, it has now shifted to a peripheral position and this poses a new challenge to the (re)construction of European identity (114). It is in this light that projects intended to fashion new stories for Europe should be evaluated. The less Europe is able to define itself as a center (and the less it is able to define its own center), the more in need of a new story the "we" posited by the ECF seems to be, but also, the more difficult the construction of such a story (with clearly defined narrators, actors and events) becomes. Indeed, the guiding questions of "Narratives for Europe" reveal what the ECF's interest in storytelling is really about: "Are there emerging European Narratives – new visions – that can connect people across Europe? What's Europe's position in today's global world? What will be its future role?" The equation of narrative with "vision" ties storytelling to imaginations of the future, designed to address the fears about this future (and Europe's diminished role in it) signaled in the final question. To imagine but also to legitimate a future in which Europe's central, rather than peripheral, position in a globalizing world is secured, both present and past need to be put firmly in place. And what better way to tie past, present and future together than through stories.

Another implication of "Narratives for Europe" is that stories would help European citizens to define themselves as specific actors, "Europeans," who share a specific quality, "Europeanness." The ECF's webpage expands on the role of storytelling in processes of identity construction, articulating in one sentence both a diagnosis of Europe's problem and the remedy at hand: "the disconnection between Europe and its citizens is being filled with new versions of old nation-based narratives." From what follows the implication is clear: national stories are old stories; hence the "urgent need" for "new narratives for Europe – for today and tomorrow."[3] "Narratives for Europe," then, is presented as a restorative project which builds on the relation between story and history. It not only considers history as a textual and discursive formation in a way that evokes the work of Hayden White (or Frank Ankersmit), but it also extends the causal relationship of narration to nation, most famously theorized by Benedict Anderson and Homi Bhabha, to that of narration to the formation of the larger imagined political community of Europe. The future of Europe, in this interpretation, hinges on its ability to connect (with) its citizens.

---

3   www.culturalfoundation.eu/content/narratives-europe. This website is no longer available, but can be recovered in a version from 23 July 2013 at https://web.archive.org/web/20130723080605/http://www.culturalfoundation.eu/content/narratives-europe.

While "Narratives for Europe" responds to the prevalent concern that Europe is "lacking a story," not everybody considers this lack negatively. For the Dutch journalist and philosopher Rob Wijnberg it is even a positive sign. The story of Europe, he argues, is a story of what is no longer part of the story, of what we would only notice if it was no longer there: peace, freedom, safety, prosperity. Through this somewhat awkward rhetorical gesture, Wijnberg of course constructs his own unifying and progressive narrative of Europe, cleverly employing the idea of a lacking story to actually denote a story with its core narrative elements firmly in place. Sociologist Monica Sassetelli refers to Europe's lack of a story as well. In the "Imagining Europe" special of the Dutch magazine *De Groene Amsterdammer*, she heads her contribution with the question "Has Europe lost its plot?" In what follows, Sassetelli argues for a new European story that would take the EU motto of "unity in diversity" as its starting point, with a narrative structure that both accommodates diversity and conveys a shared cultural heritage. She is aware of the difficulty this involves: too much emphasis on unity would overpower the variety of "our" European cultural heritage, while too much emphasis on diversity would suggest that, in reality, there is no singular story to tell. However, her proposed solution, an institutionally determined, top-down narrative frame, which can be filled bottom-up with different narrative elements, does not consider the tensions and hierarchies at play in the *relation* between the (transnational) narrative frame and the (national) elements that fill it.

"Europe" is no more a story than it is a proper name denoting an economic, political or cultural entity. That European institutional bodies seek to fashion a narrative for Europe should, therefore, arouse our suspicion. If we do cautiously agree to view Europe in narrative terms, we should do so by asking the questions that stories and storytelling evoke. For example, if "Europe" can be read as a narrative, who are its addressed readers? If "Europe" is written, who are its authors? If "Europe" is a story, how exactly is this story written? But also, who feature as subjects and who feature as objects in this story? And what is made central and what is made peripheral to, or even left out of, "Europe: The Story"? With these questions in mind, let me turn to the first cultural project of my focus: the House of European History.

"Building a House of European History"

The House of European History is scheduled to open in 2016 and will be located in the Parc Léopold, or, as the information page on the website of the European Parliament informs its visitors: "in the heart of the European quarter in Brussels."[4] Through this subordinating conjunction of place, emphasizing the museum's location, the museum is directly associated with the neighboring institutions of the European Union. That the House of European History seeks to connect culture and politics is already apparent from the fact that it was Hans-Gert Pöttering, at that time President of the European Parliament, who, in 2007, initiated it. Pöttering, now Chair of the museum's Board of Trustees, envisioned the House of European History as "a locus for history and for the future where the concept of the European idea can continue to grow" (Conceptual Plan 2008).[5] The interpretation of the past in the light of the future thus serves the purpose of providing historical and moral ground for the process of unification and integration. It is important to recognize that the House's exhibition plans are inevitably subject to the political agenda that constituted its raison d'être to begin with. As Kaiser, Krankenhagen and Poehls stress, the lack of a "legal construction in the form of an independent foundation that could secure increased autonomy for the curators," means that the museum's exhibition plans "will most likely come under considerable political pressure from within the EP [European Parliament] and beyond" (151).

Although setting out to construct a transnational historical narrative that would decenter national historical narratives, ironically this cultural project makes use of similar principles and methods to nation-building processes in the late eighteenth and nineteenth century. It presents a shared past that informs and helps to shape Europe's (political) future, and it instructs that European integration is not a coincidence, but the result of a deliberate historical process. Correspondingly, the initial Conceptual Plan explains: "[t]he overcoming, to a large extent, of nationalisms, dictatorship and war, coupled with, since the 1950s, a willingness to live together in Europe in peace and liberty, a supranational and civil union – those should be the key messages conveyed by the House of European History." The exhibition should make it clear, furthermore, that "in a world of progress, a united Europe can live together in peace and liberty on the basis of common values." The words used here – "progress," "peace," "liberty," "common values" – remind of the key ingredients in national identity rhetoric. However, as Kohli argues, it is problematic for European identity to take its clues from national identity, not only because this implies an essentialist understanding of identity, but also because it ignores the different, possibly conflicting attachments (regional, national, transnational and global) that European identity comprises (117, 126). The narrative

---

4 http://www.europarl.europa.eu/visiting/en/visits/historyhouse.html.

5 The Conceptual Plan was composed by an international committee of experts, headed by Hans-Walter Hütter, President of the House of German History (Settele 4).

presented by the House of European History does not allow for such a self-reflexive and multi-layered understanding of identity.

Pöttering wished for the House of European History to become "a place in which the European Idea comes alive" that would present Europeans from all parts of the continent with "a chronologically based narrative that helps them understand historical events and processes." The various lemmas listed which events should be addressed in such a narrative, from the "high culture" of the Greco-Roman world to the enlargement of the European Union with ten new member states in 2004, when "the division of the continent had finally been overcome" (Conceptual Plan). In this story, every narrative element has a function in the development of a linear plot, climaxing in the integration of Europe. These original plans, however, seem to have caused debate on what a shared history for all the EU member states would look like, for a flyer from 2012 suggests that the history on display would start not in Roman times, but in 1946. The peace won after the Second World War would thus not only become the starting point but also the moral ground for a united, integrated Europe. European identity would be affirmed by creating what Kohli describes as a "symbolic temporary boundary," distinguishing between the negative past and the positive future in which Europe has overcome its conflicts (127).

The most recent plans, developed by an Academic Team in 2013, can be found in the PDF document "Building a House of European History" on the website of the European Parliament.[6] The story presented there consists of six thematic chapters. The opening chapter, "Shaping Europe," seeks to display Europe's common cultural heritage. The subsequent five chapters are titled "Europe Ascendant," about Europe's entry into modernity in the 19th century; "Europe Eclipsed," about its descent into war and destruction in the early 20th century; "A House Divided," about the Cold War era; "Breaking Boundaries," about an increasingly united Europe; and "Looking Ahead," inviting visitors to reflect on the Europe of today and tomorrow (37). In two of the chapter headings, telling metaphors are used. Representing the tragedies of the twentieth century as an eclipse, first of all, suggests a diminishing of light that is darkening yet only temporarily so, implying that the shining light of "Europe Ascendant" ultimately remains unchallenged. Secondly, within the context of a "House of European History," which evokes the idea of Europe as a house in which different Europeans live together as a family, sheltered and protected from what lies outside, "A House Divided" similarly points

---

6 http://www.europarl.europa.eu/visiting/en/visits/historyhouse.html. The Academic Team was chaired by the Slovenian Taja Vovk van Gaal, the future director of the House of European History (Settele 4).

to a temporary crisis; a crisis from which the European house was strong enough to recover and which could ultimately be contained within the walls of the house. Despite the tragedies presented, then, collectively the first five chapters present a united Europe as the end point of a tumultuous history. This progressive narrative movement is enforced by the exhibition's literally upward route, starting on the second floor and taking the visitor to the top floor.

Despite this teleological trajectory, with the story of European integration strongly tied to its purpose of bringing peace and prosperity, the last chapter/top floor is not intended to offer a conclusion or closing. Instead, visitors are invited to ask questions about the future of Europe and to debate the role and position of the European Union, which challenges Pöttering's earlier insistence on "the European Idea" as an established fact. Indeed, according to the latest plans, the House's permanent exhibition will be based on "a dichotomy of objectives," not only conveying a "coherent historical narrative," but also "rais[ing] awareness of the existence of a variety of different historical interpretations, points of view, nuances of perception and memory, so as to stimulate reflection and debate" (22). Still, the singularity of a "coherent historical narrative" and the plurality of "different historical interpretations" do not sit comfortably together. Moreover, visitors to the House will ordinarily not reach the top floor without first having been presented with a progressive story of Europe, a story likely to frame any subsequent critical reflections they might engage in.

The European Parliament webpage informing visitors about the House of European History addresses a number of Frequently Asked Questions. The answer to the most important question, "Why have a house of European History?" reads as follows: "The generation of people who experienced the tragedies of the 20th century and went on to build the European Communities is disappearing," so that it is now high time "to record their stories and memories to allow future generations to understand how and why today's Union developed as and when it did," because "[i]n times of crisis, it is particularly important to articulate the crucial role of culture and heritage and to remember that peaceful cooperation is not to be taken for granted."[7] There is something unsettling about the way in which the specific "tragedies of the 20th century" are tied to the generalized and pluralized "in times of crisis." Are we at present in times of crisis and is this why we need a House of European History to begin with? If so, what does the reinterpretation of history as a pacifying story imply? And what is suggested in the belief that current crises (which, problematically, remain

----

7   http://www.europarl.europa.eu/visiting/en/visits/historyhouse.html.

unspecified) are best addressed by appealing to a shared heritage? As Ann Rigney states:

> As we reel from one Euro-crisis to another and governments struggle to control the financial markets, the contours of a new narrative about the rise and erosion of the social democratic welfare state in postwar Europe may already be emerging, along with an anti-immigration narrative, purportedly going back to the Middle Ages, centered on a European crusade against the Islamic world. In view of such shifting perspectives, stabilizing European memory in a single master-narrative conveyed through the bricks and mortar of a monumental museum may not be the best way forward.
>
> RIGNEY 615–16

Rigney not only pinpoints the actual crises at play, she also warns of the danger of using these to legitimate a single European master-narrative. Indeed, it was the use of similarly dominant and unified narratives (that of fascism, for example) that caused Europe's twentieth-century crises, so that any such Narrative should immediately give us pause.

Instead of seeking to create a collective memory narrative by appealing to an exclusive past, argues Rigney, there should be a more dynamic, less monolithic, more future-oriented way of looking at the relationship between memory, citizenship and culture (616). The House's Academic Team does express awareness of the difficulty of establishing a shared memory for a very diverse population: the House should portray "different memories and opposing interpretations of history," so that the visitor will learn that "history is a construct defined by individual values and perceptions." At the same time, however, the concept of "shared memory" will form the basis for the narrative of the museum's main exhibition, pointing to the way in which, in Rigney's words, "'memory' has come to be used in public debates as a way of designating an affective, citizen-centred relationship to the past that is distinct from history as such and linked to identity" (608). Thus considering a "shared memory" as the foundation and core of "Europeanness" either falsely presumes that all European citizens (can) have a common heritage (ignoring, among other things, the complex histories of migration to and from the European continent) or excludes the many Europeans whose story of "Europe" may not commence with, say, the end of the Second World War. Although citizenship is never explicitly mentioned, implicitly classifying as "European" only those people whose family ties go back seven decades or more creates a hierarchy of citizenship, with some of us being considered more "European" than others, or, to employ the problematic metaphor of the "house" (used both in the exhibition section "A House Divided" and in the museum's name), with some of us being more entitled to live in this house and feel at home in it than others.

A critical reflection on "European History" necessitates calling attention also to those stories and memories that do not neatly fit the central(izing) narrative on display. Precisely the gaps and silences, the contrasting memories, the peripheral stories are crucial to consider in a truly critical reflection on "European History." But, as Veronika Settele concludes, it apparently remains difficult for the museum to make its exhibition more inclusive (8). Settele calls attention, for example, to the chapter on Europe's progress in the nineteenth century. While "Europe Ascendant" acknowledges that "[t]he sheer scale of imperial expansion bolstered the self-held European sense of superiority to the rest of the world" (European Parliament 2013: 33), it fails to include any memories of those affected by colonialism, a legacy not only pervading the family histories of many people who live in the former colonies, but also those of many European citizens, whether from French or Algerian, from Dutch or Indonesian descent. Similarly, notes Settele, the only reference to migrants is to the guest workers of the 1970s. Clearly, the House has not (yet) succeeded in giving room to the diversity that it considers Europe's "defining feature" (Conceptual Plan). This underscores Kohli's observation that Europeanization may have succeeded in diminishing aggressive nationalism, but "there may be a new 'European nationalism' turning outwards, or inwards against those who represent the outer world" (128). Immigrants from outside Western Europe, he continues, confront national populations with "the question of multiple identity and inclusion – of whether and under what conditions to allow 'them' to become 'us'" (128–29). While this confrontation is especially relevant within the present context of the so-called "refugee crisis," within the walls of the House of European History, this confrontation is avoided.

The absence of marginal stories and memories jeopardizes the House's intention, as explicitly expressed in the latest plans, to involve the visitor in an "active questioning process" both about "the shared responsibility for important decisions and choices that continue to shape the history of Europe and its relationship with the rest of the world" and about "how Europe deals with diversity, nationalism, human rights" (37). It is an even more surprising absence in light of the chosen "recurring leitmotiv" of the exhibition: "centre and periphery." This concept, the plan explains, is "central to the debate about the development of the European Union," because "[o]ver time, different parts of Europe have occupied the role of the centre or the periphery, spatially and psychologically" (30). The acknowledgement that "Europe has developed mainly through these processes of shifting borders, centres and powers," involving messy processes and coincidental changes rather than a neatly linear progression, reflects a major shift of perspective from the 2008 Conceptual Plan, which still portrayed European integration as a linear story progressing towards peace and prosperity. At the same time, however, while attentive to the fact that "[t]he sense of belonging or of marginalisation is important for every European individual" (30), the plans ultimately fail to sketch a more inclusive history that would give room to the many different experiences of marginalization that are lived and remembered in Europe. As Settele concludes, such an "inclusion of exclusion" will be no easy undertaking in a project funded by political authorities (10).

It remains to be seen how the House of European History's main exhibition, once realized, will negotiate contrasting and conflicting ideas of what "European History" should signify, and how it will mediate its objectives of building a unifying narrative while safeguarding a plurality of memories, stories and identities. Will the House succeed in giving room to the diversity it considers the core of European identity, the diversity that the EU, as expressed in its "unity in diversity" motto, seeks to protect? And how much room for debate will be left once an overarching, progressive European narrative is in place? These questions are not only relevant to the House of European History, but also to the Via Regia Cultural Route, the second project I focus on.

"To Build Europe While Travelling"

The Via Regia is one of the touristic trajectories laid out by the European Institute of Cultural Routes, a non-profit organization installed in 1997, following a political agreement between the Council of Europe and the Government of Luxembourg, where it is located. The Institute's website promotes the cultural routes as "European diagonals" that are tracked along "geopolitical diagonals" and that "touch on the history of North–south relationships," as well as on "the co-operation of professionals from the west and the east."[8] These routes, then, are portrayed as able to connect all parts of the continent, also those that were disconnected for decades during the Cold War. The most striking phrases presented on the website are "repairing Europe" and "restoring continuities," evoking the image of a Europe that is broken and needs to be mended.

---

8   http://www.culture-routes.lu. Recently, the website has been updated: http://culture-routes .net/. Much of the text remains the same. My analysis is based on the previous website, which can be recovered in a version from 7 May 2015 via https://web.archive.org/web/ 20150507234210/http://www.culture-routes.lu/php/fo_index.php?lng=fr&dest=ac_oo_ooo& lng=en.

The suggestion is of returning Europe to some kind of primordial unity, which would legitimate Europe's current process of unification: we are becoming whole again and shared narratives help us retrieve what was lost. In light of the many histories of conflict and war, such discourses of a loss of wholeness should be examined critically. The Institute's motto "to build Europe while travelling" goes even further, implicitly presenting travel not only as a way to unite what was previously divided or repair what was previously broken, but to build what previously did not exist: Europe.

The routes promoted by the European Institute of Cultural Routes evoke Europe as a geographical entity and join it to an historical idea. Among the many routes that have been formalized since the Institute's foundation are the Way of St. James to Santiago de Compostela, the Via Francigena between Rome and Canterbury, the European Mozart Ways between Milano and Salzburg, the Vikings Route, the Don Quichote Route, and the Hansa Route.[9] The specific route of my focus here, the Via Regia (Latin for the King's Way), is introduced as follows:

> Taking as a starting point the observation that, within the Europe of [the] European Union, the majority of information regarding history, tourism, economics and journalism is more concerned with Western Europe, and that, as a greater focus is put on the East, prejudices increase and the knowledge of the citizens decreases, the project-leaders aim to make the Via Regia a way of "allowing the Europeans to rediscover Europe."

The emphasis, then, is on "rediscovering," through travel, those Eastern parts of Europe that the traditional privileging of the West has tended to ignore or render peripheral. The employed rhetoric of "a journey of discovery" sounds euphemistic, not only in light of the violent history of the Iron Curtain that divided Eastern and Western Europe from the end of World War II until the end of the Cold War, but also in light of the widespread discrimination against and maltreatment of Eastern European laborers in Western European countries such as The Netherlands. (Perhaps this is the contemporary reality to which the word "prejudices" is intended to refer.) There is, additionally, no mention of the main reason why stimulating the local economies of Eastern European countries (through tourism, for example) is so terribly important, namely that many Eastern Europeans live in poverty and that in many rural

---

9   The websites for these routes can be found via http://www.via-regia.org/kulturstrasse/pdf/ websites.pdf.

parts of Eastern Europe poverty is, in fact, on the rise.[10] That story would in all probability not sell.

Visitors interested in "rediscovering Europe" can subsequently travel to a corresponding website (see figure 9.1), devoted solely to the Via Regia route.[11] The English version of this website explains that "Via Regia" has several meanings. The first meaning, explicit in the route's logo (a crowned figure on top of what looks like a medieval carriage, see the top right in figure 9.1), refers to the term's origin, which has to do with the legal status of particular medieval roads. "In the Holy Roman Empire of the German Nation," it says, "when kings were still strong and powerful, they could guarantee the protection of roads." This description reduces a very complex and continuously changing political organization (which commenced in 800 AD with the alliance between Pope Leo III and the Frankish king Charlemagne and which, after decades

FIGURE 9.1   *Via Regia: Cultural route of the Council of Europe.*

10   http://www.ruralpovertyportal.org/region/home/tags/europe.

11   www.via-regia.org. This website too has been updated; my analysis focuses primarily on an earlier version of the site.

of political shifts and conflicts, finally dissolved after the defeat of Emperor Francis II by Napoleon at the Battle of Austerlitz in 1806) to a simple, almost fairy-tale like story, "when kings were still strong and powerful." Moreover, in light of the Via Regia's promotion as a route that bridges the divide between Eastern and Western Europe, the emphasis on the Holy Roman Empire, which comprised a complex of lands in Western and Central Europe only, is rather surprising. The foundational history thus evoked in effect excludes the very regions the route seeks to include.

From the protection of powerful Kings, the story of the Via Regia then moves on to another positive association of its name: solution. After all, in German, the site explains, Via Regia is also used "as a metaphor, especially in sciences and politics, and means 'king's road', 'golden trail', a way for optimal problem solving." Indeed, the word "*Königsweg*" in common German means something like the best, shortest, most preferable route to something, often used in relation to solving problems. This metaphoric explanation resonates strongly with the restorative story evoked by the House of European History. There, as I explained earlier, it is implied that remembering a shared European heritage may help in "times of crises"; in the case of the Via Regia, this (supposed) shared heritage leads all the way back to the Holy Roman Empire. It remains unclear whether website visitors are expected to draw connections between the idea of "optimal problem solving" and the political organization of the Holy Roman Empire and, if so, whether the Holy Roman Empire, uniting a complex of territories, peoples and ethnicities, is supposed to serve as an analogy for the European Union.

The final clarification of the term "Via Regia" is that it refers to "an economic, cultural, tourist network, which embraces the different meanings of the term." On the website's opening page (figure 9.1) it further says that it "is the name of the oldest and longest road link between the East and the West of Europe," that it "exists since more than 2.000 years," that it "connects 8 European countries through a length of 4.500 km" and that its "modern form is the European Development Corridor III at present." This route, then, not only connects East and West, but past and present as well, tracing back one of the ten Pan-European transport corridors (defined in 1994 as routes in Central and Eastern Europe that required major investment) not just to the Holy Roman Empire, but even further. For "the history of the Via Regia in Europe surely began before the time of Jesus Christ," because "when Gaul was occupied by Romans, there were stable provision roads between Paris (Lutetia) and the South of France." The word "surely" is significant, because it reveals the voice of a narrator who elsewhere remains unidentifiable, but who at this particular point in the narrative (with a sense of bravura) attempts to convince the website's visitors. Here, we get a glimpse, then, of what elsewhere remains more difficult to trace: a particular point of view reflecting a particular interest. The presentation of ancient Rome as the foundation and legitimation of contemporary Europe should convince visitors to the website of the Via Regia's potential as a "symbol for European unification."

The Interactive Map to which the Via Regia website redirects (figure 9.2) is worth some attention as well. There, visitors are invited to take the famous Catholic pilgrimage city of Santiago de Compostela not as a destination, but as the starting point of a European trajectory that, when "read" from left to right, leads all the way to Kiev. Though it would be interesting to consider the selection of all the places denoted as "sites" on this route, let me focus for now on one implication of beginning this European trajectory/story with Santiago de Compostela, which places emphasis on this city's religious importance to European culture and heritage. Santiago, after all, has its origin in the shrine of Saint James, who, according to legend, appeared to Christian troops fighting the Moorish army in 844. St. James, nicknamed "the Moor-slayer," subsequently became the symbol of the *reconquista* that ended Islamic rule on the Iberian Peninsula. Placing Santiago, a famous site of Western Christian heritage, at the left (starting-) point of the Via Regia and Kiev, often considered the cradle

FIGURE 9.2 *Via Regia: Cultural route of the Council of Europe (Interactive Map).*

of Orthodox Christianity, on the right, invokes Europe's Christian legacy in a way that is relevant to current debates on how "Europe" should define itself and which groups are, as a result of this, marginalized. The significance of this debate is clear, for example, from the 2004 controversy about an eighteenth-century statue of St. James housed in the Cathedral of Santiago de Compostela, which depicts St. James hacking off the heads of Moors. Immediately after the bomb attacks on Madrid trains in 2004, plans were made to relocate the statue to the secular space of a museum, so as to avoid further tensions. This decision caused such upheaval, however, that the statue remained in place. In the words of Javier Domíngues García, the resulting political and cultural debate about the legitimacy of St. James's representations illustrates the "multiple perspectives that collide in the medieval iconography of the apostle" (2009: 72–3).

To zoom in on this particular statue is important because for a traveler along the Via Regia, especially if this traveling only takes place on the virtually presented route on the website, it depicts one of the narrative elements (potentially even the narrative opening) that he or she could encounter. Within the context of Spain, the statue is an element supporting a dominant national myth of origin. Enveloped within the supranational context of Europe, through the framework of the Via Regia route and narrative, the Moor-slaying St. James could equally be read to promote a particular idea of Europe: a Europe in which "Europeanness" is equated with Christianity. Similar to the House of European History, a generalized notion of European identity is tied to a particular cultural heritage. European citizens of other religious persuasions or with other cultural backgrounds are thus excluded. With regard to the route's ambition to reconnect Eastern and Western Europe, too, the emphasis on Christianity is relevant, for it proposes a very particular understanding of "Eastern Europe," excluding, for example, regions such as Bosnia and Herzegovina or Albania, which have Islam as their largest religion. From this perspective, we have not traveled very far, it seems, from the Europe envisioned by the French poet and thinker Paul Valéry who, at the start of the twentieth century, named only those who have undergone the influences of Greece, Rome *and* Christianity, "true" Europeans (322).

Notably, Santiago and Kiev acquire very central positions in the European narrative that the Via Regia route constructs. This is especially interesting (but also ironic) when we consider the (semi-)peripheral status of Spain and Ukraine in current economic and political debates. The Eurozone crisis has pushed Spain further to the economic margins of the EU, with at present one quarter of its population unemployed. This contemporary "status" stands in an awkward relation with its privileged cultural and historical position in the European narrative of the Via Regia route. Ukraine, on the other end of the route, has a very complicated political history with its neighboring European Union. The urge to envelop Ukraine in a narrative that constructs it "as European" seems to rise now that Putin has annexed Crimea and Ukraine is "under threat" by Russia. In a sense, this political crisis also constitutes a narrative crisis. That the story of Europe needs to be put firmly in place again, with clear friends and enemies (or, in terms of A.J. Greimas's semiotic model, helpers and opponents), is clear from the speech held by Guy Verhofstadt, Liberal and Democrat Group Leader in the European Parliament, to the protesters on Kiev's Maidan Square in February 2014. With Dutch politician Hans van Baalen (representing the Dutch People's Party for Freedom and Democracy) at his side, Verhofstadt told the protesters: "You are defending European values and European principles and democracy." The protesters' fight, then, was considered to be not just about Ukraine, but about Europe; it was, in fact, a fight for "Europeanness." In a sense, the story of the Ukrainian protesters was adapted to and encapsulated in a European story.

How do these recent political developments stand in relation to Kiev's place on the European Cultural Route of the Via Regia? What does it mean to draw Kiev into the story of Europe and make it the farthest point of a progressive story of Europe (and European integration)? If anything, it demonstrates that a route such as the Via Regia is not only a project of "repairing Europe," but also of securing Europe from what is perceived to lie beyond its borders. Ukraine's interest to the European Union is primarily due to its function as a borderland and buffer zone; it was precisely its peripheral location, it could be argued, that informed Verhofstadt's centralizing rhetorical gesture. A rhetorical gesture, one might add, with great affective force: you, the people of Ukraine, are defending all that we, the people of Europe, consider to be at the core of our culture, identity and civilization. At the same time, the plural "you" addressed here is not really included in the "we" that is evoked, so that the speaking "center" effectively places the listening "border zone" in an ambiguous, in-between position.

The above example shows the need to critically examine the relationship between Europeanizing narratives and the existing narratives on which they draw. After all, as Ashworth and Graham argue, "the successful integration of Europe might demand an iconography of identity that would transcend national and regional identities" and would "involve the manipulation of heritage, demanding the addition of new layers of meaning to built environments and landscapes that are already fundamental symbols within national or regional iconographies and narratives" (382). A good example of the complex relations between regional, national and European heritage is, again, the interactive map on the Via Regia website, which tellingly redirects visitors who click on "Santiago de Compostela" to Santiago's city council website. There, the city is promoted as the cultural capital of Galicia; there, in other words, regional identity comes first. Perhaps this could be interpreted as an illustration of the tendency of European political and cultural bodies to bypass the nation-state and, with a transnational agenda in mind, emphasize the regional, the "more local" instead. Still, the Europeanization of Santiago de Compostela also reinforces its prestige as a *national* symbol of Spain, in a similar way as the "Unesco World Heritage" label does. So, in that respect, the elements drawn on in overarching Europeanizing narratives also challenge the unifying, centralizing process of Europeanization they are intended to bring about (Ashworth and Graham 382). We could read this negatively, in that the process of Europeanization may lead, against all odds, to the fragmentation of Europe, but also positively, in that the (narrative) elements drawn on are still able to maintain an external relation to the narratives that contain them and as such help to safeguard a plurality of stories and identities. Clearly, then, the position of Santiago (or Kiev or any other place on the Via Regia route) on the axis between "peripheral" and "central" is far from static and will shift according to the narrative purpose it is supposed to serve. The Via Regia reveals, in other words, that the peripheral is not so much a designation of place as it is a point of perspective and, perhaps most importantly, a mode of use.

Drawing this chapter to a close, let me emphasize that in the above investigation I have only scratched the surface of what are complex narrative processes. My aim was to make a start at analyzing what stories of/for Europe these cultural projects construct and what political implications a close reading of these stories could reveal. Naturally, I am not against the use of stories; that would be a preposterous position to take, as stories and storytelling are crucial to our daily existence and to our identity formation, both as individuals and as national, European and global citizens. There has always been and there will always be a need for stories. But stories also demand careful consideration, because as innocent as it may sound, storytelling is never a neutral activity. I am calling, then, for more critical attention to the stories of and for Europe that have been and that are continuously being constructed. By this I do not just mean the explicit Europhilic or Eurosceptic stories that circulate with increasing speed (and, at times, venom), but particularly those stories that travel across more subtle routes. Because the less explicit stories are, the more they are in need of explicit dissection.

Works Cited

Anderson, Benedict. *Imagined Communities: Reflections on the Origins and Spread of Nationalism.* London: Verso, 1983.

Ankersmit, Frank R. *Narrative Logic: A Semantic Analysis of the Historian's Language.* The Hague: Mouton, 1983.

Ashworth, G.J., and Brian Graham. "Heritage, Identity and Europe." *Tijdschrift voor Economische en Sociale Geografie* 88.4 (1997): 381–88.

Bhabha, Homi, ed. *Nation and Narration.* New York: Routledge, 1990.

European Parliament. *House of European History, Conceptual Plan by a Committee of Experts.* Brussels: European Parliament, 2008.

———. *Building a House of European History.* Brussels: European Parliament, 2013.

García, Javier Domínguez. "St. James the Moor-Slayer, a New Challenge to Spanish National Discourse in the Twenty-First Century." *International Journal of Iberian Studies* 22.1 (2009): 69–78.

Greimas, A.J. *Structural Semantics: An Attempt at a Method.* 1966. Lincoln: U of Nebraska P, 1983.

Kaiser, Wolfram, Stefan Krankenhagen, and Kerstin Poehls. *Exhibiting Europe in Museums.* New York, Oxford: Berghahn Books, 2014.

Kohli, Martin. "The Battlegrounds of European Identity." *European Societies* 2.2 (2000): 113–37.

Rigney, Ann. "Transforming Memory and the European Project." *New Literary History* 42.4 (2012): 607–28.

Valéry, Paul. "But who, after all, is European?" *The Collected Works of Paul Valéry: History and Politics.* Trans. Denise Folliot and Jackson Mathews. Princeton: Princeton UP, 1971.

White, Hayden. "Historical Text as Literary Artifact." *Narrative Dynamics: Essays on Time, Plot, and Frame.* Ed. Brian Richardson. Columbus: Ohio State UP, 2002. 191–210.

Wijnberg, Rob. "Europa is wat Europa niet is." *De Correspondent.* De Correspondent, 6 May 2014. Web. 7 Feb. 2016.

CHAPTER 10

The Rise of the Peripheral Subject: Questions of Cultural Hybridity in the Greek "Crisis"

Geli Mademli

Field Measurement

In the two-dimensional world of mathematics, the periphery of any given shape is the basis for the calculation of the area it includes; it is the only element and piece of information that is needed in order to perceive and express the extent of a surface in terms of space. Interchangeable with the neighboring notion of the perimeter as the sum of distances around something or the total length of an outline, the periphery was primordially established as an entity of measurement of physical and virtual spaces, and was implemented in the context of the imperative of the ancient world to find models of organizing externality in standardized units. The etymology of the word not only indicates its derivation from a Greek root (περί+φέρω), but also encloses a particular movement – as the proposition *peri* (around, circa, regarding, approximately) couples the palpable articulation of bearing, supporting, sporting, carrying (*phereia<phero*).

When taking the dictionary entry as a starting point, we are prompted to perceive periphery as in itself an arc of significations, showcasing the emphatic importance of circulating meanings and suggesting the necessity of a wandering subject, roaming through its reference field. As Tatyana Skrebtsova explains, in linguistics the term has been used to denote the borders of the semantic field (*Bedeutungsfeld*). Leonard Bloomfield describes the periphery as the "unitary domain of meaning," a space divided into smaller units with distinctive inner and outer boundaries that correspond to individual word meanings (Skrebtsova 146). Günther Ipsen, in turn, parallels the term to a mosaic, in that it involves an act of taxonomy that consists in the orderly placement of solid units, but at the same time reveals a different picture when examined from a distance (Skrebtsova 147). In that regard, and according to Jost Trier's work, peripheries are defined as the borders of semantic categories, indicating the necessity of moving away from a "core" – that is, from a rigid, unyielding attribution (Skrebtsova 147). The contribution of the study of the concept of the periphery to theories of the linguistic field is invaluable due to this recursion: not only does it prove that the concept only gains meaning through multiplicity (even within the definition of the word itself, "peripheries" of meaning only exist in plural form), but it also questions the validity of borders by rendering peripheries as gray zones in a vast territory of arbitrary actions.

To see how the general definition of the periphery in the linguistic context is translated into its function in the contemporary Greek one, it is helpful to consider its definition in the *Greek Modern Dictionary*. The analysis of the word's meaning and function, and the comparison of a general (and to a great extent constitutional) schema to a localized articulation, provides valuable particulars that prompt me to analyze how the notion of periphery works in the contemporary context of the "Greek crisis." Looking at the linguistic variation recorded in the *Greek Modern Dictionary*, the term "περιφέρεια/peripheria" was reintroduced only three decades ago, as an official term for the new "decentralized" administration divisions of the country's territory (with the exception of the autonomous polity of Mount Athos). These administrative units were formally established by Law 1622/1986 on "Regional Administration-Peripheral Development and Democratic Planning" (Presidential Decree 51 [6/3/1987] on the division of the country into 13 peripheries), which was followed by the publication of a series of statutes modifying its operational framework until reaching its present legal form in 1997. Interestingly, the enactment of this division did not result from a process of strategic planning within the country, but was linked to the policies of the predecessor of the European Union, the EEC/European Economic Community. Greece, a member state of the Union since 1981, could only make use of the outlays from operational programs and structural funds if it applied a specific decentralized model and channeled resources through the smaller clusters of peripheries, a policy soon to be elaborated in the European Community Support Framework.

Paradoxically, in a different example of a recursive double bind, the act of the modelization of the periphery (widely applied in European Union discourse as a managing tool facilitating the circulation of people and means within a rigidly bordered geographical area), while constituting the cornerstone of equitable administration, profitability and concordance, raises questions about the relation between different decision "centers" that displace the effect of the decision towards the outskirts. The example of the use of the notion of the periphery in the European paradigm is of particular interest, as it challenges binary oppositions in post-capitalist economies and state formulations. To name just a few of these bipolar entities, the periphery prompts us to challenge the distance between urban and rural, modern and traditional, old and new, enlightened and barbarian, productive and non-productive. Inside Greece, the division into peripheries has substituted governance through fragmentation with governance through classification. At the level of external affairs and on a global scale, the title "periphery of Europe" was given to Greece in order to underline the distance between the economic centers and the deflection points, between the decision-making hub and the implementation field, and, consequently, between the vision of Europe and its dark spots and side effects.

The 2001 EU document *Unity, Solidarity, Diversity for Europe, Its People and Its Territory: Second Report on Economic and Social Cohesion* includes an informative map of the center-periphery model within the margins of the European Union (Vol. 2: 10).[1] On this map, we can see the governmental boundaries of the continent's countries, as on conventional political maps, but there are no indications of the names of countries or major cities. We can, however, easily distinguish the boundary lines that divide each state's mainland into concrete administrative units. The key of the map indicates that its domain is divided into three categories: *central* regions include individual countries (the Netherlands, Belgium, Luxemburg) and parts of countries (North-Eastern France, Western Germany and England, apart from the North East and South West regions), and are highlighted in green; *peripheral* countries include the Baltic, the Balkan region, the Scandinavian countries belonging to the EU, the Iberian Peninsula, Ireland, Poland, Slovakia and the Eastern Czech Republic, and are highlighted in a red color that a semiotician would associate with a high-risk zone. Yellow highlighting marks EU countries identified as *other*.

Cultural geographers have highlighted the statement regarding the intention of the authors: "to give practical content to the concept of center-periphery, an index of accessibility has been developed, which measures for each region the time needed to reach other regions weighted by their economic importance" (Nemes-Nagy, Szabó and Németh n. pag.). In the context of what is recognized today as the European debt crisis, the notion of accessibility is transformed from a spatial and temporal feature to a term denoting capability. Thus, the notion of the periphery is transformed twice: first from a geographical and spatial unit into a political-financial term, and second reclaiming its dimension as a social position. This demonstrates not only how decisions in the European context can be centripetal rather than centrifugal, but also how they are literally *ec*-centric (strange, peculiar, erratic and irregular, as they fail to pivot on a consistent center), causing a complex genealogy of cultural identities to manifest in the peripheries of decision-making.

In what follows, I will reflect on the non-linear evolution of the role of the term "periphery" in Greek public discourse since the birth of the Greek nation-state, and I will argue that the inclusion of the word "periphery" in the

---

1   http://aei.pitt.edu/42147/1/2nd.v.2_report_social_cohesion.pdf.

terminology of a European Union administration model has gradually triggered a need to reconsider Greek cultural identity. At the height of the European debt crisis, this need was channeled through domestic mass media and expressed through a set of implied questions on governmentality, the politics of relation and self-determination. I consider the Greek bailout referendum, held on 5 July 2015, as a milestone that revealed the *ec-centricity* of current EU politics, while also discussing the paradoxes in the century-long bilateral cultural relation between Greece as a *topos* in the periphery of the Western world and Europe as an abstract, fuzzy center. First, I will frame and contextualize the "Greek Crisis" in light of recent political events in Greece. Second, I will draw a comparison between the recent declaration of insolvency and an earlier one in the late nineteenth century. Third, I will analyze the coverage of the referendum in Greek domestic media, seeking to show how the discourse on the "periphery" is crystalized in varied news articles on the Greek and EU political agendas. In conclusion, I will point out how the interpretation of these elements emphasizes the complexity of the "peripheral" and its importance in revealing the inadequacies of the center.

Parameters of Crisis / Perimeters of Crisis

The ready-made label of "European debt crisis" was quickly appropriated by popular media in Greece after the formal request for an international bailout for Greece in April 2010, encouraging the manifestation of Greek cultural identity as a European Other. This overemphasis on the Greek angle on the problem fueled radical ideologies from across the political spectrum – from fascist extreme-right groups and radical leftist parties volunteering to take the helm of political power to different "peripheral groups" promoting an apophatic political agenda that by and large consisted in the rejection of austerity measures rather than proactive planning. In the field of discourse, this stance would affectively translate into "no matter what Europe is, if this is how the 'center' reacts to its periphery, then Greece will not be a part of it," suggesting a dilution of the "centrality" of the European administration through an energetic embrace of the role of peripheral actor in the network of European relations. The view from the periphery would reveal what is *not* Europe, what is *not* democracy and what is *not* crisis, thus disrupting the line of vision and the focus of global attention. Here, the notion of the periphery is not appropriated to express anxiety about the loss of locality in the face of a homogenized (that is, globalized) European culture, but rather constitutes an autoimmune reaction by a "saturated mass society."

This apophatic argument, both as a component of intrinsic controversy (revealing a convention that can only be perceived in terms of what is not recognizable) and as a vigorous call for the rise of a decisive political subjectivity (*apophasis* is the Greek equivalent of the word "decision"), was best conceived in the question posed in the Greek bailout referendum implemented on 5 July 2015 by the Syriza-ANEL government:

> Should the agreement plan submitted by the European Commission, the European Central Bank and the International Monetary Fund to the Eurogroup of 25 June 2015, and comprised of two parts which make up their joint proposal, be accepted? The first document is titled "Reforms For The Completion Of The Current Program And Beyond" and the second "Preliminary Debt Sustainability Analysis."

The referendum, the media coverage of which will be analyzed below, was announced in the small hours of 27 June 2015, in response to the bailout conditions proposed during the negotiations with delegates of the three institutions (European Commission, European Central Bank and International Monetary Fund). Regardless of the parallel discourse on the validity of the procedure (different legal entities in Greece, including the Council of State, challenged the compatibility of the referendum with the Constitution) and the specificity of the question involved (the creditors' proposals were no longer on the table and when they had been presented in the form of a working paper on 25 June 2015, one day before the official proclamation of the referendum in Greece, they were accepted by a part of the Greek delegates), and despite the efforts of the government to disassociate the referendum question from the larger question of whether Greece should remain in the Eurozone, the voting body by and large interpreted the referendum as concerning national sovereignty and the relation between the centrality of Europe's administration and the peripheral imperative of its implementation. Thus, in voting "no" (as 61.31% of voters did), it could be seen to claim an energetic political subjectivity not in spite of but by means of Greece's peripheral identity. In this way, the periphery entered the symbolic order, diverging from its regular use in the standardized terminology of the European Union.

The distinctive dismissal of European identity and the partition of Greece into two contrasting entities "pro" and "con" its organic position in Europe do not merely constitute hallmarks of the present day or side effects of austerity measures in the age of neo-liberalism. On the contrary, this ambivalence towards Europe is vocalized as a palpable cultural expression following convulsions of administrative dominance and challenges to state sovereignty.

In Greece, the cultural expression of a certain "peripherality" has been discernible at regular intervals since the late Ottoman occupation and the early dawn of the War of Independence. During the short period of the First Hellenic Republic (1828–1831), the first political parties (which remained active in Greek territories) openly stated their support for greater political power on a continental level in being named after the "Great Powers" of the time. Each of them, however, established a very different set of relations between the center and the periphery of the modern idea of Europe: the Russian Party, strongly affiliated to the Orthodox Church, the state apparatus, noted leaders of the military and affluent families in the South of Greece, propagated the ideal of a centralized government. Their political rivals were the moguls of the Greek navy, associated with the emerging business class, who found their anchor in the circles of the British Party. This party was "the smallest of the three, counting on the support of some Hydriot leaders and learned men, such as historian of the Greek revolution Spyridon Trikoupis. It was the party which favored liberal reforms, and as such was closer ideologically to the monarchical government" (Koliopoulos and Veremis 35). Supported by the *Phanariotes*, the prominent cosmopolitan Greek families of merchants residing in Constantinople, and the *Philhellenes* of the West and of Russia, who expressed the "extravagance of Western Liberalism," the popularity of the British Party among Greeks was, however, minimal (Petmezas 126). Finally, the French or Constitutional Party had an important base of followers, primarily in the central region of the Greek territory, among retired captains of the revolutionary war, liberal intellectuals and supporters of a constitution that would have expansionist undertones and promote a purist nation-state.

In 1854, during the Crimean War, fought by an alliance of Great Britain and France against Russia for sovereignty of the Middle East and the outlet to the Mediterranean, the Russian authority became affiliated with the Orthodox Greek populations in the Ottoman Empire. Otto, the first king of the modern Greek nation-state (originally a Bavarian Prince, he ascended the throne while still underage), openly supported the opposition of the Greek populations to the European forces as a means of subverting Ottoman rule. At the same time, the intellectual legacy of King Otto's Prime Minister (and founder of the Russian Party) Ioannis Kolettis revolved around the irredentist claim of the *Megáli Idéa* (Great Idea), according to which a newly formed Greek state would include all the areas inhabited by Greek (or, rather, Greek-speaking) populations. This fueled revolts in the regions of Epirus and Thessaly on the mainland of the Balkan Peninsula, in response to which Anglo-French army troops occupied Athens for five months until the Greek government repudiated its support for the revolutionary movements on the continent. The Anglo-French troops brought cholera, resulting in the deaths of three thousand individuals (at the time a tenth of the population of Athens). The aftermath of the disease found the Greek population divided between supporters of the European policy, which guaranteed a level of stability in the area and would pave a path to independence in the long run, and partisans of the Russian policy, which promised the immediate conditions for a transitional stage.

By the end of the nineteenth century, the question of whether to perceive European political and financial support as an alliance or as a paternalistic gesture (that is, the question of the sort of peripheral identity Greece possessed) was condensed in the political rivalry between two opposing parties, which, from 1875 until 1905, alternately governed the fragile Greek democracy. The first was the New (or Modernist) Party (*Neoteristiko Komma*), led by Kharilaos Trikoupis, an open supporter of a reform agenda along "Western" standards and a promoter of the interests of the Greek diaspora and the landholders in the interior of the country (who had formerly supported the British Party). The second was the Nationalist Party (*Komma Ethnikofronon*), led by Theodoros Deliyannis, a conservative politician who campaigned as a spokesperson for the lower middle classes, primarily pledging to cut taxes. Whereas the former "sought to establish the country's international credit worthiness, to encourage incipient industrialization through ... a costly program that entailed increased taxation," the latter opted for the promotion of Greek autonomy through an aggressive, warlike policy against Turkey that could potentially drag more European countries into war, thus dividing the coalition of the "center" of Europe (Clogg 63).

In the meantime, new loan agreements were made possible due to the death throes of what Eric Hobsbawm describes as the Age of Capital, "a world of a continuous and accelerating material and moral progress" in which "the institutions of the world would gradually approximate to the international model of a territorially defined 'nation state' with a constitution guaranteeing property and civil rights" (13). Between 1879 and 1890, seven European loans with a name-value of 630 million drachmas were contracted between Greece and the European creditors, amounting to one third of the country's revenues. The notorious "currant crisis," which saw the annihilation of world demand for the main Greek export product, concurred with the official bankruptcy of the state in 1893 and arguably led to a "retention system," as explained by Greek economists of the era (Andreades). Trikoupis prioritized the maintenance of a strong, combat-ready army over a balanced government budget and the army's operations in the Greek-Turkish war of 1897, during Deliyannis's government, led to the engagement of a war indemnity that had to be paid by Greece, which skyrocketed the state's debt and led to the formulation of an International Financial Commission, heralding the loss of fiscal sovereignty.

The analysis of the formulation of new political forces in the shape of parties in the aftermath of the Revolution and onwards is indicative of the particularities of the modern Greek political ethos. The notion of the periphery as an interchangeable as well as unassailable reality was embraced as a feature of a self-sufficient political identity that could promote the different, often contradictory but frequently matching claims of social groups in a territory whose borders were liquid yet solid and impossible to dismiss altogether. Arguably, this model of a persistent appropriation of a peripheral identity *par excellence*, where the periphery is always fixed, but the center to which this periphery refers is perpetually in flux between different poles, is a recurring theme in modern Greek history. In that respect, the notion of periphery in the Greek context is not so much a denominator in the scheme of the dependency theory or transition from feudalism to capitalism implied in Immanuel Wallerstein's *World-Systems Analysis*, which conceives new, non-binary spheres of impact and control in a power-hierarchy dependence. The concept of the core-periphery distinction, Wallerstein notes, was itself developed as a tool of controlling through defining: "it was developed by the United Nations Economic Commission for Latin America" (11). In addition, it was based on a premise of economics: "some countries were stronger than others [the core] and were therefore able to trade on terms that allowed surplus-value to flow from the weaker countries [the peripheries] to the core" (Wallerstein 12).

Wallerstein's critique is based on the conviction that no political revolt could effectively serve as a pressure point for equal economic regulation. The paradigm of Greece in the modern age is compatible with this train of thought, revealing the complexity of the borders between economic, political, social and cultural relations, and demonstrating how the narrative of a common peripheral cultural identity functions as a unifying device that subdues inherent antinomies. Furthermore, it suggests how a paradoxical cultural role model resists framing and classification, thereby challenging the center as "a phenomenon of the realm of values and beliefs, which govern society" because "authority is thought to possess a vital relationship to the center" (Shils 3). If the center is an authoritative construction that branches out into the periphery, could establishing a cultural identity that challenges the notion of periphery as a derivative of an ultimately arbitrary center open up a perspective of autonomy? Is the peripheral an embodiment of a dualistic ontology or does it embed its counter-effect? If the foundation of modernity is accompanied by the predominance of dualism as the basic formulating schema, can the rupture of another binary model become a means of transgressing geopolitical power structures? What are the connotations of the "peripheral" in this transition from the Age of Capital to the Post-Capital Age? And how is it culturally expressed in the complex European mediasphere, "this dynamic system of complex ecosystems reorganized by and around a (single) dominant medium," the Internet (Debray 26)?[2]

A Dilemma as a Non-Binary Event

In July 2015, the Greek bailout crisis monopolized the international headlines, which were updated every other minute and which revolved around neighboring or conflicting notions of negotiation and agreement, solutions and feasibility, deadlines and alternatives, compromises and developments, credits and debt, bailouts and reforms. At the same time, domestic media in Greece followed a similar stance, while constantly reframing statements of members of the Greek parliament that made extensive use of words and concepts such as "dignity," "abominable," debt, morality and ethics. These words and concepts were linked to financial and juridical terminology, building a new discourse around the familiarity, ostensible proximity and accessibility to the "periphery," and echoing what Richard Sennett defines as the "ideology of intimacy [that] transmutes political categories into psychological categories" (259). Within this context, the periphery emerged as a site of shared articulations of social memory and culture, articulations that proceeded through difference and through the remembrance of the common "center," and that were aimed at creating an "agentic self," addressing every person within Greece's borders as an agent of historical change.

A month earlier, in June 2015, different groups of Greek citizens flooded Parliament Square in the center of Athens every other evening, in a way that resonated with the blooming period of the Occupy movement. They were making alternate claims regarding the positioning of the government in relation to the country's European peers. Two contrasting blocks were formed in these public performances of national sentiment: one concentrating movements against the memorandum, which paradoxically ran the gamut of the political spectrum, from the extreme right to the far left; the other bringing together previously apolitical currents under the umbrella of *Menoume Evropi* ("we stay in Europe"), a title all too reminiscent of television shows and popular entertainment ads. I am tempted to observe a peculiar dichotomy of Greek cultural identity and speculate on the importance of stimulating collective memory:

---

2   The French media theorist Régis Debray divides the history of Western civilization into three distinct chronological unifiers. The first is the *logosphere*, which is identified with societies before the advent of typography, the second is the *graphosphere*, where printed text imposes its rationality on the whole of the symbolic milieu, and the third is the *videosphere*, which is associated with the dawn of the Industrial Revolution.

public discourse in Greece appears to be based on either a "pro-European" or an "anti-European" rhetoric – and never on an actually *European* one.

The aforementioned tendencies culminated in the announcement of the referendum regarding the creditors' suggested austerity measures and were crystallized in a wide range of media reports and opinion articles, a selection of which is analyzed in Table 10.1 below. The table shows data collected through

TABLE 10.1 *Coverage of the referendum in domestic Greek media between 27 June and 13 July 2015.*

	Kathimerini	Ta Nea	Ethnos	Avgi	Naftemporiki
Total number of articles containing the word "referendum"	455 (100%)	742 (100%)	638 (100%)	625 (100%)	77 (100%)
Total number of articles published before the results of the referendum	210 (46.15%)	568 (76.54%)	404 (63.32%)	482 (77.12%)	41 (53.24%)
Opinion articles	101 (22.19%)	89 (11.99%)	94 (14.89%)	147 (23.52%)	10 (12.98%)
Greek delegates statements	89 (19.56%)	115 (15.49%)	98 (15.36%)	102 (16.32%)	30 (38.96%)
European delegates statements	53 (11.64%)	76 (10.24%)	69 (10.81%)	72 (11.52%)	16 (20.77%)
Republications of International Media	12 (2.63%)	9 (1.21%)	10 (1.56%)	7 (1.12%)	5 (6.49%)
Comparison to similar instances in Greek history	8 (1.75%)	3 (0.4%)	2 (0.31%)	15 (0.24%)	0
Analysis of the proposal / content of the referendum question	4 (0.87%)	3 (0.4%)	3 (0.47%)	2 (0.32%)	1 (1.29%)
Articles evaluating the EU strategy	59 (12.96%)	93 (12.53%)	82 (12.85%)	109 (17.44%)	11 (14.28%)
Articles evaluating the government strategy	84 (40.43%)	94 (12.66%)	96 (15.04%)	246 (39.36%)	8 (10.38%)

TABLE 10.1   *Coverage of the referendum in domestic Greek media between 27 June and*
            13 July 2015 (cont.)

	Kathimerini	*Ta Nea*	*Ethnos*	*Avgi*	*Naftemporiki*
Commentary on the outcome of the referendum	49 (3.95%)	46 (6.19%)	37 (5.79%)	141 (22.56%)	5 (6.49%)
Comparison to other countries in the EU (in terms of alliance / compliance)	52 (11.42%)	20 (2.69%)	11 (1.72%)	47 (7.52%)	9 (11.68%)
Overall stance YES / NO / N/A	YES	N/A	N/A	NO	N/A

the websites of the five most influential newspapers in Greece, three of them representing the biggest media corporations in Greece (*Ta Nea, Ethnos* and *Kathimerini*, the latter outspokenly critical of the Greek government formed after the elections of 25 January 2015), one officially attached to Syriza, the main party in the Syriza-ANEL government led by Alexis Tsipras (*Avgi*), and one financial newspaper (*Naftemporiki*). I collected the data over a period of two weeks, from the official announcement of the referendum on 27 June 2015 until the official contracting of an agreement between Greece and the European Union on 13 July 2015. My choice to use web sources not only affirms the Internet as the dominant media sphere, but also alludes to the issue of accessibility. In this two-week period, print newspapers in both urban centers and provincial areas were chaotically distributed, to a large extent because of the difficulties in effectuating monetary transactions after the imposition of strong capital controls recommended by the Bank of Greece and assessed by the Greek government on 28 June 2015. Moreover, the density of the events on a social and political level could only be followed by online media. Lastly, the open comment forums of these newspaper websites enabled active (and often high-pitched) discussion among Greek citizens.

The purpose of this survey was to probe the dominant discourse in the most influential domestic Greek media on the question of the position of Greece in relation to the European Union and on the issue of the position of the periphery towards a distinguishable yet remote center, addressed implicitly in the ballot and expressed through the media agenda of newspapers of similar impact, readability and circulation, but completely different political stances. I gathered the data using the keyword "referendum" as my basic filter. After aggregating the articles, I set the date of voting (5 July) as a milestone, intending to examine whether the political orientation of each newspaper would alter the extent of the coverage in view of the voting result. Surprisingly, the *Avgi* newspaper, which is openly positioned as supporting the Syriza-ANEL government, did not scale up the number of articles presenting the results as an election victory. *Kathimerini*, which is closer to the opposition, also kept the coverage at the same level.

Next, I formulated a set of different criteria by distinguishing the type of article, the general focus, the selection of sources (Greek or EU) and the way the result was evaluated. The first surprising observation of this analysis is that, despite the clear social-economic content of the question of the referendum and the financial consequences of its result, none of the monitored media focused on analyzing the proposal (even the financial newspaper *Naftemporiki* only devoted 1.29% of its coverage to content analysis). Instead, the main focus of the articles on the referendum was on questions of politics and cultural identity (with the question "do we belong to Europe?" often able to be read between the lines). Yet, by far the most interesting conclusion that is to be derived from the analysis is that, regardless of the political orientation of each newspaper, the variance of the data in each entry field is in fact rather small. This lack of big divergences implies an overall balanced positioning between the two poles of the EU and Greece, of the center and the periphery.

Most referendums are based on a binary logic of accepting or not accepting a given statement. This was also the case with the Greek referendum of 5 July 2015. Its formulation was based on the hypothesis that the "core" of the question of the referendum, regarding the terms of Greece's position in the Union and the limits of control, cooperation, and sovereignty, was expressed through the adoption of a peripheral point of view, disputing the authority of an EU decision and of its role as an administrative center. Yet, this schematization of a complex network of actors, factors and relations in a binary opposition is dissolved through a set of different associations between the European and the Greek delegation, and their role in the crisis negotiations. Despite their political predisposition, all five newspapers agree on a de-centralized image of Europe and interpolate (and therefore hybridize) the space between the opposing sides. They all emphasize the Greek policy in negotiating a "bailout" program with softer terms with EU delegates as a way of converting the dynamics within the European Union and note the importance of maintaining a distance from the centers of media attention by avoiding extensively republishing interpretations of the "Greek bailout issue" by foreign media. This possibly also explains the lack of analysis of the content of the referendum question and the absence of any historical references to comparable events in Greece's past: this periphery insists on defending itself against the center.

In the past few decades and especially in relation to the Euro crisis, the contribution of the media to the configuration of peripheral subjectivity in Greece has been crucial. Peripheries have come to be regarded as spaces for "reporting" the peripheral experience to the center. When discussing the need to defend the practice of theory and to intercept the global circulation of cultural stereotypes, Homi Bhabha brings forward the notion of cultural translation as a way of conveying "an 'interstitial' articulation that both holds together and 'comes between'" (qtd. in Mitchell 82). In the vein of Bhabha's suggestion, the peripheral subjectivity developed in the Greek context dismantles the stereotype of the European "periphery" by encouraging us to translate the bipole "center-periphery" as interstitial. Similarly, Ross Chambers defines the peripheral subject as one who "not only reports on life at the margins for the benefit of those who inhabit the center," but who "is also in an excellent position to acquire a relativized knowledge of life at the centre of things ... and to report ... on the deficiencies of that life, which are of course those of self-enclosure, blindness, and the exclusions and marginalization – the ignorance of the other that these give rise to" (61). In this sense, the alleged danger of creating "peripheries" in the "central" parts of Europe[3] reveals itself as harboring an open and valuable potential for creating knowledge through interstitiality.

Reading Chambers's theory together with Stuart Hall's "What's the Culture in Multiculturalism? What's the Difference of Identities?" further illuminates how the notion of the periphery is exploited in the context of public life in Greece. At the beginning of his article, Hall states that it is "written from a position basically sympathetic to the claim that modern identities are being de-centred" (274). Moreover, in his three-fold schema tracing the development from the enlightenment to the sociological to the post-modern subject, the main ontological question is related to the nature of the subject's "core," to its existence or disappearance. The enlightenment subject was entitled to the potentials of free reasoning and action, and maintained an inner, solid core. However, in becoming sociological, the subject reflected the growing complexity of the modern world and the awareness that this inner core was not autonomous and self-sufficient, but formed in relation to "significant others" (peripheries) that functioned as mediators of values, meanings and symbols. In that sense, Hall describes identity as a process of constant de-centralization and hybridization within volatile borders. With the transition

---

3   http://www.cnbc.com/2014/10/21/are-these-countries-the-new-periphery-in-europe.html.

to the post-modern subject, this otherness is conceptualized entirely as a periphery, as a Hemingwayesque "moveable feast,"[4] continuously formed and transformed in relation to the ways in which we are represented or addressed by the cultural systems surrounding us. The peripheral subject manifests as a transit identity between stages of transformation, persistently pushing the borderlines between them.

During two crucial weeks in the recent political history of Greece, domestic Greek media captured a significant twist in the (self)realization of contemporary Greek cultural identity, crystallizing this transit from a fixed set of certainties with a consistent center to a process in flux. The data I gathered imply that, despite the polarization, public discourse in Greece translated the perspective of (another) dichotomy into a vital questioning of the "center" and its deficiencies from the vantage point of the periphery.

Peripheral Conclusions

Peripheral vision, taken literally, is weak in humans, as opposed to in many other living beings. However, humans are trained to practice their peripheral vision when central vision becomes weaker, such as in conditions of absolute darkness, when different receptor cells are called to take up the mission of the reinforcement of movement. In the bleakness of times of economic crisis and political turbulence, arguably not only central vision is hindered, but also the capacity of the human gaze to distinguish forms and draw connections between visual stimuli off-center. A careful look at the representation of the most recent installment of the Greek bailout crisis in domestic media challenges the appropriateness of a classical reading of international relations according to a center-periphery model, as it indicates that the priority in Greek public discourse was not the maintenance of a fixed binary schema, but the quest for a cultural identity that is necessarily constantly negotiated and re-negotiated in terms of geography, economy and history (i.e. in terms of space and time).

In this text, I have tried to shed light on an off-center space by linking quantitative data to a cultural interpretation of the "periphery." Different conceptualizations of the term "periphery" across the disciplines (from mathematics to optics, from linguistics to sociology, but mostly in the field of

---

4 *A Moveable Feast* is the title of the memoir Hemingway wrote when he was living in Paris in the 1920s. In it, he describes his experiences as an expat far from his central cultural reference system.

cultural studies and the work of Ross Chambers and Stuart Hall) offer valuable insight into the possibility of imagining a periphery in a dynamic relation to a center. The peripheral subject in Greece relates itself to shifting centers and reminds us of the uncanny recurrence of historical circumstances, even as recent Greek history is undervalued in public discourse. In lieu of the mathematical calculation of remedies against public debt (austerity), tracing the notion of the periphery to the field of mathematics suggests that the costly credit of the European debt crisis could give birth to the wandering peripheral subject, roaming through the standardized borders and limitations of the allocated European territory and bearing the responsibility of reporting on the nature of the borders and the qualities of the surface of this entity, without forgetting the need to struggle in order to measure its depths.

Works Cited

Andreades, Andreas. "The Currant Crisis in Greece." *The Economic Journal* 16.61 (1906): 41–51.

Chambers, Ross. *Loiterature*. Lincoln: U of Nebraska P, 1999.

Clogg, Richard. *A Concise History of Greece.* 1992. Cambridge: Cambridge UP, 2013.

Debray, Régis. *Media Manifestos: On the Technological Transmission of Cultural Forms.* Trans. Eric Rauth. London and New York: Verso, 1996.

Hall, Stuart. "What's the Culture in Multiculturalism? What's the Difference of Identities?" *Modernity and Its Futures: Understanding Modern Societies, Book IV.* Ed. Stuart Hall, David Held and Tony McGrew. London: Polity Press, 1992. 273–316.

Hemingway, Ernest. *A Moveable Feast.* 1964. New York: Scribbler, 2010.

Hobsbawm, Eric. *The Age of Capital, 1848–1875.* London: Abacus, 1975.

Koliopoulos, John S., and Thanos M. Veremis. *Modern Greece: A History since 1821.* Hoboken: Wiley-Blackwell, 2010.

Mitchell, W.J.T. "Translator Translated (Interview with Cultural Theorist Homi Bhabha)." *Artforum* 33.7 (1995): 80–84.

Nemes-Nagy, József, Pál Szabó, and Nándor Németh. "Centre-Periphery Relations on the European Periphery: The Case of Hungary." Conference Paper. Entre Espace Schengen et Élargissement à l'Est: Les Récompositions Territoriales de l'Union Européenne. CEGUM – Université de Metz, France, 17–19 Jun. 2002.

Petmezas, Socrates D. "From Privileged Outcasts to Power Players: The 'Romantic' Redefinition of the Hellenic Nation in the Mid-Nineteenth Century." *The Making of Modern Greece.* Ed. David Ricks and Roderick Beaton. Farnham: Ashgate, 2009. 123–36.

Sennett, Richard. *The Fall of Public Man.* 1977. London: Penguin, 2002.

Shils, Edward. *Center and Periphery: Essays in Macrosociology, Selected Papers of Edward Shils, II.* Chicago: U of Chicago P, 1975.

Skrebtsova, Tatyana. "The Concepts 'Centre' and 'Periphery' in the History of Linguistics: From Field Theory to Modern Cognitivism." *Respectus Philologicus* 26.31 (2014): 144–51.

Wallerstein, Immanuel. *World System Analysis: An Introduction.* Durham: Duke UP, 2004.

PART 4

Peripheral Aesthetics

∵

CHAPTER 11

Remains to be Un/Seen: Envisioning the Disappeared in Willie Doherty's *Ancient Ground* and Patricio Guzmán's *Nostalgia for the Light*

Paula Blair

> Between what is visible and what is intelligible there is a missing link, a specific type of interest capable of ensuring a suitable relationship between the seen and the unseen, the known and the unknown, the expected and the unexpected; and also of adjusting the relationship of distance and proximity between stage and auditorium.
>
> RANCIÈRE 2007: 112–3

The Atacama Desert in Northern Chile is marketed to Anglophone holiday-makers as a "haven," an "unspoilt environment" and "a place of tremendous natural beauty" (www.atacamadesert.co.uk). The peat bogs in County Donegal, Republic of Ireland, are similarly described as "a symbol of hope and success" (www.gleanncholmcille.ie).[1] These sparsely populated rural sites, which until the late twentieth century were primarily locations for scientific discovery and extracting natural resources, are becoming popularized and thus more central by the tourism drives afforded by neo-liberalism. In the past, however, the Atacama and the borderland Irish peat bogs were not only geographically peripheral to the centrality of populated urban spaces; during times of political violence in the 1970s and 1980s, these now touristic beauty spots were implemented as exclusion zones harboring the insidious secrets of troubled pasts. In these cases, therefore, tourism, or the process of centering the peripheral, can facilitate the forgetting or whitewashing of uncomfortable truths. This chapter examines cultural outputs that draw attention to the spectral psychic legacies of these sites, specifically the "disappeared" of General Augusto Pinochet's regime in Chile (1973–1990), and of the Northern Ireland conflict (1969–1998), thought to be buried in the desert and bogs. Chilean filmmaker Patricio Guzmán's personal documentary *Nostalgia for the Light* [*Nostalgia de la luz*] (2010) and Northern Irish artist Willie Doherty's video installation *Ancient Ground* (2011)

---

1   Notably, the Gleann Cholm Cille bogs are distinguished as "a place apart," a term which carries negative connotations when applied to the conflicted UK region of Northern Ireland as it denotes a place peripheral to both Irish and British politics and national identities.

pose a resistance to systems of official forgetting by using their respective media platforms to centralize marginal themes, people and spaces. Working in forms peripheral to dominant, mainstream moving image production, these filmmakers show how modes such as the essay film and the video installation can be used to highlight the trace remains of memories that trouble official histories and to facilitate the wider recognition of peripheral issues relating to conflict that fester unresolved in post-conflict societies.

Nostalgia for the Light and *Ancient Ground* have high production values, but the forms of critique that emerge from these works uphold the transgressive impetus of Third Cinema (a form of revolutionary filmmaking originating in Latin America) and early video art in the 1960s, both designed to "activate" spectators to engage critically with the world around them. While the films' audiences are not substantial, they are global, and perhaps attracted by the works' high-quality photography married with the scenic locations they feature. In centering marginalized spaces and issues, the works ensure that difficult pasts and truths are not buried along with the missing, while their circulation further expands a global network of shared traumatic experiences. As such, these works contribute to an alternative form of globalization in which what is traditionally peripheral in terms of location, social status, media practice and commercial enterprise can connect globally, in part by emulating the techniques of the corresponding centers. Given its global dominance, Hollywood's systems, conventions and economics are the center in relation to which art cinemas, documentary and national/regional cinemas beyond North America are generally peripheral. *Nostalgia for the Light* and *Ancient Ground* present multiple layers in their peripherality: their modes lack commerciality; they are examples of national/regional cultural production only exhibited in specialist circumstances, which are relatively under-examined in academia; and they deal with a topic involving minor groups that are often met with denial and exclusion.

The problem of the disappeared lingering in many post-conflict and post-dictatorship countries is particularly distinctive in that the nature of the disappearances means that it is relatively easy for state authorities working in conjunction with mass media to suppress both official historical accounts and the personal testimonies of families and survivors. The assumed reasons behind why an individual was disappeared are often linked with informing or demonstrating resistance to oppression, meaning that public references to the disappeared tend to be met with denial and social exclusion. Moreover, as Teresa Meade explains, most survivors are simply too traumatized to communicate the extreme torture they experienced and to which they were forced to bear witness (134–5). It is the arts where the most substantial accounts seem to emerge, given the ability of documentary and fact-based fiction to tread the precarious line between evidence and testimony. As practitioners, Guzmán (b. 1941) and Doherty (b. 1959) have been establishing a gaze on behalf of the socio-political periphery which can be turned back on the center in their respective home regions. In drawing their works together, I identify the possibilities that arise when common sociocultural themes and issues connect across space and time. The affinity drawn here between Chile and Northern Ireland is a starting point in illustrating how marginal issues in peripheral places or situations can form synergies beyond the dominance of globalizing capitalist systems. This is mirrored by practitioners working against the tide of populist commercial media supplying a consumer demand that apparently stems from freedom of choice, but is in fact engineered to maintain depoliticized passivity (McChesney 111–3). In shedding light on the subtle form of globalization developing through the circulation of connective experiences, this chapter points towards the broader significance of the arts and humanities in transcending borders to contribute to conflict transformation and transitional justice. These works and their critical analysis promote space – including global pockets of connected spaces – for the long overdue dialogue and intervention needed to enable social change.

The Disappeared and Post-Conflict Northern Ireland

Doherty's eight-minute video installation *Ancient Ground* is a conceptual audio-visual poem comprised of a series of views of rural pathways and bog marshes framed in different proximities and filmed in different focal lengths using high-definition telephoto lenses that carefully scrutinize the surface of the Donegal landscape. On the soundtrack, a woman's voice describing acts of searching conjures further images of what may lie concealed beneath the seemingly unspoiled surface. As the sequence progresses, however, the images increasingly reveal past human interactions with this place: the tarmac path (figure 11.1), sodden ditches, an abandoned car door, netted piles of peat blocks (figure 11.2). The unidentified disembodied voice is soft and melancholic with a grain indicating age as she lists feelings and objects related to what can be understood as a body she is looking for, apparently buried in the peatland. In the form of a minimal poetic testimonial, she claims to walk the same paths every day, hoping to see shifts in a landscape that has taken millennia to form, which would reveal what has been hidden. As she speaks, the shots reveal surface details and the lighting illuminates the muddy depths of the bog water. In close-ups coinciding with her descriptions of "looking for a sign," the texture of weathered rocks half exposed on the surface is photographed in haptic detail while the grass in the back, sides and immediate foreground of the frame appears in varying degrees of soft and blurred focus. The images slowly change between different characteristics of the bog (soil, moss, grasses, mud, pools, rocks, roots, insects, flowers, and so on), and without the voice-over narration could easily be mistaken for a slide set of nature photography. The shots are indeed moving images, but collapse the boundary between stillness and movement. For example, in a later shot of the sedimentary layers in the exposed ridges where peat cutting has taken place, the focus is pulled and shifts between the details of roots and grains at different proximities to the camera's probing gaze. Performing these changes to the focus in the cinematography and editing reflects how the viewer of any lens-based work is at the mercy of externally controlled shifts in vision and perception. The detail in the focus and the downwards tilt in many of the shots also give a sense of a careful and intimate vigil from a subjective point of view, as if the scene is viewed through this woman's eyes during her daily search.

The monologue evokes issues known to have affected the families of those disappeared during the Northern Ireland conflict, which are aligned with the passing of time: "The seasons. The passing years. The whispers. The shame. The punishment. Beyond words" (Doherty 54–5). An almost ekphrastic allusion to Seamus Heaney's bog poems, particularly the graphic "The Grauballe Man" (1975), emerges when the woman utters, in conjunction with images of dank surface water and the ridged cuttings: "Hooded. Bound. Weighted down.

FIGURE 11.1 *Pathway,* Ancient Ground.
REPRODUCED WITH PERMISSION OF THE ARTIST.

FIGURE 11.2 *Peat cutting,* Ancient Ground.
REPRODUCED WITH PERMISSION OF THE ARTIST.

Discarded. Unmarked. The callousness" (Doherty 58–60).[2] Given the Heaney connection, these terms evoke the ancient preserved bog bodies often found bound, hooded, weighted and buried with no shrouding, ceremony or possessions other than the clothes they wore, which were also largely preserved by the bog. The callousness of the unmarked graves indicates that this burial method was reserved for wrongdoers. The practice was revived during the Northern Ireland conflict as punishment for suspected transgressors and informers, or served as a warning to others to comply or face the consequences.

In the 1970s, the Provisional Irish Republican Army (IRA) kidnapped, murdered and secretly buried suspected informers. Most known victims were from Catholic/nationalist areas and the IRA has claimed responsibility in most of these cases, releasing only vague details of burial sites. This has led to extensive and only partially successful digs since 1999. Out of at least sixteen known bodies, six remain missing.[3] The ten that have been found and identified were

2   The title *Ancient Ground* is mindful of Heaney's *Opened Ground* anthology in which many of
    his bog poems are reprinted. Explicitly, they depict the preserved remains found buried in
    bog marshes across Europe of people who, centuries before, had been executed for a transgression. In 1970s Northern Ireland, the bog's powers of preservation became a significant
    symbol. In the post-conflict period, notions of dumped bodies, burials and traces of violence
    scarring the landscape recur persistently in Doherty's work, indicating how little resolution
    there has been regarding victimhood in the conflict.
3   On 25 June 2015, the remains of at least two bodies were found in a bog land in Meath, a
    border county in the Republic of Ireland. It is believed these are the bodies of Séamus Wright

discovered on the liminal spaces/landscapes of beaches, peat bogs and fields, largely in areas along the border between Northern Ireland and the Republic of Ireland, that is, the geopolitical frontier between the UK and Ireland, which also splits the province of Ulster. Given the rumors about informing, often professed by the IRA, the families have been met with denial and shame within their own communities. It was only with the ceasefires in 1994 that space began to slowly open up for them to confront what had happened and to ask for answers, but this still often led to their social exclusion (Dawson 75–6). In *Ancient Ground*, the frustration of endless concealment and waiting emerges clearly in the aged voice reciting the sparse lines as close-ups of muddy water are penetrated until the darkness reveals no more: "The small details. Half remembered. The dank smell. The forgetting. The regret. The silence" (Doherty 73–4). Some wider shots reveal the overcast grey sky as the stillness of the scene reflects the lack of development in this woman's burden year by year. Here, the loop feature of the installation becomes a politicized aesthetic feature in that it reflects the repetitiveness of this endless, unchanging cycle and the stagnant conditions of the situation. Her closing words, "the silence," implicate the spectator, and speak directly to the networked political, social and media establishments' complicity in maintaining the air of silence hanging over these disappearances.

The Disappeared and Post-Dictatorship Chile

A similar silence burdens many citizens of post-dictatorship Chile. Upon first glance, Patricio Guzmán's documentary *Nostalgia for the Light* is a personal account of the director's lifelong interest in astronomy. However, according to Patrick Blaine, the film "constitutes the most complete attempt in any medium to document Chilean national life before, during, and after the Pinochet dictatorship" (114). Guzmán's ninety-minute film, produced by his partner Renate Sachse, is a complex meditation on memory, time and the cosmos, used to explore multiple levels of metaphor for absent presence as denoted by the trace. This all takes place under the stark clarity of the skies over the Atacama Desert, where ancient civilizations left thousands of geoglyphs (works of art made by arranging stones or earth), which remain largely preserved in the otherwise barren and arid landscape. The meanings of these markings have long since been lost and they are now merely self-referential abstract traces

---

and Kevin McKee, who were disappeared by the IRA in 1972. At the time of writing, forensic testing to confirm their identities is taking place.

indicating that this activity happened at all. The film's rumination on the distant past also includes mummies that pre-date the European discovery and colonization of the Americas, the preservation of which bears similarities with the bog bodies implied in Doherty's *Ancient Ground.*

The film's introduction consists of Guzmán's voice-over narrating a personal account of his childhood interest in astronomy, noting that at the same time as "a revolutionary tide swept [Chile] to the centre of the world ... science fell in love with the Chilean sky." At 10,000 feet above sea level, the Atacama is the driest desert on Earth and boasts some of the clearest skies and greatest visibility of the stars, making it a huge draw for astronomers who search the heavens using the world's most powerful telescopes. They discover stars that are long dead, but the traces of which remain visible as their light takes millennia to reach Earth. The starlight, thus, is a visible trace of something no longer there, no longer alive, of what was and is no more. Deepening this symbolism, the film also reveals the women searching the Atacama for traces of loved ones who were among the three thousand disappeared during Pinochet's regime. It follows them as they excavate the dehumanizing mass graves where the remains lie in an attempt to find the tiniest fragments of bodies or possessions. The tension between extremes of in/visibility is threaded throughout the film, as are traces of the ancient indigenous civilizations highlighting the gaps between the known and the unknown, the mysteries of the ancient past and the secrets of a difficult present.

When asked by Guzmán what he thinks of the women searching the desert, astronomer Gaspar Galaz voices his concern at the reticence of a society that understands astronomers much more than people trying to find their dead. He says that in a way their quests are similar, except that he and his colleagues are untroubled by their excavations of the sky. It transpires in the film that the calcium that falls to Earth from space is identical to that which formulates our bones. The discoveries made about the elements of the universe are thus paralleled by the women combing the desert for bone fragments. They are investigating the mysteries of the past in space, connected at a fundamental level to the mysteries of the present by the very elements that make all of us who we are. While a Steadicam, in a full shot, follows one of the women carrying a spade and crunching along the desert in glaring sunlight (figure 11.3), Guzmán's voiceover explains that, to avoid the bodies ever being found, "the dictatorship dug them up and disposed of the remains elsewhere or threw them in the sea." The sense of this misdirection pervades the rest of the sequence. The woman stops and the camera catches up with her, remaining behind to her left side and watching as she scans the landscape. A cut to a static wide angle shot with a long depth of field shows another woman as a tiny speck moving across the plain in the central horizontal axis of the frame. Her body is engulfed by the rocky plain in the foreground, the arid hills in the distance and the cloudless azure sky filling the top half of the frame, as the wind is heard blowing steadily across the expanse (figure 11.4). The sequence visualizes Galaz's comparison of the Atacama to the vastness of space and demonstrates the futility of the women's search with poignant efficacy. Guzmán's narration deepens this by explaining the stretches of time the women of Calama have spent searching. Many searched for twenty-eight years until 2002, but since then only a few have continued. As is the case in Ireland, traces and fragments of bodies are still being found, and several of the now elderly women have devoted their lives to not giving up hope.

In the same sequence, Guzmán explains that, during filming, the body of a disappeared female prisoner was uncovered in another part of the desert. In the detail that the woman in *Ancient Ground* yearns for, Guzmán's camera probes the surface of the dig to show the ghostly yet all too real fingertip and nail emerging out of the compacted sand. It is photographed in the center of the frame in such clarity that the lines of the fingerprints are displayed, showing the extent of the preservation (figure 11.5). This shot is followed by two more brief stills taken as the body was uncovered. The first shows the feet, still wearing sandals, their position indicating that she was buried face down and uncovered. The second shows her shriveled hands crossed at her outstretched wrists protruding from what appears to be sacking cloth. Notably, the spectacle of showing the body in full is avoided. The three emotive close-ups ending the searching

FIGURE 11.3 *The search,* Nostalgia for the Light.
REPRODUCED WITH PERMISSION OF THE ARTIST.

FIGURE 11.4 *The Atacama Desert,* Nostalgia for the Light.
REPRODUCED WITH PERMISSION OF THE ARTIST.

FIGURE 11.5 *Preserved remains,* Nostalgia for the Light.
REPRODUCED WITH PERMISSION OF THE ARTIST.

sequence communicate both the gravity of the situation and the women's reasons for continued hope.

Two of the women are interviewed at length, both delivering moving and difficult testimonies. Vicky Saavedra relates her memories of receiving fragments of her brother José Saavedra González, including his foot still in shoe and sock, and how for her this was a reunion. At the time of filming, Violetta

Berríos had found no trace of the person she was looking for, but was determined to keep searching for as long as she can. She was told by the authorities that the bodies were excavated, bagged and dumped in the sea, but she questions this, declaring: "At this point in my life, I'm 70, I find it hard to believe what I'm told. They taught me not to believe." She talks of the struggle to keep going, but says she and Vicky pick themselves up every day and return to the desert more hopeful than the day before, "and more impatient to find them." Her pain and desperation are clear, but so is her formidable strength. These are women who refuse to be victims, who simply want rightful burials for their dead.

At once hidden beyond vision and gone without trace, the physical disappearances are mirrored by processes of state-sanctioned forgetting. The dissolving of all evidence of what had existed causes a loss of meaning and connection over time, just as is the case with the geoglyphs on the landscape and the stars in the sky. The geoglyphs and stars embody a fissure between states of being visible and invisible: the geoglyphs can be seen, but what is seen is inaccessible; and the stars must be probed with technologies that expand vision in order to be understood. This lack of communicability reverberates through the experience of loss through disappearance. In contrast to the women's need for figurative light to be shed on the desert, the astronomers gaze at objects that cannot be discerned with the naked eye in daylight. It is the darkness of night and the vastness of space that facilitates astronomical discoveries, while the shroud of secrecy and denial continues to hide the disappeared bodies.

Alternative Globalization in the Margins

The sensitive issue of the disappeared of Pinochet's regime is easily cast to the nation's social, cultural and political peripheries, lest the current economic stability and prosperity of neo-liberal Chile be disrupted. Today, Chile leads Latin American nations in human development, competitiveness and income per capita. On the surface, it is in a state of peace with economic freedom enjoyed by the majority, although its indigenous populations continue to experience social, economic, cultural and political exclusion alongside those who have suffered directly from Chile's recent torturous past. Patricio Guzmán's personal history intersects with the events that have transpired there since the 1970s. As a political filmmaker from the outset, Guzmán's career has played out on the far reaches of the margins of populist commercial production and distribution. Notably, though, the circulation of his work has been dependent on networks he formed in Europe, and indeed on his own exile there since the 1973 military coup d'état.

In 1970, while Guzmán was studying film in Madrid, Salvador Allende was elected president of Chile. The allure of a Marxist head of state was too compelling for him to stay abroad, so he returned to Santiago. As part of a likeminded group, he filmed the revolution happening in conjunction with Allende's governance, initiating a life-long filmmaking career centered on political inquiry. His crew on *The First Year* [*Primer año*] (1972) was young and the equipment modest, filming on 16 mm black and white film. They were disorganized but enthusiastic, as emerges in the film's positive propaganda about social change across the provinces of Chile. When finished, it was transferred to 35 mm in Buenos Aires. In France, renowned Left Bank filmmaker Chris Marker heard about the work and this opened up Europe to Guzmán. He took the negative and soundtrack to Paris, where it was redubbed in French. The voices were provided by popular actors as a favor to their friend Marker, which drew in Francophone audiences to see it and led to the film winning European film festival awards. This transatlantic connection was fundamental in ensuring the circulation of Guzmán's continuing work as events in Chile took a dramatic turn following the coup (Guzmán).

Guzmán was targeted and the negatives of his early films were destroyed by the military as Chile's history underwent revision. Guzmán felt compelled to film the events, but his access to equipment was severed. In 1974, Guzmán's cinematographer Jorge Müller Silva and his partner were among the thousands who were disappeared by Pinochet's regime. Guzmán wrote to Marker about the severity of the situation and soon received a package containing high-quality film stock. For the first time, he could record with synchronized sound, which made the spontaneous filming of the events appear more real and urgent (Guzmán). With all this happening during the epoch of *cinéma vérité* in Europe, Direct Cinema in North America and Third Cinema in Cuba and Argentina, Guzmán not only joined the political revolution in Chile in resistance to the dictatorship, but also participated in radical shifts in global independent documentary production, which more than ever directly intersected with everyday life.

In filming what would become *The Battle of Chile* [*La batalla de Chile*] (1975–79), Guzmán had to learn fast how to work economically within constrictions (the crew posed as a French news team) and how to select the most indicative examples of the events that unfolded. What was needed was a robust theoretical framework to focus the filming and a sense of chronology. The result had to be distinctive from state-controlled news broadcasting and propaganda. The crew was able to film every day while conserving the limited supplies provided by Marker (Guzmán). As a result, *The Battle of Chile* reveals invisible truths, providing evidence for the atrocities committed by Pinochet's government and his concealment of the detrimental impact that his about-turn renationalization schemes had on miners and factory workers. It was also the film that forced Guzmán into exile. He moved back to Francoist Spain in 1973 and edited the film with the help of the Cuban Cinematography Institute in 1974. *Chile, the Obstinate Memory* [*Chile, la memoria obstinada*] (Guzmán, 1997) depicts Guzmán's return from exile to screen *The Battle of Chile*, which had been banned under the dictatorship. *Chile, the Obstinate Memory* places the testimonies of people's lived experiences of the regime in dialogue with the young people of the postmemory generation, who, through the facilitation made possible by the screenings, began to learn about the violence being cleansed out of history, including the more than three thousand dead and disappeared.

Unlike the coverage of Northern Ireland's disappeared, which is beginning to emerge in mainstream media as described below, to date, *Nostalgia for the Light* has not received a theatrical release in Chile and has only ever been shown on television during the night (Guzmán).[4] In addition, apart from brief availability on the SKY satellite company's pay-per-view service around 1999–2000, *The Battle of Chile* has also rarely been screened there. Thomas Miller Klubock points out that it took the intervention of a multinational corporation that has played a significant role in the globalization of telecommunications services to screen such films – that is, through their commodification, and only to a limited number of households. He states: "In Chile's neo-liberal democracy, memory and history are subject no longer to the censorship of military dictatorship; today they are commodities contingent on the vicissitudes of the market and decisions made by multinational corporations" (Klubock 279). Whereas Pinochet's government actively diminished press freedom of speech, subsequent democratically elected governments have sustained a passive silence concerning the past. Although the torture and disappearances were acknowledged by the left-wing *Concertación* government (the Coalition of Parties for Democracy, in power 1990–2010), for example, its refusal "to press for reparations or to hold the military responsible for human rights violations, allow[ed] them to govern without confrontation" (Meade 136). This suggests that access to unofficial histories is only available to those willing and able to pay for it. The more radical arts may find ways of ensuring that the ghosts of the past will not die, but they remain reliant on global distribution and screening networks to maintain the presentness of the past.

---

4   Even when it was televised in the UK, the usually progressive Film4 screened it late at night and ran minimal advertising for this internationally acclaimed, award-winning film.

An example of how the persistence of the more niche arts can pressure mainstream media into acknowledging marginalized issues emerges in the Northern Irish context. On 4 November 2013, a co-produced documentary on the disappeared aired on BBC1 Northern Ireland and RTÉ in the Republic of Ireland. Its director, Alison Miller, has made many television documentaries that mine marginal stories in Northern Irish society and culture, indicating that there is interest in accessing lesser known issues more generally amongst filmmakers and audiences alike. "The Disappeared" includes testimonies from the victims' families, some members of which were speaking publicly for the first time. It took four decades for this sensitive topic to be given any real airtime on mainstream regional – not national – television.[5] Given the novels, poems, paintings, music, photography, video art, plays, community arts and even experimental operas that have kept the issue present to some degree, the break in silence in mainstream mass media was inevitable. In this more mainstream appearance, the significance of the arts confronting this issue is evident in the program's inclusion of excerpts from Heaney's bog poems. Like Heaney, Doherty is another artist who has become high profile due to critical acclaim and the prize culture in the art world. In a similar way to Heaney's, too, important messages that society and politics in Northern Ireland remain reluctant to confront lie beneath the fine art veneer of Doherty's works.

A uniting factor between Guzmán and Doherty is that despite their political messages, they do not make work expressly for didactic purposes. Rather, the issues are there to be teased out by what Rancière would describe as the "emancipated spectator" who is prepared to engage critically with the form and content. The sparse poetic language in the voice-over monologue in *Ancient Ground* evokes ghost stories deriving from Irish traditions of oral storytelling, and establishes a link to another kind of disappearance, namely the mass loss of population during the Irish potato famine in the mid-nineteenth century. These cultural codes are mapped onto images that at first glance look like idyllic picture postcards, a method which allows such sensitive topics to overcome the implicit silencing of free speech by either the state or paramilitary organizations. In both contexts, the authorities maintain an air of silence, waiting for victims and survivors to die so the problem will die with them. In defiance of

---

5   However, cable providers in the UK tend to supply customers with the regional versions of mainstream channels such as BBC1 and BBC2. Together with the channels' online catch-up services, it is possible that the program achieved a wider reach than the limited viewership in small and relatively sparsely populated Ireland and Northern Ireland. There was little social media activity beyond these regions to support this, though. A quantitative study would need to be conducted to provide certainty.

dominant discourses, works such as *Nostalgia for the Light* and *Ancient Ground* hold these individuals and their stories in posterity; they remain as spectral, visible, circulating presences, the distribution of which is at once hindered and facilitated by their marginal, non-commercial modalities.

Many of Doherty's video installations can be read as critiques of media representations of events and of general problems with mediated versions of memory and history. He is drawn to the shared cinematic experience of being in a desensitized room, and his use of film language plays with the generic aesthetic codes of horror and thriller fiction. This is reflected in his exhibition techniques; his moving image work is always screened in a blackened, muted space lit only by the screen, with the viewer having to blindly turn at least one corner to enter the space. He consistently plays with vision and enforced lack of vision; often, what is seen onscreen merely draws attention to that which viewers are prevented from seeing, situated beyond what seems to be revealed, or at least implied, in the frame. In drawing out performative acts that deny the passive spectatorship found in commercial cinema, viewers are also invited to question the recalcitrant political authorities that ultimately control the field of vision to which the public has access. This is the manifestation of my earlier claim that Doherty has constructed a gaze which returns and disrupts that of the controlling center; in adopting some of the methods of the center, his installations give the viewer an opportunity to see peripheral issues through alternative frames, and to open up a path of vision back to the center. It is the critical, active viewer who will see beyond the protective idyllic veneer of a work such as *Ancient Ground* and become aware of those denied social justice.

As an established and successful international fine artist in the 2000s, Doherty has been able to acquire crews and increasingly better quality equipment to make his work, and, as is the case with *Ancient Ground*, tends to use 35 mm film (now rare in the film industry and reclaimed by artists) transferred to HDCAM. Just as the video grain reflected the spontaneity and closed-circuit feel of covert surveillance in earlier pieces such as *Blackspot* (1997), the high definition camera and high-key lighting arrangements in *Ancient Ground* capture durational shots of the landscape in all proximities with nuanced focal depths to scrutinize the objects in the frame in forensic detail. The aesthetic effects of both techniques draw attention to what is not in frame that perhaps ought to be. In the earlier surveillance-themed work, this would be an authoritative search for transgressive behavior. In *Ancient Ground*, the searcher represented by the ageing woman's poetic monologue and the more subjective cinematography is indicative of the families' hope that shifts in the – political as well as physical – landscape will reveal the remains of the supposed transgressors (figure 11.6).

FIGURE 11.6 *Ditch,* Ancient Ground.
REPRODUCED WITH PERMISSION OF THE ARTIST.

Doherty's video works may now have high production values which afford the intense scrutiny of the landscape seen in *Ancient Ground*, but in terms of equipment and production had more modest beginnings in the 1990s. Even still, his first foray into video, the two-channel *The Only Good One Is A Dead One* (1993) was nominated for the 1994 Turner Prize, a prestigious award for contemporary artists living and working in the UK. Although today the video form experiences increasing recognition as a fine art that places it at a far remove from its counter-cultural beginnings in the 1960s, it is still mainly accessed by niche gallery audiences. *Ancient Ground* is an example of high-end production in video afforded by Doherty's international acclaim as a video artist, photographer and educator. Although his body of work is substantial and many solo exhibitions and publications have been dedicated to it, his videos and photography are often merely footnotes, if acknowledged at all, in contemporary arts scholarship beyond Ireland. Chilean documentary is also under-acknowledged in international film studies, with Guzmán, again, appearing as a minor reference to exemplify the nation's output in documentary texts with an international focus.[6] He is discussed more (but still much less than his French counterparts) in scholarship concerning the essay film, which is defined by Paul Arthur as "a meeting ground for documentary, avant-garde, and art film impulses" (62).

---

6   A rare instance when Guzmán and Chile are referenced in global documentary scholarship occurs in Ana Amado and Maria Dora Mourão's "Images from the South: Contemporary Documentary in Argentina and Brazil."

The subjective, do-it-yourself, personal intellectualism, set against the transnational production backdrop which can further characterize this mode, sets the essay film apart from other forms of non-fiction filmmaking and it is also largely accessed by specialist viewers only.

While the city symphony, *cinéma vérité* and the archive compilation are widely divergent forms, they are all clearly identifiable as documentary, and films associated with these modes are firmly part of the documentary canon. Given the essay film's ability to marry objective nonfiction with self-reflective/reflexive poetic avant-garde approaches to cinema, it is hard to label this method beyond articulating a sense of the personal as the political. A convergence with video art takes place in that many gallery films take the essay form, such as, for example, the installation practices of Chris Marker and Jean-Luc Godard. Video art in particular generally experiences cycles of financing, distribution and marketing different to feature-length films of any kind. Taking mainstream film industries such as Hollywood as the center, independent video production and experimental forms of documentary both operate on the margins of moving image production more broadly. Yet many individual works, including the films under discussion, are circulated worldwide and often depend on international support to fund and facilitate their production and exhibition. While this peripheral yet global network may find collaborative, transnational ways in which to operate, a problem arises when negotiating between producing a marketable product and dealing with traumatic issues with sufficient sensitivity to those affected.

The Ethics of Dealing with Marginalized Pasts

The ethical dimensions of dealing with the pain of others are much debated in trauma and memory studies, and artistic engagements with sensitive issues do risk reducing them to aestheticized images. Both films discussed here find a balance between aesthetic production value and facilitating the release of testimony, the delivery of which creates the potential to generate affective connections and to extend the live archives of unofficial attempts to attain social justice and conflict resolution. *Ancient Ground* and *Nostalgia for the Light* are visually rich works internationally marketable as fine art and a documentary masterpiece, respectively. Doherty's video was first screened alongside an accompanying photographic series and some older work in the *Disturbance* exhibition at Dublin's Hugh Lane Gallery in 2011. Many of the photographs featured traces of unnatural human interference with the bogs, including the ditches where peat has been extracted for fuel and the red door of a car becoming consumed by the grass growing through it. The latter image invokes similar scenes in Doherty's earlier photographic works, such as *Border Incident* (1994), featuring a burnt-out car highlighting the ambiguity between images of "ordinary" criminal activity and paramilitary signs of control along Northern Ireland's border with the Republic of Ireland. These ambiguities transfer a responsibility to construct meaning onto the viewer, testing our pre-conditioned assumptions based on how news media and generic fictions frame such images. This onus on viewers to negotiate between different viewpoints and to actively determine meaning, then, includes an ethical responsibility for their response to the issues the works present and to how they present them.

In both works under discussion, the women giving testimony make a verbal or physical allusion to there being no words for how their situation affects them. The danger here is that this failure of language has facilitated and sustained the success of statewide silence. However, while these works do not claim to directly represent the feelings or experiences of this kind of pain, their aesthetics and the performative acts of telling they present do communicate a sense of what spoken language fails to, particularly in terms of marginalized or peripheral vision. In showing what should not be shown and in drawing attention to the authorities' acts of whitewashing, they indeed say what should not or cannot be said. Thus, these works confront their sensitive subject matter with integrity. At the same time, it should be recognized that it is Guzmán's and Doherty's eventual success as award-winning internationally distinguished artists that allows them to continue working in more niche fields; to explore their at once intellectual, political and emotional curiosities about their home regions; and to provide interstitial, global platforms to communicate the incommunicable.

Although it is a concern for Doherty that his practice is more easily marketed at home and abroad as Irish landscape art, the way this traditionalism masks sensitive socio-political issues allows him to creatively avoid pressure or censorship from state authorities keen to promote "forgetting the past and moving on," or indeed from paramilitary groups. The distribution and screening of Guzmán's films, which directly intersect with politics, has been more problematic. His films are undeniable critiques of the Chilean state, past and present. They are also complex and multi-layered. As a result, they are considered by production companies to be unsellable. When Guzmán first began circulating his script for *Nostalgia for the Light* to European and North American television companies, he and Sachse were met with only rejection for two years. The reason given was that the narrative had too many threads and that understanding their interrelationships would require deep thought and repeat viewing. Television companies tend not to expect viewers to want to make this effort, leading them to favor narratives that can be understood immediately. Presenting human rights stories alongside astronomical and archaeological discoveries apparently does not comply with the conventions of the marketable television documentary. Guzmán explains that "when something is different, it's a problem" and that it is the responsibility of the documentarian to confront this problem by making the work regardless. The result is that the process is slow, as demonstrated by the long gaps between the release dates of his films (Guzmán). This is worth it, though, when the result is a film like *Nostalgia for the Light*, as its careful consideration, integrity and earnestness are felt in every beat. It is a polished and pristinely beautiful film whose production value masks its difficult journey from conception to finished article, and which carries the tremendous pain of the many told through the testimonies of the few.

Conclusion

The women's acts of scouring the unforgiving landscape for remains (figure 11.7) links *Nostalgia for the Light* and *Ancient Ground* most strongly, exploring the notion that it is primarily marginalized women who carry the burden of predominantly male conflicts centered on power, ownership and control. The works' position of "between-ness" as they shift from the margins to the center is refracted in their forms, content and aesthetics. Both take a poetic and subjective approach to dealing with a similar theme and both interrogate the landscape, albeit in different ways. Using the latest film technologies and resulting aesthetic

FIGURE 11.7 *Elemental forces,* Nostalgia for the Light.
REPRODUCED WITH PERMISSION OF THE ARTIST.

effects to disrupt the impenetrable nature of the landscapes where the disappeared may be found, they un/recover the problems placed beyond vision, as represented by the notion of unearthing the physical corpses. The lingering gaze on the landscape in both films is loaded with the implication that there is – or was and is no longer – something there worth looking at regardless of the state's misdirection of vision. It poses an invitation to the viewer to scrutinize and excavate what might lie beneath the surface rather than simply accepting the surface image. In disrupting the idyllic Irish landscape or the vastness of the Chilean desert, an insidious presence is discovered to be lurking. This presence is not necessarily only that of the bodies, but also that of the hand of the state cleansing the memories of the past while refusing to acknowledge the reality of the material remains that linger out of sight, if they have been preserved at all. Moreover, the bodies function as metaphors for the psychic legacies of violence experienced in any place, not just their own.

It is the persistence of the niche arts that has kept the issue of the disappeared and others alive the world over, and there is every indication that this will continue. In Northern Ireland, the mainstream media are at last beginning to take notice and news coverage has increased since the BBC documentary was aired. However, in 2015, arts and education in the region have experienced severe funding cuts delegated by the Northern Ireland Assembly (managed specifically by arts and education ministers who are members of the nationalist party Sinn Féin) at a time of conservative austerity in the UK. Worryingly, the grassroots community organizations that have facilitated the most healing have been most affected. On the part of the consociational devolved government that Northern Ireland currently has, there is an urgency to preserve the status quo and to not rock the boat lest the peace process be dismantled. The stifling of voices resulting from this contributes to official forgetting and ensures that the past stays in the past to the detriment of psychic healing and social justice. The story is reset and the loop begins again in real life. Circling that loop will always be the few who refuse to forget the people and issues excluded from official narratives. Guzmán's and Doherty's careers demonstrate that dogged resistance to silence can, however gradually, work towards visualizing the invisible and centralizing the marginal.

Works Cited

Amado, Ana, and Maria Dora Mourão. "Images from the South: Contemporary Documentary in Argentina and Brazil." *The Documentary Film Book*. Ed. Brian Winston. London: BFI, 2013. 228–54.

Ancient Ground. Dir. Willie Doherty. 2011. Single-channel video installation.

Arthur, Paul. "Essay Questions: From Alain Resnais to Michael Moore." *Film Comment* 39.1 (2003): 58–63.

The Battle of Chile [*La batalla de Chile*]. Dir. Patricio Guzmán. Icarus Films, 1975–79.

Blackspot. Dir. Willie Doherty. 1997. Single-channel video installation.

Blaine, Patrick. "Representing Absences in the Postdictatorial Documentary Cinema of Patricio Guzmán." *Latin American Perspectives* 40 (2013): 114–30.

Blair, Paula. *Old Borders, New Technologies: Reframing Film and Visual Culture in Contemporary Northern Ireland.* Oxford and Bern: Peter Lang, 2014.

Chile, the Obstinate Memory [*Chile, la memoria obstinada*]. Dir. Patricio Guzmán. Icarus Films, 1997.

Dawson, Graham. *Making Peace with the Past? Memory, Trauma and the Irish Troubles.* Manchester and New York: Manchester UP, 2007.

"The Disappeared." *Storyville.* Pres. Darragh MacIntyre. Dir. Alison Miller. BBCNI and RTÉ. 4 Nov. 2013.

Doherty, Willie. *Border Incident.* Dublin: IMMA, 1994. Photograph.

———. *Disturbance.* Dublin: Dublin City Gallery The Hugh Lane, 2011. Exhibition catalogue.

"Fáilte!" *Glencolmcille.* Donegal Webit, 2013. Web. 9 Sept. 2015.

"Films." *Patricio Guzmán.com.* Web. 9 Sept. 2015.

The First Year [*Primer año*]. Dir. Patricio Guzmán. Escuela de Artes de la Comunicación de la Universidad Católica de Chile, 1972.

Guzmán, Patricio. "A Lecture by Patricio Guzmán." Parliament Hall, St. Andrews. 3 Apr. 2015.

Heaney, Seamus. *North.* London: Faber and Faber, 1975.

———. *Opened Ground: Selected Poems 1966–1996.* London: Faber and Faber, 1998.

Keogh, Elaine, and Colin Gleeson. "More Than One Body Found in Dig for 'Disappeared.'" *Irish Times.com.* 26 June 2015. Web. 26 June 2015.

Klubock, Thomas Miller. "History and Memory in Neoliberal Chile: Patricio Guzmán's *Obstinate Memory* and *The Battle of Chile.*" *Radical History Review* 85 (2003): 272–81.

McChesney, Robert W. *Rich Media, Poor Democracy: Communication Politics in Dubious Times.* Urbana: U of Illinois P, 1999.

Meade, Teresa A. "Holding the Junta Accountable: Chile's 'Sitios de Memoria' and the History of Torture, Disappearance, and Death." *Radical History Review* 79 (2001): 123–39.

Nostalgia for the Light [*Nostalgia de la luz*]. Dir. Patricio Guzmán. New Wave Films, 2010.

The Only Good One Is A Dead One. Dir. Willie Doherty. 1993. Double-channel video installation.

Rancière, Jacques. *The Emancipated Spectator*. Trans. Gregory Elliott. London and New York: Verso, 2009.

———. *The Future of the Image*. Trans. Gregory Elliott. London and New York: Verso, 2007.

"Welcome to the Atacama Desert." *The Atacama Desert*. Atacama Desert.co.uk, 2015. Web. 9 Sept. 2015.

CHAPTER 12

Shaping "Common Places": Post-Soviet Narratives beyond Anti-Utopia in Ksenia Buksha's *The Freedom Factory* and Igor Saveljev's *Tereshkova is Flying to Mars*

Ksenia Robbe

Perhaps the strongest force behind the disintegration of Soviet political, economic and social structures was the gradual decline of a general belief in utopian ideals and of trust in the power of the state to realize them. Much of the "underground," semi-official and émigré culture, which could be called "post-Soviet" even before the end of the political system, contributed to the historical undoing of clichéd ways of thinking and acting that, by the 1980s, were surviving mostly as empty signifiers. Along with the stylistics of Sots art,[1] which ironically deconstructs the metaphors dominating popular consciousness, the genre of anti-utopia came to the fore on the wave of rapid transformation and disillusionment of the 1990s. Creating phantasmagorical worlds that allow one to trace the paradoxical logic of Soviet myths and their mutations, anti-utopian imaginaries span the novels of Vladimir Sorokin, Tatyana Tolstaya, Vladimir Makanin and Victor Pelevin, among others. Against the backdrop of increasing conservatism in the post-Soviet public sphere, the genre's critical role and popularity (at least, among the intelligentsia) continues into the present. Reworking the legacies of early Soviet utopian imaginaries or positivist calls for creating "utopia factories" in 1960s America (as propagated by Alan Toffler), much of contemporary Russian literature can be seen as an "anti-utopia factory" (Chantsev), producing warning images and trying to awaken readers conceived as zombified by commodity culture.

Together, the onset of commodification in the public sphere since the 1990s and the depth of critical deconstruction have created a void that has

---

1 Sots art is a genre or style of conceptual art initiated by non-conformist artists in the Soviet Union in the 1970s which, similarly to Pop Art, relies on clichés of mainstream discourses and representations, using the material of Socialist rather than Western mass culture. Drawing on the stock images of socialist realism, Sots art reproduced them in an ironic way, thus revealing the incongruities of Soviet life.

recently started to be filled in by neo-traditionalist discourses. According to Mark Lipovetsky, the coexistence of deconstuctive (postmodern) and neo-traditionalist tendencies (often employing elements of socialist realism) has resulted in "a virtual war of discourses," in which these tendencies crisscross and produce hybrid forms (192). While the more extreme types of discourses seeking to revive Soviet aesthetics and to shape identitarian politics[2] have received their share of criticism, some of the more hybrid forms, which often involve innovative themes and styles, deserve more attention.

One of the reasons for the above-mentioned void is the fact that ways of organizing social existence and everyday life during the Soviet period have been, too quickly and unambiguously, pushed to the *peripheries of public discussion and collective memory*. This went hand in hand with the emergence of *physical peripheries* – within the country (former industrial towns, rural areas) and, on a smaller scale, within cities (abandoned districts) – to which large groups of socially marginalized people have been displaced, facing conditions of poverty or precarity as a result of neo-liberal restructuring and deindustrialization. While early post-Soviet literature and film were mostly aimed at dissecting old myths, Russian cultural production of the last decade, I suggest, engages the myths of the present that are based on selective remembering (the "glorious moments" of Soviet history) as well as selective forgetting (mostly the routines of everyday life and their continued existence). Through examples of such textual and visual narratives, a certain nostalgia for a belief in the possibility of "commonality" emerges, mixed with confusion experienced at the sight of the decaying material structures of the utopia – not so much the monuments aimed at commemorating socialist heroes, but more "commonplace" artifacts as well as ways of narrating the "common."

It is the intersection of such peripheral imaginary and material sites of social habitation and their role in contemporary (re)constructions of the common that I will focus on in my reading of two novels by young Russian writers: Ksenia Buksha's *The Freedom Factory* (2014) and Igor Saveljev's *Tereshkova is Flying to Mars* (2012). In interrogating the signs of (re)imagining the common in these narratives, I am drawing on Svetlana Boym's (1994) critical exploration of "common places"[3] in her eponymous book. In particular, I am guided by the multilayered meaning Boym gives to this expression. Firstly, common places

---

2   See, for instance, the works of Alexander Prokhanov, as well as some of the novels by Zakhar
      Prilepin and Sergei Shargunov.

3   From here on, "common," "common places" and "commonality" are employed with reference
      to their conceptual meanings as outlined by Boym. Since they appear throughout the text, no
      quotation marks are used.

refer to the structures of the myths that organized Soviet life (in this sense, common is close to normative, denoting values that are shared and represented without questioning). Secondly, the commonplace invokes sites of ordinary, daily life that often unfolded against the grain of the common places of Soviet ideology (simple, trivial ways of expression as opposed to the elevated style of Soviet rhetoric). Thirdly, common places point to the spaces of imagining and enacting the common as an ideal – from the idea of the "common wealth" to the Soviet *communalkas* – that emerges from utopian thought, which is nostalgic in its very origin as it refers to places and realities that never existed in this imagined form (Boym 11–19). All these meanings can be read as intertwined, evoking both kitsch and innovation, both nostalgia and futurism.

Boym's interpretation of the common (place) as "a mythical site from which intellectuals perpetually displace themselves, only to write elegies to the lost communality" (19) is, then, not unlike the peripheral, read as an assemblage of imaginary and material forces. This multilayered semantics of the common also invokes the double notion of periphery as an area bound to the center and a space that, while being subjected to dependency, can generate alternative visions that contest the hegemonic structure. The power structures involving common places as normative guidelines and the commonplace as improvisational site of everyday life can, however, be re-thought as dynamic and changeable, drawing on postcolonial and decolonial developments of the periphery-center model formulated in dependency theory.[4] These developments stress the insurgent potential of peripheralized knowledges (Dussel 1998) and demonstrate the presence of "central" colonial epistemologies within the "peripheries" (Chakrabarty 2000).

In their present condition, the common places of the Soviet period are more like ruins than monuments of the past. Taken in the normative sense, some of them are occasionally resurrected by "official" or right-wing ideologues to evoke a sense of collectivity without reforming discourse; these are the symbols that circulate in what is usually thought of as post-Soviet nostalgia. The two other senses of Boym's common places – everyday practices and utopian/futurist imaginaries – refer to what has been peripheralized and disremembered by mainstream discourses. These become spaces of what Boym

---

4 In particular, I am referring to Immanuel Wallerstein's world-systems theory, which analyzes global divisions of labor in terms of the world's division into "core," "semi-periphery" and "periphery" countries. As a contestation of modernization theories, this vision has provided plural and de-centering approaches to the history and future of societies from a global perspective. It has, however, been critiqued for its schematism and its simplification of global relations of power.

calls "reflective nostalgia" – practices of "deep mourning that performs a labour of grief both through pondering pain and through play that points to the future" (Boym 55). Signs of such deep mourning can be found in many post-Soviet discourses that involve longing for an imagined communality that was, in certain forms, experienced and enacted by earlier generations.

My reading of Buksha's and Saveljev's novels will examine the ways in which positivist discourses of the past are re-collected as peripheral presences while being divested of essentialist forms and turned into positive – engaging and relevant – narratives that attempt to develop a language for speaking about the past, particularly for new generations. The common places of the Soviet they invoke – both material (factories that worked for the defense industry developing space and rocket technologies) and imaginary ones (ideals of freedom practiced in a Soviet state "free of discrimination" and the "global leader" in the space race) – have become peripheral spaces of the present: still existing and functioning, but largely neglected and discarded. This essay will argue that, compared, on the one hand, to restorative practices of nostalgia that simply recreate the ideals that once inspired faith in the moral righteousness of Soviet structures and, on the other, anti-utopian imaginaries of the future that re-invoke common places of the past in their most terrifying forms, the two examples of post-Soviet narratives re-imagine common places of the past as provisional spaces for building commonality in the present. In so doing, they occasionally involve restorative reminiscing, which can be interpreted as a marketing strategy (hence, they are not unambiguous examples of reflective nostalgia). In the most interesting episodes, however, these texts attempt to breach the discursive gaps between institutionalized amnesia, restorative nostalgia and aphasia,[5] experienced particularly by the younger generations, whose relationship to the Soviet past is limited to early memories, remembrances of (grand)parents and media representations.

The remembering and re-creating of common places by authors born in the 1980s can be interpreted as a reaction to an overwhelming privatization and atomization in all spheres of life, and as a strategy of imagining a tentative continuity between the ideals of communality from the past and the disenchanted present. This also involves imagining continuity between generations, which, at its best, does not rehash old narratives, but produces new forms for speaking about both past and present. In search of this new language, both narratives bring to light pieces of what is generally regarded as rubbish and waste,

---

5 I am using this term with reference to Serguei Oushakine's theorization of post-Soviet aphasia, which defines it as the inability to speak in a language adequate to the changed socio-cultural situation.

to re-collect the former lives of objects and ideas now relegated to the peripheries of social imaginaries. My discussion will consider how peripherality functions in the two novels, starting with the chronotopical structures that conjoin peripheral(ized) spaces and times. It will proceed by exploring the functions of Soviet spaces and symbols, and the ways these are remembered in the texts' reflections on the present. These rememberings have a peripheral quality as they involve protagonists' fleeting childhood memories of everyday life and images of "forgotten" Soviet novels and films that are similarly unstable and open to interpretation. Bringing together these time-spaces, symbols and memories, I will argue, produces a sense of alternative common places of speech and imagination, which can become idioms of a new symbolic language.

Places Out of Time

In a provincial Russian town[6] of the late 2000s not much has changed compared to the early post-Soviet or even the late Soviet period. This, at least, is the impression one gets when starting to read Saveljev's *Tereshkova is Flying to Mars*. Old schools and community centers are rented out to scam companies trying to sell their products to a new class of "successful people." Certainly, whole new districts composed of mansions for the new rich have appeared, separated by muddy roads from the town centers, but the old residential areas seem to have been conserved, only looking shabbier every year. Saveljev's descriptions do not amount to more than brief strokes, mentioning *khrushchyovka*[7] apartments with "lavatories right near the kitchen" (39) and the smell of "some kind of wettish desolation" (60), and hospitals with "depressing ... corridors, lumps of linoleum, indifferent lamp shades and the ominous rumble of urinals coming from a far end" (209).[8]

Put together, however, these recognizable details create an atmosphere of desolation: the physical presence of the old that does not vanish but only grows older prevents the characters from taking any action. Most of them attempt to escape reality, albeit in different ways. Natasha, the protagonist's girlfriend, realizes that she needs a degree from a university abroad and, putting great effort into learning English and overcoming bureaucratic hurdles,

---

6 The provincial town in which the action of Saveljev's novel takes place is modeled after the author's home town Ufa.

7 Three- to five-storied concrete apartment blocks were built en masse during the 1960s, following Nikita Khruschev's project of providing families with individual flats.

8 Since neither of the novels has been translated into English yet, all translations are my own.

leaves for Pittsburgh. Pavel, the protagonist, experiences her departure as being left behind, but also as a challenge to do something with his life. The narrative opens with Pavel's ruminations about his state of confusion and follows his life over the next few months. The events of the novel are triggered by the appearance of Pavel's cousin Maxim, who offers the depressed protagonist a job in a company that organizes flights to Moscow for VIP clients. For readers familiar with the realities of domestic flights in post-Soviet Russia, it comes as no surprise that the praised planes are in fact written off samples made in Kazakhstan. The growing number of clients virtually zombified by Maxim's motivating speeches are happy to be deceived, however, for the privilege of being members of an exclusive club. For an artful impostor like Maxim, creating a world of business schemes becomes a way of escaping the reality of his lower-class, rural background.

The temporalities organizing the representations of the characters can be divided into three types. First, the novel evokes the time of business elites, which is based on the submission of private time to the demands of profit and a sustained focus on the present. Second, there is the time of the former Soviet intelligentsia, represented by the parents' generation, who continue to live with the ideals of the past, only slightly adjusting them to contemporary realities. Caught between these two temporalities and spheres of post-Soviet existence are the younger characters, born in the 1980s, who are trying to carve out ways of life oriented towards the future, but who mostly end up either harking back to the utopian worlds of their parents or buying into the pragmatic fantasies represented by the new elites. The latter track is taken by Maxim and, in a different way, Natasha. However, the physical places with which these fantasies are associated – Moscow as the business center of Russia and America as a global factory of self-making – bring nothing but disillusionment. The Russian capital, to which Pavel travels twice, is depicted as a place of faceless crowds and endless traffic jams. The world abroad is imagined by Pavel as entirely different from Russia, seemingly offering a dream and a purpose, but in his imagination and in Natasha's experience this other world appears not worth leaving home and family for (as confirmed by Natasha's decision to return from Pittsburgh at the end of the novel).

The time inhabited by Pavel and his two friends Igor and Danila can be described as "provincial" and "peripheral" in relation to both the new and the old public times, as well as to the time of aspiration that characterizes the "central" spaces of the national and international. All three young men still live under the protection of their parents and grandparents: Pavel's studies at a faculty for the humanities and social sciences, and his decision to pursue a PhD are directed by his mother's fear that he would otherwise be drafted into the military; Igor is, in Pavel's words, "feeding off" his parents, who are happy to see him as an editor and doctoral student, even if he is not financially independent; Danila, saved by his grandmother from juvenile prison, still lives in her old flat, spending his time in a community of role players. The "in-between" time they are living in is a characteristic of any young generation, but compared to their peers in Russian metropolitan centers, their lives are certainly less accelerated. They seem more rooted in the memory of Soviet utopias and more confident in their locality, often disregarding a Western cultural symbolic. Even the friends' project of sabotaging the work of the scam airline seems anachronistic, especially as the narrative reveals its futility. Their use of disruptive tactics such as distributing leaflets revealing facts about the company's machinations is reminiscent of romantic depictions of Soviet youth brigades and thus alludes to the persistence of certain styles of thinking and acting on the peripheries of post-Soviet social consciousness.

In contrast to Saveljev's, the narrative of Ksenia Buksha's *The Freedom Factory*, which is a collage of short sketches featuring a variety of perspectives, is organized entirely around and by one place: the Freedom factory, located in an old industrial district of St. Petersburg.[9] The novel traces the history of the plant from the post-World War II period up to recent times, giving life to this once very important and now dying industrial giant. The first stories allow the reader to remember the enthusiasm with which young people once worked at the factory and shows how formative the factory's social networks were for them. Episodes featuring such forward-looking temporalities (aligned to a space perceived as productive) give way to narratives capturing the rash marketization and devastation brought about by privatization in the 1990s and 2000s, when the lack of further state commissions and funding quickly makes the majority of employees redundant. Only the most devoted or those who have nowhere else to go stay on the sinking ship, with the episodes narrated from their perspectives revealing how much the factory has become a part of them.

The Freedom Factory emerged as a follow-up to Buksha's work as a journalist making promotion materials for the factory's new management. Interviewing workers in this capacity made her curious, and she set out to imaginatively explore the personal histories of the people, old and young, who identify

---

9   The Freedom factory in the novel is based on one of the existing factories in the Kirov district of St. Petersburg. Built during the industrialization of the late nineteenth century, these factories became major centers of heavy industry in the 1930s and continued working mainly for the defense industry after World War II, slowly diversifying their production since the 1970s. At present, most of them still operate, although at a very low capacity.

themselves with the factory. This genesis of the project partly explains the novel's style and structure: each chapter presents an anecdotal story or an impression narrated and focalized by one or several subjects. The constant change of perspectives and narrative styles, sometimes within the same chapter, creates a feeling of confusion. Once the reader gets used to this type of oral and associative narrative, however, the mosaic of individual styles of speech comes to be seen as a chorus of interconnected voices. Similarly, on the story level, patchy impressions flow into a common plot and into what could be read as a collective account – not only of this particular factory, but, synecdochically, of the whole post-Soviet industrial sector. In this way, spaces like those alluded to by the image of the Freedom factory, which have turned into physical, social and imaginative peripheries in what are now poor and criminal districts of cities like St. Petersburg, become characters in their own right.

Individual stories focused mostly on everyday, seemingly insignificant events are put together and create a fragmented chronicle of the factory. In this sense, the novel forms an alternative to official Soviet records and contemporary stereotyped rememberings of factories as spaces of social oppression, as well as to the complete erasure of such places and histories from public memory. While it can be read as a reflection on the post-war history of the larger society, in this reading I focus on the way Buksha's narrative gives life to peripheralized spaces and experiences – both by resurrecting styles of speaking and acting, and by making the narrative dynamic and lively, thus updating old forms for younger readers. Featuring attitudes and social dialects[10] recognizable to Russian readers of different generations, the narrative of *The Freedom Factory* captures particular times: the forward-looking times of the 1950–60s, the more pragmatic 1970s and 1980s, and the times of despair and nostalgia in the last decades. It makes these times more concrete through the characters' association with the specific and almost unchanging place of the factory. Seen through the oral histories of commonplace situations, the factory grows into a common place embodying collective identities: individuals of different backgrounds who would otherwise not associate with each other become, as the narrative proceeds, part of a community. This community survives for the few members of the "old guard" and newcomers who are able to relate to the outdated place. This could be interpreted as a return to the *topos* of the factory as used in Soviet industrial novels from the 1950s, but the fragmented style of the narrative and its fluctuation between ironic and lyrical modes render

---

10 Here I am referring to the Bakhtinian notion of language as stratified into socio-ideological dialects or ideolects, including languages of social groups, professions and generations, as well as genre- and period-bound literary languages, etc. (Bakhtin 288–93).

such a (re)turn more complicated. Underpinning a narrative that highlights the peripheral sides of Soviet styles of acting and speaking (commonplace and critically attuned to the clichés of socialist realism) are what I want to call chronotopes[11] of *persistence*, bringing together still existing yet peripheralized spaces and times of remembrance that help one to endure. Reading the unity of time and space in these representations through the concept of the chronotope, I want to suggest that these narratives attempt to create new genres of dealing with the persistence of the past in the present.

In her discussion of temporalities (chronotypes) of post-Soviet postmodern literature, Marina Balina (2000) focuses on examples of prose and poetry characterized by a reworking of the "absolute" time of socialist realism, involving either ironic exaggeration (acceleration) or distancing (retardation). In Saveljev's and Buksha's novels, the absolute time of Soviet ideology is displaced by the time of the market. The work of a factory or the life of a provincial town, which in a socialist realist novel would reflect "objective time" (Balina 58), in these novels, particularly in Buksha's narrative, become "subjectivized." In fact, these personalized depictions of places are often more interesting than the characters' subjectivities. The way in which the peripheralized ("forgotten") temporalities in both novels engage the anachronistic persistence of places "out of time" (both outdated and seemingly timeless) can be read as disrupting the dominant post-Soviet temporalities of chasing after material success and moving to the centers of present-day economic and cultural capital. On the other hand, these chronotopes of persistence provide an alternative to the models of time-space in post-Soviet anti-utopian narratives: they focus on the continuing lives of discarded objects, ideas and subjectivities not in expectation of an ensuing catastrophe, but in terms of a positive re-imagining of living with the past.

Soviet Myths as Peripheral Presences

The discussed chronotopes of the factory and of a provincial town in the two novels are partly formed by structures of imagination and narration dating back to Soviet times. Examples of such structures are typical Soviet myths such as the narrative of unsurpassed achievements in space exploration,

---

11   The term "chronotope" was coined by Mikhail Bakhtin to describe "the intrinsic connectedness of temporal and spatial relationships that are artistically expressed in literature" (84). The leading role in this unity, according to Bakhtin, belongs to temporalities (or forms of time) that interact with spaces significant for the particular period depicted.

community imagined as a "great family" and a belief in the ability of this community to unite and transcend limitations in critical situations. How can we make sense of the continuing presence of these myths and tropes? What is their function in the novels' present times? Do they signal a return to the past or an endorsement of still existing stereotypes? Are they approached from an ironic distance or with a sarcastic attitude? Given the stylistic difference of the two novels from earlier postmodernist literature, the latter is less likely. The former hypothesis, however, needs a detailed interrogation. In the following reading of mythical structures in the novels, I will propose that the way in which these myths are remembered – as spectral[12] peripheral presences – reveals the self-reflective quality of these re-writings and constitutes an invitation to re-inhabit spaces full of ghosts without chasing the shadows of the past away.

The play with the meanings invoked by the title of Buksha's novel is an interesting example of the ambiguity of attraction and repulsion present in dealing with ghosts. The first chapter opens with a casual anecdote: "A wise mother was once teaching her first-grader son: when you see the letters white on red, don't read – that's all rubbish, but don't ever tell anyone what I've just told you. White on red, over the factory stands 'Freedom': that's all rubbish" (9). The narration picking up the perspective of the boy conveys the incongruence between aspirations and reality. The apparent conflict between the mother's instructions and the prohibition to voice such ideas openly, between the pompous name and the ordinariness of the red fabric on which the name of the factory is written, and between the ideals of space exploration and the reality of a working district becomes an underlying motif of many stories. Reflecting the irony of the typical post-Soviet habit of giving tendentious names to compulsory activities[13] (and perhaps the incongruence of Soviet life as such), the oxymoronic title also involves nostalgia for past imaginaries of freedom and the way they could find expression in the spaces of factory life. This optimistic remembering runs counter to the dominant imagination of the factory in contemporary literature and film, where it usually appears as a

---

12   Here I am referring to Derrida's conception of the spectral as an alternative understanding of historicity that displaces "onto-theo-archeo-teleological" scripts by foregrounding the deconstructing forces of "supplementarity," the "trace" and the "promise" (74). I read spectrality also along the lines suggested by critics who have focused on the spatial dimensions of haunting and on the disempowering aspects of "ghosting" often represented through figures of displacement and dispossession (Blanco and Peeren 10).

13   Names such as "Freedom" were commonly used for factories during the Soviet period. Most of these factories have not been renamed, thus remaining common landmarks of the post-Soviet space alluding to Soviet imaginaries.

symbol of meaningless monotonous work, of a lack of future perspective and of poverty and violence.[14]

Buksha's novel, through the confidential tone of the narration, invites readers to re-experience details of Soviet everyday life and makes the dark, inhospitable spaces of the factory more homely. Its directors, even in their authoritarian behavior and bourgeois manners, are remembered fondly as those most devoted to the factory (such as director V,[15] who attempted to commit suicide after losing an election). A whole series of episodes relates stories of factory employees who decide to stay despite having more attractive career options. Out of such episodes, an image emerges of people from different backgrounds and occupying various positions forming a community and a family of sorts. Invoking the topos of the "great Soviet family," this depiction, however, also reworks the old myth by focusing on its peripheral presence, indicating that this common place might not really exist, except as a remembered symbolic value.

Another myth can be traced through the recalled stories of legendary achievements: producing a record number of airplane details within a few days, or a new model of a radiation meter as an immediate response to the Chernobyl catastrophe. Such stories, certainly, bring to life the mythologies of the Russian people's great efficiency in the face of an emergency. But by allowing the characters to speak for themselves, in their own dialects (mostly about their youth), the author also distances her own voice from the myths, at times breaking into the narrative to challenge these often exaggerated or sugar-coated rememberings. Rather than recreating the tendentious styles and magical resolutions of socialist realist fiction, Buksha's narrative, due to its fragmented structure and its reanimation of local, no longer privileged speech styles, reads more like a compilation of urban legends, which are both commonplace and incredible. A similar impression is created by the author's drawings, which accompany the narrative: blurred black-and-white images of faces and figures, like shadows or memories in the process of fading away, interpellate the reader, reminding him or her of their continued but precarious presence.

The legendary figure of Tereshkova[16] appears in Saveljev's novel in a somewhat similar way, as a ghost-like yet meaningful presence. Her name is

---

14   Some recent examples include the image of the factory in Natalia Meschaninova's *The Hope Factory* (*Kombinat "Nadezhda"*) and Andrey Zvyagintsev's *Leviathan* (*Leviafan*).

15   All characters' names are reduced to a Latin initial, alluding to the regime of secrecy that characterized Soviet industrial plants.

16   Valentina Tereshkova (b. 1937) is the first woman astronaut to have reached space in 1963 on board of the Soviet spacecraft Vostok 6. After the successful flight, Tereshkova became

first invoked when Natasha explains to Pavel why she is leaving for the US: the thought of living like her mother, who dreamed of becoming an astronaut but ended up a schoolteacher, makes her want to emigrate. Mentioning the name of the first woman astronaut makes Natasha's reasoning understandable for post-Soviet youth. The utopias of the past are perceived as a deception that never allowed the generation of their parents to succeed. Further in the novel, Tereshkova becomes a topic of conversation between Pavel and other characters reading an interview with the astronaut in honor of her seventieth birthday. Reacting to Maxim's bursts of laughter as he reads a journalist's ironic rendering of Tereshkova's wish to organize a flight to Mars, Pavel defends her as an old lady who "has a dream which she dared to share. A goal with which she has lived all her life" (197). In Igor's interpretation of the interview, it appears as an anachronistic, even surrealist narrative: something that was normal within the romantic utopian imaginary of the past sounds incoherent and phantasmagorical now. He quickly turns this incongruence into an idea for an anti-utopia:

> I've just made up such a plot, might even write it down. A grand anti-utopia. A story about how old symbols are not compatible with our time, they just cannot exist now, it is unreal, you see? ... So a story about how they are celebrating [Tereshkova's] anniversary and ceremonially launch her to Mars, as she wished. There is broadcasting of the launch on TV, lots of fuss and celebrations. And everything as though it's just the way things are.
>
> 155

Pavel, however, greets this idea with skepticism; following the conversation about Tereshkova, he becomes more concerned about Natasha's mother, visiting her in hospital and thus attending to "real" problems. The two friends' reactions can be seen as expressing two different attitudes to the past. Igor's response is more distanced and aestheticizing, while Pavel's could be described as more immediate and ethical. The latter does not consider myths of the past as strange othernesses; rather, he attempts to accept their continued existence and to re-imagine a commonality between the phantoms of the past and the inhabitants of the present. Another example of this is the association Pavel draws between the romantic enthusiasm of the 1960s generation, expressed in the popular literature of the time, such as the novels of Granin and Golovnin (184), and the excitement of the new business travelers traversing the post-Soviet

---

a prominent public figure representing the Soviet Union in a number of international forums and councils.

space (183–5). Crucially, both Igor's and Pavel's reactions, aesthetic and ethical, anti-utopian and neo-utopian, resist Maxim's cynicism.

Processes of imaginative materialization are an important part of dealing with Soviet symbols and their present-day transformations in these novels. Old planes, for instance, which used to embody liberating futures and Soviet achievement on the world scene, are losing their symbolic power; or rather, they have become symbols of an imagined security for a small group of people only. This symbolic permutation is revealed to be absurd in the face of the planes' actual material dilapidation. Still, these objects carry symbolic power for Saveljev's protagonists: they inspire the young generation in the provinces longing for meaningful work and for the possibility to pursue ethical causes. Similarly, the image of the factory in Buksha's novel, seen at the end as "magnificent and scuffed" (235), a "museum which ... can be built ... endlessly but ... does not bring either profits or losses, nothing ... " (228), invokes a profound ambiguity. The formerly glorious giant is dying, yet it continues to exist and serves for the new generation of employees as a symbol of enthusiastic commitment and commonality – for the new director, it is "a continuation of [his] father and many other things" (229). The factory's name, often approached tongue-in-cheek, also invokes memories of earnest beliefs that produce not only nostalgia but also inspiration to think about what can be changed.

Materialization also occurs at a textual level in Saveljev's novel, for instance when Pavel reflects on his life while roaming around Moscow:

> Nothing to look back at. And what is ahead?
> Ahead is a yard of a multistoried block of flats, strangely empty, and the second floors have stretched weird trawls under the windows, catching in the iron nets maybe garbage or maybe some repenting members of the CC [Communist Party Central Committee]. A tube is sticking out of an air conditioner pegged into a wall, water dripping onto one of the memorial boards, mourning a desolately obscure hero of socialist labor – at least the glamorous name of Roman Karmen was not telling for Pavel.
> And all of us are like mankurts.
> SAVELJEV 27–8

The sense of being lost in time, in this episode, is rendered in spatial terms through the metaphors of looking back and ahead, and the abstract future (ahead) is concretized as the typical yard of a Soviet block of flats. Time thus materializes into space like memory has materialized into monuments such as the memorial board. Combining irony and lyricism, the description of this commonplace monument evokes mourning – not of the forgotten heroes, but as a feeling of being united in remembering them.

Remembering the Peripheral

Pavel's emphatic "mankurts" (*mankurty*) at the end of the above quote refers to a word coined by the Kyrgyz writer Chingiz Aitmatov in his novel *The Day Lasts More than A Hundred Years* (1980) to refer to someone who has forgotten his history and roots, and can therefore be easily manipulated.[17] In their novels, Saveljev and Buksha are precisely trying to come to terms with processes of forgetting and selective remembering. Serguei Oushakine (2000) has characterized post-Soviet practices of speaking about the past and present, particularly by young people during the late 1990s (the same generation as the authors of the novels discussed here), as a state of aphasia. Aphasia, in Oushakine's reworking of the medical term[18] along the lines of Roman Jakobson's linguistic analysis of speech behavior, refers to "a compensatory type of discursive behavior, in which the lack of new creative symbolic production ... is to be filled by complex patterns of usage of the symbolic forms acquired during the previous stages of individual and societal development" (995). This discussion of re-using old symbolic forms that do not reflect changed realities carries a medical term, through the analysis of individual language use, over into a project of scrutinizing collective speech/thought during a specific historical period.

Can the two authors' use of the Soviet symbolic be regarded as a symptom of such aphasia? Certainly, some signs of it are present in both novels. For example, Buksha recreates specific discursive practices and delivers them to her readers in almost raw form. However, the novels' engagement with the question of how the past is remembered, how old symbols are reused and mediated (as my readings will show), makes them *representations* of aphasia rather than forms of this discursive disorder. In representing aphasic practices, Saveljev's text, for instance, tends to develop a critical consciousness in relation to the demobilizing effects of using "empty signifiers" to relate to contemporary realities. Buksha's novel, on the other hand, attempts to envision new frameworks to mediate between the experiences of older and younger generations.

The narrative of Saveljev's novel, told from Pavel's perspective, repeatedly registers the comforting effects of reading and watching examples of old literature and films that have not been included in post-Soviet canons. Along with Pavel's sensations of remembering his reading of romantic novels from

---

17   *The Day Lasts More than A Hundred Years* (1980) is a Soviet classic.

18   As a medical term, aphasia denotes various speech disorders occurring as a result of brain damage.

the 1960s, it is Danila's discovery of his grandfather's collection of *Ogonyok*[19] magazines from the same period – "what a sophisticated meal!" (128) – and Olga's (Pavel's short-lived romantic interest) passion for old movies that the novel represents as ways of escaping the reality of the present. Pavel's defense of Lyubov' Orlova's acting in a late film[20] in a conversation with Olga might also be interpreted as a symptom of aphasia.[21] However, the protagonist's appreciation of Orlova as a personality, in spite of her poor acting and the film's unintended culmination in self-parody, is also an indication of attachment to discarded and largely unknown – peripheral – productions of the Soviet film industry. When paralleled with his expression of respect for Tereshkova, there seems to appear, behind Pavel's nostalgia, an ethical discourse of defending those who believed in a cause, even when it is seen as having failed.

Compared to Igor, who, as a writer, believes in the power of imagination, Pavel, towards the end of the novel, is portrayed as striving for a more hands-on attitude as he debunks Igor's idealistic plans of building an underground resistance movement that would bring to light the illegal operations of the town's scum companies. This criticism of Igor's living in the world of phantoms and never-ending adventures (174), which Pavel compares to Maxim's adventurism, can be read as a sign of a deeper critique of the young generation's inability to step out of old narrative and symbolic frames involving both utopian and anti-utopian elements. That this constitutes a significant undercurrent of the novel is evidenced by Pavel's longer reflection on the reasons why the numerous clients of Maxim's company (and more generally, mass media consumers) let themselves be fascinated by romantic narratives about aircrafts and flights. He relates the "special excitement" of the nouveau riche "ladies and gentlemen" gathering at the airplane stairway to the sensibilities generated by Soviet novels of the 1960s that were "boiling with the mixture of wide-eyed enthusiasm about technology, sky and friendship, of literary modesty and special, intoxicating risk" (184). I read this reflection on perpetuating myths from the 1960s into the present as a sign of the protagonist's emerging

---

19   *Ogonyok* is one of the oldest illustrated magazines in Russia; it was particularly popular during the perestroika years.

20   Lyubov' Orlova was a famous actress who played her main roles in the Soviet classics of the 1930s and 1940s. The film discussed in the book, *Starling and Lyre* (1974), was considered a failure and was not released until the 1990s.

21   Or, more specifically, of what Oushakine, drawing on Jakobson, refers to as "expressive aphasia" by which he describes his informants' inability to decode the notion of the "post-Soviet." Instead of using metaphors to explain it (through comparison), they tended to "metonymically displace it onto other signifiers" within the same field of signification (Oushakine 999). According to Jakobson, such linguistic operations indicate the loss of a metalanguage or, in Oushakine's terms, of a meta-context (1000).

critique of post-Soviet aphasia. It becomes an indictment of the contemporary social establishment's looking at the world through the prism of new-old myths, as well as of his own, his friends' and his whole generation's peripheral existence "out of time" (living in the imaginaries of the past or the future) and "out of place" (not engaged in activities that could bring about change). Thus, the narrative moves beyond aphasic attachments to old forms, via a critique of commodifying the past in anti-utopian narratives (such as Igor's plot of a novel about Tereshkova), towards attempts to develop new "common places" of a language to talk about the Soviet past as a valuable resource for idioms, which, however, need to be translated into new forms to suit the changed realities. Remembering peripheral, non-canonical artefacts and discourses of the past, similar to dwelling on peripheralized times and spaces, can thus be read as a strategy of starting to imagine new commonalities through invoking what is now seen as outdated and failed – not to celebrate and monumentalize such examples, but to examine both the potentials and limits of old common places.

Buksha's text, although it does not involve any direct reflection on Soviet fiction, certainly relies on the material of Soviet literature and films in its recreation of the past. This material – from lyrics of a bard song (which give the title to Chapter 23) and typical phrases and gestures from post-war films to the styles of children's literature from the 1960s – are scattered throughout the book, recognizable to Russian readers. The novel's impressionistic narrative moves on the borderline between personal and collective memory (as mediated by almost forgotten Soviet films, literature and songs), trying to re-create the sensations and senses of the past through juxtaposing details of speech and imagery rather than through re-writing historical narratives. The narrative's reflections on its own mediated quality (its reliance on remembering), particularly evident in the chapter "May Day," are among the most interesting aspects of Buksha's project.

The narrative of "May Day," which depicts a viewing of footage from a May Day demonstration, weaves together three voices: that of a person who took part in the event and is commenting on it, the voice of a commentator in the film, and the voice of the "author"[22] reflecting on what she sees. The voices constantly interchange, picking up on and flowing into each other. Nonetheless, one can clearly distinguish the official tone of the commentator, the reminiscing voice of the participant recalling personal details about his colleagues, and the author's thoughts pondering the incongruences between the grand narratives and private recollections. Her curiosity about the latter,

---

22   By the "author" or meta-narrator, I refer to the fictionalized figure speaking to and interviewing the factory's employees.

combined with attempts to remember her own childhood impressions of such demonstrations or of what she heard about them, make the commentary voice sound unreliable, de-centering its authoritative position. Against the background of numerous details, the participant-narrator starts to reflect on the feeling invoked by watching-remembering: "But why such a sad impression, since the sadness occurs not because this is a communist demonstration and not a free people's festivity and the people there are in fact not free people. Not because of that. And not because we were young then and are old now" (113). The thought is picked up by the author's voice: "No, this is an internal sadness of the film itself, aesthetic, it is the sun that enhances it, it seems, because I know that in spite of the sun there, in the festive streets there is cold May, hands are freezing and getting dry in the wind ... and the black-and-white film cannot depict red flags, carnations and multicolored balloons ... " (113).

This narration, together with similar episodes, suggests that recollections dwelling on minor, peripheral details may provide multifaceted insights into stereotypical depictions of the past, allowing one to discover a commonality between them and present-day sensibilities. This imagining of a commonality (young people comprehending what earlier generations must have experienced) through peripheral signs and memories can be seen as a step towards developing a new language, beyond the aphasic reliance on older centralist frames which Oushakine observed in everyday speech and media representations of the 1990s (and which has dominated public discourse until now).

Conclusion

In sum, the temporal-spatial and symbolic structures, as well as the patterns of remembering the past in these two novels, show a tendency towards focusing on peripheral perspectives and now marginalized narratives and objects that used to be common places defining Soviet everyday life. Searching for new places of the common, they do not simply go back to what was once considered normative and absolute, as in Boym's first sense of the word. Rather, they confront the ruins of common places (in the imaginary and material sense) in their status as peripheries of former and contemporary dominant time-spaces, as undersides of the currently dominant regimes of being. In confronting these times, spaces, symbols and practices of representation, these narratives generate ways of remembering the peripheral that enable a re-thinking and re-actualizing of common places (and commonplace signs) of the Soviet. As such, they aim, as I have argued, to create new languages for speaking about the past, present and future that neither disregard nor

essentialize continuities. Providing an implicit critique of practices of restorative nostalgia and socio-cultural aphasia, these narratives zoom in on
peripheralized signs of the past and find in them the potential for creating
new common places as sites of new collective identities.

Such re-actualization, in most cases, does not imply any straightforward
nostalgia for the past or a conformist project of upgrading styles and symbols
of the past for the younger generations. Rather, what matters is the peripheral
status of the almost forgotten imaginaries, which foregrounds their persistence on the margins, their ongoing life against the backdrop (and in spite)
of neglect. The novels' reliance on the peripheries of Soviet commonplace
imaginaries for developing new symbolic frameworks might be seen as a way
of creating new utopias. I would argue, however, that both authors find more
subtle and perceptive ways of relating to the signs and discourses of the past.
They both show the potential of perpetuating old myths and constructing
new ones in the current Russian public sphere, which lacks new narratives.
The move of these texts away from the anti-utopian narratives of post-Soviet
literature that dwelled on and deconstructed Soviet utopias might be a sign of
a more positive approach to conceiving new narratives out of the ruins of the
past. A good example of this is the ending of Buksha's novel, which presents
the story of the young engineer N coming to the factory – an ordinary graduate
of an unremarkable institute, who always did what he had to do and "always
felt a lack, a meagerness of life forces" (231). It is his confrontation with the
factory that turns him into a more determined person, standing behind a new
project and feeling part of the factory's community and even its surroundings: "The feeling of lack, the feeling that was dominating him his whole life,
has suddenly, as though with an invisible turn of a key, illuminated the world;
something was still lacking, but it was beautiful" (237). The way in which this
passage develops the metaphor of lack conveys the idea that a void bearing
the signs of the peripheral exists not to be filled by a new centralist narrative,
but rather to be lived with and through in order to have a value of its own.
By relating a perception of what is lacking to the peripheralized remnants of
the past surviving in the present, the narrative suggests that a new language
can potentially develop in which one can speak about the past and present
through new symbolic forms that bear visions of another future.

Works Cited

Bakhtin, Mikhail. "Discourse in the Novel." *The Dialogic Imagination*. Ed. M. Holquist.
    Trans. C. Emerson and M. Holquist. Austin: U of Texas P, 1981.

Balina, Marina. "Playing Absolute Time: Chronotypes of Sots-Art." *Endquote: Sots-Art Literature and Soviet Grand Style*. Ed. M. Balina, N. Condee and E. Dobrenko. Illinois: Northwestern UP, 2000, 58–76.

Blanco, María del Pilar, and Esther Peeren. "Introduction: Conceptualizing Spectralities." *The Spectralities Reader: Ghosts and Haunting in Contemporary Cultural Theory*. Ed. María del Pilar Blanco and Esther Peeren. New York: Bloomsbury, 2013.

Boym, Svetlana. *Common Places: Mythologies of Everyday Life in Russia*. Cambridge and London: Harvard UP, 1994.

———. *The Future of Nostalgia*. New York: Basic, 2001.

Buksha, Ksenia. *Zavod "Svoboda."* [*The Freedom Factory*.] Moscow: OGI, 2014.

Chakrabarty, Dipesh. *Provincializing Europe: Postcolonial Thought and Historical Difference*. Princeton: Princeton UP, 2000.

Chantsev, Alexander. "Anti-Utopia Factory: Distopian Discourse in Russian Literature of the mid-2000s." [Fabrika Antiutopij: Distopicheskij diskurs v rossijskoj literature serediny 2000kh.] *New Literary Review* 86 (2007): n. pag.

Derrida, Jacques. *Specters of Marx: The State of the Debt, the Work of Mourning and the New International*. Trans. P. Kamuf. New York and London: Routledge, 1994.

Dussel, Enrique D. "Beyond Eurocentrism: The World System and the Limits of Modernity." *The Cultures of Globalization*. Ed. F. Jameson and M. Myyoshi. Durham: Duke UP, 1998. 3–31.

Lipovetsky, Mark. "Post-Soviet Literature between Realism and Postmodernism." *The Cambridge Companion to Twentieth-Century Russian Literature*. Ed. E. Dobrenko and M. Balina. Cambridge: Cambridge UP, 2011. 175–94.

Oushakine, Serguei. "In the State of Post-Soviet Aphasia: Symbolic Development in Contemporary Russia." *Europe-Asia Studies* 52.6 (2000): 991–1016.

Saveljev, Igor. *Tereshkova Letit na Mars*. [*Tereshkova is Flying to Mars*.] Moscow: Eksmo, 2012.

CHAPTER 13

The Heterotopic Closet: Spectral Presences and Otherworlds in *La Revue Monstre* and Michael James O'Brien's *Interiors*

Matthieu Foucher

"Homosexuality haunts 'the normal world,'" writes Guy Hocquenghem in the introduction of *Homosexual Desire*, before quoting the Austrian psychotherapist Alfred Adler:

> The problem of homosexuality hovers over society *like a ghost or a scarecrow*. In spite of all the condemnation, the number of perverts seems to be on the increase ... Neither the harshest penalties nor the most conciliatory attitudes and most lenient sentences have any effect on the development of this *abnormality*.
>
> qtd. in HOCQUENGHEM 1993: 50, emphasis added

After arguing that "capitalist society manufactures homosexuals just as it produces proletarians, constantly defining its own limits" and thus avoiding the confrontation with its own homosexual desires, Hocquenghem analyzes the discourses used by "the normal world" to create the repulsive figure of the homosexual, suffering from all kinds of vices (1993: 50). In the chapter "Anti-Homosexual Paranoia," he dedicates an entire section to "Homosexuality and Crime" (1993: 67). If he recalls that "homosexuality is first of all a criminal category," he also insists that legal repression has slowly been replaced by psychiatry and therefore by the *internalization of guilt*: pathologizing discourses have increasingly marginalized homosexuality by linking it to delinquency and criminality, and, if homosexuality *per se* is no longer a crime, "every homosexual is a potential killer" (1993: 68). As Gustave Macé, chief of the Paris Sureté of the third republic, wrote: "there is but one step from blackmail to crime, particularly since the sodomite is always hidden ... All sodomites are intelligent, but their minds turn to evil" (qtd. in Hocquenghem 1993: 68). The French queer theorist goes on, quoting "the Spanish law on social diseases":

> Clause I, paragraph (i). The following categories of persons are declared to be social dangers: (1) vagrants, (2) pimps, (3) homosexuals ... (7) the mentally sick who, for want of medical attention, constitute a peril

to society ... (9) drug peddlers ... (11) those who unite in gangs and whose intent is clearly criminal.

qtd. in HOCQUENGHEM 1993: 68

The relationship between homosexuality and crime, then, is longstanding, and, within this discourse, if homosexuals sometimes suffer from these troubled alliances, it is only because of their actual connections with criminals. To Hocquenghem's genealogy I want to add here the nineteenth-century French medical examiner Ambroise Tardieu, who noted that if "examples of pederasts assassinations are not very rare," it is strictly because "the satisfaction of their monstrous desires" can only be found in "the foam of the vilest world" (133).[1]

"Homosexuality is not just a delinquent category, it is a pathological one," continues Hocquenghem (1993: 69), referring to both psychiatric and physical senses: indeed, drugs and homosexuality often appear together in official reports, and venereal diseases play an important role in such paranoia. "The anti-homosexual measures of 1960 were legitimized by a press campaign which dragged out the old bogey of a resurgence of syphilis," writes Hocquenghem, before quoting the French Minister of Health, M. Chenot:

> In fact, the causes may be divided into two categories: the increasing immunity of viruses to antibiotics and the considerable development of homosexuality in every country ... How can we fight this recrudescence? By increasing the penalties in force against homosexuals.
>
> qtd. in HOCQUENGHEM 1993: 70

In both cases – the relationship established between homosexuality and crime, and that between homosexuality and disease – the pathologizing discourses of the nineteenth century charted by Hocquenghem were still highly present in people's minds during the 1960s and 1970s, and kept influencing media comments, court judgments and medical reports, as he demonstrates. Needless to say, this figure of the homosexual as killer and infectious carrier was reactivated during the AIDS crisis, as noted by Leo Bersani in *Is the Rectum a Grave?* Making a connection with the perception of female prostitutes in the nineteenth century, Bersani comments ironically that "women and gay men spread their legs with an unquenchable appetite for destruction" (18).

---

1 "Les exemples d'assassinats pédérastes ne sont pas très rares. [Ces assassinats] ont révélé avec éclat la fin cruelle à laquelle peuvent être réservés ceux qui ne peuvent trouver que dans l'écume du monde le plus vil ces liaisons inavouées auxquelles ils vont demander la satisfaction de leurs monstrueux désirs."

Having this in mind, and especially Tardieu's comment about "the foam of the vilest world," I want to focus on the collective imaginary of homosexuals as situated in peripheral space and on the way this imaginary, in accordance with Jacques Derrida's notion of spectrality, lives on in the present. After outlining how queerness and haunting have been thought together, I will discuss how the notion of the queer underworld appears in the work of Dominique Kalifa, a French cultural historian specializing in the history of crime and its representation. Then, I will question in what ways (not necessarily all negative) this peripheralization "haunts" contemporary queer cultural practices, by analyzing a series of photographs by Michael James O'Brien featured in the first issue of the French queer publication *La Revue Monstre*, provocatively titled "Back to the Closet."

Queer Hauntings

In *Specters of Marx*, Derrida points out just how blurred the lines between past, present and future can be. When, in his discussion of the heritage of Marx, he re-reads the first sentence of the *Communist Manifesto*, Derrida notes that the temporality expressed in "a specter is haunting Europe" is not the same when written by Marx in 1848 as when read in 1993. In Marx's vision, "the specter of communism" is a potentiality and an event to come, while from Derrida's point of view that same specter has already come and gone: it is now a legacy we are confronted with. How to deal with such a legacy and how to transform it back into a potentiality are the questions that drive Derrida: what if communism is still, after all, a specter yet to come? The intertwinement of past, present and future – the idea that "time is out of joint" – is what Derrida conceptualizes, in a play on ontology, as *hauntology*. This notion points to the complex interrelationships that make it impossible to cleanly separate promises of revolution in the past, memories from the past inherited in the present and the renewed possibility of a revolutionary future.

As María del Pilar Blanco and Esther Peeren remind us in *The Spectralities Reader*, since Derrida, the spectral metaphor has taken many directions across various disciplines. Queer theory has also known a spectral turn. In her book *The Apparitional Lesbian*, published in 1993 (the same year as the French original of *Specters of Marx*), Terry Castle applies the spectral metaphor to homosexual women, exploring how Western culture has constantly made lesbians invisible, even when they were renowned artists or entertainers: "Why is it so difficult to see the lesbian – even when she is there, quite plainly, in front of us? In part because she has been 'ghosted' – or made to seem invisible – by culture itself" (4). Lesbian-themed works of art have been routinely "censored and de-stroyed," and lesbians treated as "nonperson[s]" almost consistently rendered unseen (Castle 5). Even when they did become visible, they could only do so negatively: "as soon as the lesbian is named, ... she is dehumanized" (Castle 6). Spectrality, in Castle's work, is thus mainly equated to an absence of visibility and agency, but it is also tied to notions of temporality and inheritance: refer-encing the final pages of Radclyffe Hall's *The Well of Loneliness*, Castle recalls how "the melancholy heroine Stephen Gordon imagines herself surrounded by a hallucinatory 'legion' of spirits – the ghosts of all the women, past and pres-ent, who have suffered over their homosexuality" (7). The ghosts evoked here were, in their own time, marginalized "living ghosts" (Peeren 5) and their suf-fering is seen to haunt Stephen. Yet Castle views them as ghosts from the past that may also be brought back to life in a positive, enabling way by restoring them to visibility:

> Once we begin to look, we may find [the lesbian] looking back at us: mak-ing eye contact, delighted to be seen at last ... In seeking out the lesbian who is everywhere, one often finds a part of oneself. Like a ghost come back to life, or Garbo in her greatest role, the lesbian offers us new and vital information about what it is to be human.
>
> CASTLE 19

The spectral metaphor has also been applied to male homosexuality and its way of dealing with a history of suffering in American queer theorist José Esteban Muñoz's 2009 *Cruising Utopia: The Then and There of Queer Futurity*. Muñoz opens the second chapter, "Ghosts of Public Sex: Utopian Longings, Queer Memories," by discussing art historian Douglas Crimp's application of the Freudian notion of mourning to queer cruising spaces. About the HIV/AIDS pandemic, Crimp notes: "alongside the dismal toll of death, what many of us have lost is a culture of sexual possibility: back rooms, tea rooms, movie hous-es, and baths; the trucks, the piers, the ramble, the dunes" (qtd. in Muñoz 33). Muñoz's analysis of these words recalls Derrida's notion of the specter as bringing together past, present and future:

> Although the moment that Crimp describes is a moment that is behind us, its memory, its ghosts, and the ritualized performances of transmit-ting its vision of utopia across generational divides still fuels and pro-pels our political and erotic lives: it still nourishes the possibility of our current, actually existing gay lifeworld. Crimp's writing stands as a testi-mony to a queer lifeworld in which the transformative potential of queer

sex and public manifestations of such sexuality were both a respite from the abjection of homosexuality and a reformatting of that very abjection. The spaces and acts he lists represent signs, or ideals, that have been degraded and rendered abject within heteronormativity.

MUÑOZ 34

Visions of a lost "queer sex utopia" and fantasies of a forgotten past haunt Crimp's speech, which evokes nostalgia, or "queer utopian memory," as Muñoz defines it. Memory, as he explains, is "most certainly constructed and, more important, always political," and the different media used to carry on such remembrances, "film, video, performance, writing, and visual culture," have "world-making potentialities" (Muñoz 35). He then builds on Derrida to discuss the futurity of such queer utopias and their potential political function: "spectrality," he writes, "seems especially useful for a queer criticism that attempts to understand communal mourning, group psychologies, and the need for a politics that 'carries' our dead with us into the battles for the present and future" (Muñoz 47).

Both Castle and Muñoz convey a sense that acknowledging the ghosts of the past – the history of marginalization that cleaves to queerness – can lead to a different, better future. This suggests that Hocquenghem's "homosexuality haunts the normal world," in the same way as Marx's specter of communism, can be at once a threat subject to violent repression and a revolutionary promise. Yet the question that remains is what exactly of the history of queer marginalization should be taken up to fulfill this promise and in what way: should what was rendered invisible or abject in the past be rehabilitated (and, in a sense, rendered non-spectral) by being brought into the "normal world" and exposed as unthreatening, as Castle seems to propose, or is there also a potential revolutionary value to retaining it as invisible, abject and threatening of "normality"? In other words, should the spaces of the queer underworld, as enumerated by Crimp, rise to the surface or should they retain their obscurity? To answer this, it is first necessary to establish what it means to be assigned to the peripheral realm of the "underworld."

Kalifa's Queer Underworld

In his 2013 book *Les bas-fonds. Histoire d'un imaginaire*, Kalifa focuses on the construction of "the underworld": first associated with submarine spaces,[2] it is during the nineteenth century and in several European countries

---

2 "*Les bas-fonds*" in French literally means "the shallows."

simultaneously that the word acquires its social dimension of referring to the dregs of society and the seedy parts of the city.[3] According to Kalifa:

> Essentially, the underworld is a "representation," a cultural construct, born at the crossroads of literature, philanthropy, the desire for reform and moralization on the part of the elites, as well as of a thirst for escape and social exoticism, eager to exploit the potential for "sensational" emotions that, today as in the past, these milieus are the bearers of.
>
> KALIFA 17[4]

If the underworld is a representation, it is not without materiality and it acts in a performative manner: the fantasies and moral judgments associated with marginalized social practices are used to reinforce repression against "the dangerous classes" in a dialectical relationship. "In these sinister places, misery, vice and crime prosper," notes Kalifa, before adding:

> If anything, the underworld is characterized by dirt, stench and deformity. Pulled to the bottom, it is also the world of "the bodily lower stratum" in the sense given to that term by Mikhail Bakhtin. It is the realm of fat, filth, excrement and the scatological.
>
> KALIFA 42–3[5]

Along with vermin, poverty and crime, vice and perversion strongly characterize the *bas-fonds*: inherited from the biblical myths of Sodom and Gomorrah, the underworld is governed by a "bestial, transgressive sexuality" and often fueled by alcohol and drugs (Kalifa 70). Kalifa quotes Hippolyte Raynal remarking on Saint-Denis in 1834 that "the hideous mixture of infancy, decrepitude and virility" forms "a monstrous assemblage, teeming with vices and infamies" (51).[6] The vile aspects of the underworld are highlighted for those outside it in the 1860s when both the sensation novel – the "erotic dimension"

---

3   See the *Oxford Hachette French Dictionary* entry for *bas-fond*.

4   "Pour l'essentiel, les bas-fonds relèvent d'une 'représentation,' d'une construction culturelle, née à la croisée de la littérature, de la philanthropie, du désir de réforme et de moralisation porté par les élites, mais aussi d'une soif d'évasion et d'exotisme social, avide d'exploiter le potentiel d'émotions 'sensationnelles' dont, aujourd'hui comme hier, ces milieux sont porteurs."

5   "Dans tous les cas cependant, c'est par la saleté, la puanteur et la difformité que se manifestent les bas-fonds. Entraînés vers le bas, ils sont aussi un monde du 'bas corporel' au sens que Mikhail Bakhtine a donné à ce terme. C'est l'univers du gras, du sale, de l'excrément, du scatologique."

6   "'Le hideux mélange de l'enfance, de la décrépitude et de la virilité' y forme 'un assemblage monstre, grouillant de vices et d'infamies.'"

of which is "undeniable" (Kalifa 201)[7] – and the practice of undercover journalism emerge in England. James Greenwood's story "A Night in a Workhouse" (1866) is a good example of the latter, as it "clearly suggests the homosexual orgy taking place at night" (Kalifa 201).[8] In France, it is only in the 1920s that the taste for undercover journalism develops: Maryse Choisy, one of the rare women allowed in the profession, publishes several reports about her investigations of brothels, among which is the Fétiche, "a lesbian house" (Kalifa 189). Homosexuality's assigned place in the underworld is cemented when, in 1936, the American writer Djuna Barnes provides, in her novel *Nightwood*, a brutal depiction of the Parisian lesbian scene as "a dirty, marginal universe, *queer* in all the meanings of the term, ... 'a truly monstrous parade' featuring transvestites, lesbians, beggars, degenerate and imbecile children" (Kalifa 51).[9]

According to Kalifa, the representation of the underworld as a marginal, peripheral universe is what makes it fascinating and attractive to writers, poets and journalists: it is a world in which social norms are inverted, a reversed world with its own codes, signs and languages that the profane ignores (188). Partly permeated with biblical imagery, representations of the underworld often refer to it as an "Urban Hell" or as purgatory (Kalifa 131). Certain neighborhoods or specific places such as prisons, hospitals and asylums are frequently depicted in these terms and seen as populated by the living dead. Thus, Paul Bru describes Bicêtre as "a place where at night the damned came dancing their funeral, macabre dance, where ghosts wandered freely, celebrating profane Sabbaths and engaged in diabolical orgies" (qtd. in Kalifa 132).[10] Similarly, in Pierre Mac Orlan's *Rues secrètes*, it is said that "I call phantoms these human appearances one can meet in all cities, in all landscapes, and who are the true literary creations of daily life" (qtd. in Kalifa 258).[11]

For Kalifa, the underworld appears as an anti-world used by Western modern societies, troubled by the disruptions of the nineteenth century, as a "scarecrow" to better define the center and repress the periphery (373). Importantly,

---

7   "La dimension érotique de ces récits est indéniable."
8   "Le récit de Greenwood ... laisse clairement entrevoir l'orgie homosexuelle qui s'y déroule la nuit."
9   "Un univers sale, marginal, *queer* dans tous les sens du terme, ... 'une véritable parade monstrueuse' composée de travestis, de lesbiennes, de mendiants, d'enfants débiles et dégénérés."
10   "Endroit où le soir les damnés revenaient danser la funèbre danse macabre, où les revenants se promenaient librement, célébraient les sabbats profanes et se livraient à des orgies diaboliques."
11   "J'appelle fantômes ces apparences humaines que l'on rencontre dans toutes les villes, dans tous les paysages, et qui sont les véritables créations littéraires de la vie quotidienne."

although the underworld was, in the nineteenth and twentieth centuries, often approached with fascination, the processes of exclusion that produced it as a marginal space were not questioned but rather reinforced by the imaginary created.

As Kalifa explains, the need for the elites to "rethink the contours, the organization and the stratification of the social world" (373) later became less urgent and representations of the underworld slowly declined and became restricted to designating organized crime. Nevertheless, its imaginary partly persists until today in films, television series, new media, comics and video games.[12] The same applies to the representation of the deviant and criminal homosexual, as exemplified by William Friedkin's 1980s thriller *Cruising*, which depicts the hunt for a serial killer who picks up his victims in S&M and leather bars. Interestingly, this representation also features in work by queer artists: in addition to the 1983 film *L'Homme blessé* by Patrice Chéreau – the story of a young man discovering the underworld of a Parisian railway station's urinals, which results in a crime of passion – a more recent example is the 2013 thriller *L'Inconnu du lac* by Alain Guiraudie, which tells the story of Franck, a gay man spending his summer cruising by a lake where he meets Michel, to whom he is instantly attracted. One night, Franck witnesses Michel murdering his partner, whose body is later discovered in the water, but he decides to keep Michel's secret. Although the investigation that follows results in Michel killing two other men, Franck ultimately chooses his desire for Michel over his fear, calling his lover's name three times in the night in the closing scene of the film. Although the survival of the imaginary of the queer underworld as a realm of criminality and deadly desire may seem something to be regretted, I want to suggest that it could also be seen to hold a political potential. By analyzing *La Revue Monstre*'s controversial call to return to the closet and Michael James O'Brien's photo series *Interiors*, I argue that, when re-appropriated, the imaginary associated with the queer underworld offers a productive starting point for thinking the political potential inherent to peripheral spaces.

La Revue Monstre and Michael James O'Brien's *Interiors*

By digging into old archives of the now-defunct militant online magazine *Minorités.org* – headed by sociologist Laurent Chambon and activist Didier Lestrade – I discovered *La Revue Monstre*, a unique specimen in the French

---

12   "Les élites ont ressenti le besoin de repenser les contours, l'organisation et la stratification du monde social."

queer media landscape. Launched in 2009 and co-founded by Gilles Beaujard, Gauthier Boche, Thomas Cepitelli, Philippe Joanny and Timothée Madesclaire, it is a niche publication with a print run of a thousand copies, somewhere between art magazine and academic collection, which features essays, interviews and short stories, as well as paintings and photography. As explained by Timothée Madesclaire in an interview conducted by email, the founders wanted to avoid the typical gay imagery: "no rainbow flags, no pretty boys, no info on topics largely discussed by existing gay media." From the first moment, I was fascinated. *Monstre*… The name itself sounded like quite a statement – a promise in these times of demobilization and increasing attempts at respectability within the French gay movement, especially after the humiliation and apathy that came with marriage equality. The explicit focus on the monstrous led me to ask why present-day queers would want to portray themselves as creatures of the underworld, despite the homophobic connotations this might have, and why such representations were so pleasing to me. Besides its aesthetic allures, what was *La Revue Monstre* trying to say – or what did *I* want it to say?

The name *Monstre*, said to be first of all a reference to a publication's mockup (a *monstre* in French), obviously plays with the more literal meaning of the word: *monstre*, etymologically, comes from the Latin noun *monstrum*, which primarily means a warning from the gods or an omen and, by extension, a monster as something evoking both fear and wonder. The noun, it is worth noting, is itself derived from the verb *monstro*: to show. It is precisely this relationship between the monstrous that one shows or exhibits and the idea of an omen, warning or threatening potentiality that I want to highlight here. Referring back to the Derridean specter's implications for notions of agency, marginalization and temporality, I will analyze how the first issue of *Monstre* and O'Brien's *Interiors*, featured within it, play with and challenge the traditional politics of gay visibility. The latter, for example in Castle's work, equates emancipation with an emergence from the shadows, and has evolved over the years into an "imperative of gay pride" translating into an "increasingly sanitized, staid, politically vacuous, and generally boring official gay culture of self-affirmation" (Halperin and Traub 8).

Monstre is fascinated by marginal imageries. In the first issue, provocatively titled "Back to the Closet," a series of three photographs by Achim Kraemer shows him impersonating a haunting feminine creature stepping back into a wooden closet. Hardly readable, the artwork reveals, in black, stained, shadowy Gothic letters divided over the three images, the following message: "There is/no place/like home" (*Monstre* 1 65–8). A few pages further, an interview with ethnologist and photographer Ralf Marsault nostalgically discusses the lost culture of public sex, described as "a highly interesting quagmire, …

a kind of compost where one could blossom" (*Monstre 1* 93). In the third issue, titled "Undetectable" (*Indétectable*), artist Mavado Charon's four-page drawing *Toile de Jouy* replaces the innocent, playful, bucolic scenes normally depicted on these traditional French cotton fabrics with sadomasochistic celebrations, diabolical orgies and queer bacchanalias: a Sadian mixture of sex, torture and murder (*Monstre 3* 77–80). Thus, rather than rejecting the obscurity of the queer underworld, *Monstre* appears to revel in it.

The specific artwork I want to analyze here is a series of pictures by the American photographer Michael James O'Brien entitled *Interiors*, featured in "Back to the Closet" (*Monstre 1* 20–4). It portrays four distinctive Parisian back-rooms, each dominated by a specific range of colors: green and yellow; red and black; brown and yellow; and blue and black. The difference between the back-rooms is not limited to but rather accentuated by these colors, as each also has its specific "interior." The series' title encourages us to focus on the details, the materials and spatial arrangements particular to each backroom. The first one is mainly occupied by green wooden bench seats (figure 13.1). The second, with its exposed stone walls and its red-lit and tiled bed, connotes something like a

FIGURE 13.1   *Michael James O'Brien,* Interior 09.
REPRODUCED WITH PERMISSION OF THE ARTIST.

dungeon (figure 13.2). The third, with its brown leather-like sofas and old-fashioned wallpaper, looks like a traditional smoking room, although prominently featuring a non-smoking sign (figure 13.3). The last one, with its blue-lit metal staircase, concrete floor and exposed stones, is literally a cave (figure 13.4). Yet, if each interior is unique, they all serve the same purpose: the pursuit of quick, anonymous, sometimes numerous sexual encounters, the detached consumption of bodies in semi-obscurity. What is confounding is that the photographs, rather than displaying the naked bodies of the usual inhabitants, are empty of human presence; this is unusual in gay art, especially when linked to sexuality. The only reminders of human activity are the signs featured in *Interior 01* ("Every Tuesday from 9pm underpants and boxer shorts night," the round, school-like writing contrasting with the adult nature of the place) and *Interior 03* ("no smoking," a red and white notice that, in this context where many social norms do not apply, seems ironic).[13]

FIGURE 13.2   *Michael James O'Brien,* Interior 01.
REPRODUCED WITH PERMISSION OF THE ARTIST.

---

13   "Tous les mardis dès 21h00 soirée slip caleçon"/"Défense de fumer."

FIGURE 13.3   *Michael James O'Brien*, Interior 03.
REPRODUCED WITH PERMISSION OF THE ARTIST.

FIGURE 13.4   *Michael James O'Brien*, Interior 02.
REPRODUCED WITH PERMISSION OF THE ARTIST.

The *visible absence* of those supposed to populate these rooms evokes the spectral and is reminiscent of an artwork by Tony Just mentioned by Muñoz. In the chapter entitled "Ghosts and Utopia," Muñoz discusses a series of pictures of "run-down public men's rooms in New York City, the kind that were certainly tea rooms before they … were shut down because of the AIDS/HIV public health crisis" (40). Just, who scrubbed and sanitized these spaces, "documented this project through colour slides and photographs that focused on the bathroom's immaculate state and the details of such spaces," a task that, according to Muñoz, produces a haunting effect: "The urinals, tiles, toilets, and fixtures that are the objects of these photo images take on what can only be described as a *ghostly aura, an otherworldly glow*" (40, emphasis added). If Muñoz's interpretation of Just's work and his further theorization of "the ghosts of public sex" seem to focus, as noted earlier, on specters from the past and on nostalgia, a similar spectral effect can be perceived in O'Brien's pictures: the photographer puts the imagination of the viewer to work precisely by keeping bodies out of the picture. This allows for a displacement, shifting the focus onto the space itself rather than on a specific person, sexual practice, nude body part, gesture or look.

Still, it is difficult to look at these images without having in mind the kind of encounters that usually take place there. As much as the bathrooms captured by Just are "scrubbed and sanitized," the backrooms shown by O'Brien are empty of any residue one could imagine finding in such a space; yet they remain occupied by the uncanny "presence of an absence." In the words of Muñoz, "that space of emptiness is meant to make room for other worlds of sexual possibility" (42). In addition, with their colored lighting, the *Interiors* are surrounded by a similar "ghostly aura" and "otherworldly glow" to Just's work, increasing their mysterious appeal and inviting viewers to wonder about these specific queer *otherworlds*. Within the Derridean framework, this emphasis on haunting is not a call for an identical return of the past, nor simply an invitation to remember and wallow in nostalgia, but rather an incitement to question what *has been* or *could have been*, and what *could be* in the future.

The Heterotopic Closet

This invitation is made even clearer by the short text, written by the editors of *Monstre*, that presents the *Interiors* series and introduces the peripheral spaces of the backrooms in a rather provocative and idealized manner:

> *Interiors* are backrooms. Spaces whose hermetic (hermeneutic?) closure is the condition for the extraordinary liberty at play there. The extraction

from the "profane" world allows the redefinition of the relational game, of exchange logics and of self-construction. Together with others, a closet is well and truly a perpetually expanding universe.[14]

      Monstre 1 20

The references to liberty, to the "extraction from the profane world" and to the "redefinition of the relational game," besides resonating strongly with Hocquenghem's and Kalifa's descriptions of the underworld, also instantly evoke the Foucauldian *heterotopia of deviance*, a space that leaves room for otherness by reversing social norms and presenting a deviant mirror image of the ordinary world (Foucault 1986). In this light, the text could appear as an effort to claim back marginalized social practices and to salute the possibility to invent new forms of sociality away from society's center and its surveillance. The backroom is described as a space enabling a collective resistance to normative subjection and identities: it is a heterotopia, moreover, precisely because it is occupied "*à plusieurs*," an idea that echoes Derrida's proposition that the specter is always "more than one/no more one [*le plus d'un*]" (xx).

The deliberate use of the word "closet," however, first appears to suggest times of oppression rather than queer liberation. "The adroit and secret placement of homosexual claims along the edges and peripheries of moral society have been labelled as the 'closet' by the gay liberation movement," recalls Edward Delph in *The Silent Community* (158). In this light, the backrooms shown by O'Brien evoke the description given by Hocquenghem in *The Screwball Asses* of how he followed a fellow queer man into the toilets of the French Beaux-Arts:

> ... a boy takes me by the arm and leads me towards an obscure passageway. I enter into a dark, humid hovel where we wade in puddles of water and urine: the toilets of the Beaux-Arts. *Half a dozen bodies, anonymous in the dim light, are enlaced there in what complex circuitries one cannot immediately decipher.* I feel burdened by the enforced blindness, the acrid smell of piss chokes me and I recoil, feeling guilty immediately.
>
>   HOCQUENGHEM 3–4, emphasis added

---

14   "*Interiors,* ce sont des backrooms. Des espaces dont la clôture, hermétique (herméneutique?), est la condition de l'extraordinaire liberté qui s'y joue. L'extraction du monde 'profane' permet la redéfinition du jeu relationnel, des logiques d'échange et de la construction de soi. A plusieurs, un placard est bel et bien un univers en perpétuelle expansion."

Ashamed by his own shame and by the shame of those around him, Hocqueng-hem explodes in rage:

> It is as if homosexual desire could only be inscribed where repression has inscribed it. I know how many queers only have toilets in which to touch each other. It depresses me that those who have decided to come out of hiding continue to project their excitement in the miserable places that the system condescends to allow them and where the police provoke them.
>
> HOCQUENGHEM 2010: 4

There is something sinister in the obscure appearance of the "half a dozen bodies, anonymous in the dim light" depicted by the young Hocquenghem. For him, there is no doubt: such toilets are a suffocating space occupied by guilty ghosts – the proverbial "skeletons in the closet." The bodies encountered and conjured by Hocquenghem are hidden, disenfranchised specters similar to the ones described by Castle in *The Apparitional Lesbian*: bodies without faces, bodies denied identities whose sexuality can only take place clandestinely in these gloomy allotted peripheral places.

In relation to Castle's endorsement of a politics of visibility that also domi-nates contemporary mainstream LGBTIQ activism, the backrooms portrayed by O'Brien appear as disturbing remnants from the past. For anyone who has never been to one, it is easy to go along with Hocquenghem and assume that such spaces are mainly governed by shame. Moreover, *Monstre*'s reference to "the profane world" connotes the entire imaginary associated to public sex and its specific coded language charted by, for example, Bruno Proth. Significantly, the very article to which I owe my discovery of *Monstre*, written by Act-Up Paris activist Arlindo Constantino for the online political magazine *Minorités*, com-ments in extremely negative terms on the *Interiors* series. Rejecting *Monstre*'s invitation to go "back to the closet," Constantino concludes with a hostile rhetorical question: "Is *Monstre* a publication of shameful barebackers?"[15]

Spectral Politics: From World-Making to Agency

The hyperbolic tone used by the editors ("the extraordinary liberty") does not help, it is true, to understand O'Brien's series other than as a provocation. Yet, the move made by *Monstre* is an interesting one, with the entire first issue an

---

15 "*Monstre* est-elle une revue de barebackers honteux?"

explicit invitation to question injunctions to gay visibility and transparency. By describing the backroom/closet in a positive light, *Monstre* encourages its readers to consider the invisibility and anonymity that certain peripheral spaces can ensure as able to maximize sexual possibilities away from the shame induced by light, and as capable of deconstructing the identities assigned by the normative social order, allowing one to reinvent oneself beyond or in excess of them. Therefore, if the haunting elements of *Interiors* ensure that the negative connotations of the backroom do not entirely disappear from view, the series also encourages us to consider this inherent tension: the collectivity of the closet and its being peripheral to and closed off from the outside world are precisely what make it an expansive space of possibility rather than strictly a place of hiding. "Extracted from the profane world," the backroom/closet enables a kind of sociality which is not a copy or mirror image of that of the outside world, but which creates a new territory capable of transgressing class, racial and social barriers.

Such a depiction may seem idealistic when one considers the unavoidable hierarchies still at play in such places. Muñoz dedicates a section of *Cruising Utopia* to precisely this tendency to romanticize cruising spaces. Mentioning Bersani's *Is the Rectum a Grave?*, where the latter recalls that such places were far from the utopic queer spaces they are often depicted as, Muñoz writes: "Bersani rightly brings to light the fact that those pre-AIDS days of glory were also elitist, exclusionary and savagely hierarchized libidinal economies" (34). However, he adds, if public sex culture often tends to be idealized, this idealization does not have to be read negatively, but could be seen as "an example of the way in which a rich remembrance of sexual utopia feeds a transformative queer politics" and as "an act of queer world-making" (36, 37):

> I see world-making here as functioning and coming into play through the performance of queer utopian memory, that is, a utopia that understands its time as reaching beyond some nostalgic past that perhaps never was or some future whose arrival is continuously belated – a utopia in the present.
>
> MUÑOZ 37

Indeed, reflecting on Adorno's ideas on "the utopian function of art," Muñoz sees a strong political power in such a world-making practice that is often an indirect manner of criticizing the present. A similar argument appears in the French philosopher Didier Eribon's *Réflexions sur la question gay*. Mentioning how forced secrecy and clandestinity have been – and still are – sources of a certain kind of pleasure for many homosexuals, Eribon explains:

It is not rare to hear, from the mouths of homosexuals who lived part of their sexual life before the 60s, and thus before the "liberation," that they miss the time of the imposed secret and of the "game" one had to constantly invent to deceive outsiders' looks and find complicities.

ERIBON 78[16]

As he recalls, the closet has also been "a space of freedom, and a means – the only one – to *resist* and not to obey normative injunctions" (Eribon 78, emphasis added).[17] A certain "pride" could, paradoxically, be found in the closet and

it is this extraordinary feeling of *pride and liberty conquered and maintained as a secret shared with others* [*partagé à plusieurs*] that the gays from previous generations perhaps do not find any more in the liberty and pride now publicly displayed, which seems too easy to them and tasteless in a sense, having lost the taste of the forbidden game.[18]

ERIBON 78, emphasis added

This idea of the closet being also a space of liberty, a secret shared *à plusieurs*, parallels that expressed in the editors' description of *Interiors*, and the same tension, the same paradox, is at play there.

In the end, *Monstre*'s reflection on the closet through the *Interiors* series forces us to reconsider traditional assumptions about the desirability of gay visibility and to ask what is lost in the focus on being or becoming visible. What is the result of this negotiated visibility? What kind of images, practices and bodies do we sweep under the rug or pretend to forget in moving from clandestine peripheral spaces to the social center? More than a provocation, *Monstre*'s invitation to go "back to the closet" forces us to see past rigid visible-invisible, pride-shame and center-periphery dichotomies, and to embrace

---

16   "Il n'est pas rare d'entendre, dans la bouche d'homosexuels qui ont vécu une partie de leur vie sexuelle avant les années soixante, et donc avant la 'libération,' des regrets sur l'époque du secret imposé et du 'jeu' qu'il fallait inventer sans cesse pour tromper les regards et trouver les connivences."

17   "Le placard a été si souvent dénoncé par les militants homosexuels comme symbole de la 'honte' et de la soumission à l'oppression qu'on a fini par oublier ou négliger qu'il peut être aussi, et en même temps, un espace de liberté et un moyen – le seul – de résister et de ne pas se soumettre aux injonctions normatives."

18   "Et c'est cet extraordinaire sentiment de fierté et de liberté conquise et maintenue comme un secret partagé à plusieurs que les gays des générations précédentes ne retrouvent peut-être plus dans la liberté et la fierté affichées au grand jour et qui leur semblent trop faciles, et en un sens un peu fades, ayant perdu la saveur du jeu de l'interdit."

a reconnection with marginalized experiences. In its alluring portrayal of the backrooms and its evocation of the present absent bodies in it, *Interiors* not only objects to the moral judgments associated with promiscuity, but also appears as a call in favor of specific homosexual subcultures, codes and social practices that could – and to a large extent still can – only prosper out of sight from mainstream society. Paradoxically, it sheds light on the backroom to better question the force of what remains unseen: the bodies missing from the pictures and the spaces set apart from "the profane world."

Against Castle's work on the apparitional lesbian, gay ghosts are here not entirely disenfranchised creatures, but experience instead a form of spectral agency, defined by Peeren as the "idea for the ghost to come back and possess (in the sense of inhabiting and disintegrating) its conjurer" (20). What spectral agency suggests is that "exploiting one's ghostly status might be more productive than trying to deny or overcome it" (Peeren 23). Importantly, then, *Monstre*'s invitation to go "back to the closet" is not a call for the return of oppressive times as they were, but rather a call to recognize and mourn the freedom and inventiveness also enabled by one's assignation to clandestine peripheral spaces: this queer nostalgia, strongly tied to "world-making" (Muñoz 37), thus holds a strong political and transformative power.

Spectrality here implies a double, ambivalent status of disenfranchisement and agency. As Peeren writes, following Derrida, "the haunting force is effective precisely because of its undecidable nature and origin, its blurring of the active-passive dichotomy" (20). In a manner similar to Marx's prediction that "a specter is haunting Europe – the specter of communism," Hocquenghem proclaims that "homosexuality haunts the normal world" from the peripheries to which it has been assigned (1993: 50). I have sought to reactivate the revolutionary promise in this proclamation through my reading of Kalifa's queer underworld and my analysis of O'Brien's *Interiors* as presented in the "Back to the Closet" issue of *Monstre*: the underworld may be an anti-world of forceful exclusion from the normative center, but it is also a world of peripheral possibility, of hidden pleasures and deviant alliances, of "macabre dance[s] where ghosts wander freely" (Bru qtd. in Kalifa 132).

Works Cited

Bersani, Leo. *Is the Rectum a Grave? And Other Essays*. Chicago and London: U of Chicago P, 2010.

Blanco, María del Pilar, and Esther Peeren. *The Spectralities Reader: Ghosts and Haunting in Contemporary Cultural Theory*. New York: Bloomsbury, 2013.

Castle, Terry. *The Apparitional Lesbian: Female Homosexuality and Modern Culture.* New York: Columbia UP, 1995.

Charon, Mavado. *Toile de Jouy. La Revue Monstre Numéro 3: Indétectable* Jan. 2011: 77–80.

Constantino, Arlindo. "Gay, pédé ou Monstre?" *Minorités.org.* 2010. Web. 20 June 2015.

Cruising. Dir. William Friedkin. Warner Bros., 1980.

Delph, Edward William. *The Silent Community: Public Homosexual Encounters.* Beverley Hills, CA: Sage Publications, 1978.

Derrida, Jacques. *Specters of Marx: The State of the Debt, the Work of Mourning & the New International.* 1993. Trans. Peggy Kamuf. New York and London: Routledge, 1994.

Eribon, Didier. *Réflexions sur la question gay.* Paris: Fayard, 1999.

Foucault, Michel. "Of Other Spaces: Utopias and Heterotopias." 1984. Trans. Jay Miskowiec. *Diacritics* 16.1 (1986): 22–7.

———. *Abnormal: Lectures at the Collège de France, 1974–1975.* Ed. Valerio Marchetti, Antonella Salomoni and Arnold I. Davidson. New York: Picador, 2003.

Halperin, David, and Valerie Traub, eds. *Gay Shame.* Chicago: U of Chicago P, 2009.

Hocquenghem, Guy. *Homosexual Desire.* 1972. Trans. Daniella Dangoor. Durham and London: Duke UP, 1993.

———. *The Screwball Asses.* Trans. Noura Wedell. Los Angeles: Semiotext(e), 2010.

Kalifa, Dominique. *Les bas-fonds. Histoire d'un imaginaire.* Paris: Seuil, 2013.

Kraemer, Achim. *The Girl inside Me. La Revue Monstre Numéro 1: Back to the Closet* Dec. 2009: 65–8.

L'Homme blessé. Dir. Patrice Chéreau. Gaumont, 1983.

Marsault, Ralf. "Un chaos bien ordonné." Interview by Tony Plump. *La Revue Monstre Numéro 1: Back to the Closet* Dec. 2009: 93–6.

Muñoz, José Esteban. *Cruising Utopia: The Then and There of Queer Futurity.* New York: New York UP, 2009.

O'Brien, Michael James. *Interiors. La Revue Monstre Numéro 1: Back to the Closet* Dec. 2009: 20–4.

Peeren, Esther. *The Spectral Metaphor: Living Ghosts and the Agency of Invisibility.* Basingstoke: Palgrave Macmillan, 2014.

Proth, Bruno. *Lieux de drague. Scènes et coulisses d'une sexualité masculine.* Toulouse: Octarès Editions, 2002.

Tardieu, Ambroise. *Étude médico-légale sur les attentats aux mœurs.* Paris: J.B. Baillière et fils, 1859.

Name Index